Entire Sanctification

From 1739 to 1900

by

Rev. S. L. C. Coward

First Fruits Press
Wilmore, Kentucky
c2015

Entire Sanctification from 1739 to 1900 by S. L. C. Coward

First Fruits Press, ©2015
Previously published by the Pentecostal Publishing Company, 1904, c1900.

ISBN: 9781621712404 (print), 9781621712602 (digital), 9781621712619 (kindle)

Digital version at http://place.asburyseminary.edu/firstfruitsheritagematerial/108/

First Fruits Press
B.L. Fisher Library
Asbury Theological Seminary
204 N. Lexington Ave.
Wilmore, KY 40390
http://place.asburyseminary.edu/firstfruits

Coward, S. L. C. (Samuel L. C.)
    Entire sanctification from 1739-1900 / by S.L.C. Coward.
    371 pages ; 21 cm.
    Wilmore, Ky. : First Fruits Press, ©2015.
    Reprint. Previously published: Louisville, KY : Pentecostal Publishing
    Company, 1904, ©1900.
    ISBN: 9781621712404 (pbk.)
    1. Holiness. 2. Sanctification. 3. Perfection. I. Title.
BT767 .C58 2015

Cover design by Wesley Wilcox

asburyseminary.edu
800.2ASBURY
204 North Lexington Avenue
Wilmore, Kentucky 40390

First Fruits
THE ACADEMIC OPEN PRESS OF ASBURY SEMINARY

First Fruits Press
The Academic Open Press of Asbury Theological Seminary
204 N. Lexington Ave., Wilmore, KY 40390
859-858-2236
first.fruits@asburyseminary.edu
asbury.to/firstfruits

ENTIRE SANCTIFICATION

From 1739 to 1900

BY

Rev. S. L. C. COWARD,

OF THE

Louisville Conference M. E. Church, South
Author of "Perfect Love," "Young
People's Scrap Book," etc.

PENTECOSTAL PUBLISHING CO
LOUISVILLE, KY.
1904.

To

MARGARET COWARD (MY MOTHER),

WHO GAVE ME TO CHRIST AND THE CHURCH IN EARLY
CHILDHOOD, AND BROUGHT ME UP IN
THE "CHRISTIAN FAITH,"

AND

TO DORA J. COWARD, MY DEVOTED WIFE,

WHO HAS BEEN TO ME A WIFE INDEED, THIS VOLUME
IS MOST AFFECTIONATELY

DEDICATED.

PREFACE.

THIS book is a compilation. The aim has been to bring together in one volume the very best that has been written by the very best writers on the various phases of the doctrine of Entire Sanctification between the year 1739 and the present.

While many of these chapters have never appeared in print before, others have been published in the columns of various papers and magazines and in tracts and pamphlets, and are republished here with the consent of the writers.

The doctrine of entire sanctification has always had a place, not only in the theological text-books, but also in the history, biography and current literature of Methodism. The position of any branch of the Methodist Church upon this doctrine, and its attitude toward the experience implied, is not a matter of doubt when this literature of the church is read without prejudice. It has been the purpose of the author of this book to bring together a series of papers which will set forth in the most complete and comprehensive way the doctrine as taught in the Methodist Church, as experienced by Methodist people, and as it has affected the church during the period mentioned in the title.

For about twenty years there has been much contention in the M. E. Church, South, over this doctrine and experience. The claims of the so-called Holiness People have been strongly and conclusively maintained. They have proven beyond the possibility of successful controversy that the doctrine is Wesleyan; that it is scriptural; and that it is confirmed by multitudes of our very best men and women.

But the facts and arguments by which these points have been established have been widely scattered through books and papers, very few of which could be in the hands of any one person. We believe the reader will here find the most compendious statement of Methodist teachings upon this interesting teaching that can be found anywhere. We are persuaded that many persons have felt the need of a hand-book which would give them the very information herein contained and that they will approve the efforts of the author in his attempt to meet the demand.

Our thanks are due and are hereby tendered to all who have furnished papers, or have otherwise aided us in preparing the book. And now for each of our readers we earnestly pray: "The very God of peace sanctify you wholly; and I pray God your whole spirit and soul and body be preserved blameless unto the coming of our Lord Jesus Christ. Faithful is he that calleth you, who also will do it."—I Thes. 5:23, 24.

CONTENTS.

Contents.

PORTRAITS.

SECTION I.

WESLEY AND HIS TEACHINGS.

CHAPTER I.

Sketch of John Wesley, A. M.
Fellow of Lincoln College, Oxford.

BY SAMUEL L. C. COWARD.

*Rev. John Wesley was born June 28, 1703, in the parish of Epworth, Lincolnshire, England. He was descended from a long line of able ministers. "When God sets out to make a great man, He first makes a great woman." "This is eminently true in the case of John Wesley. His mother, Susannah Wesley, was a woman of strong intellect, fine culture, deep piety, and rare domestic qualities. John Wesley came of good stock. His father was a preacher before him. He entered college at the age of seventeen, and came out a distinguished graduate from one of the most famous universities of the world. His intellectual training was of the highest order. A *happy* and *thorough conversion* marked his religious experience."

Mrs. Susannah Wesley, the mother of John Wesley, was, as might be expected from the eminent character of her father, Dr. Samuel Annesley, educated with great care. Like her husband, she also, at an early

*After the printers began work on this book the work stopped till the writer could get ready this chapter. He desires to acknowledge his indebtedness to Bishop McTyeire's History of Methodism, The Life of Wesley, by Watson, and The Methodist Armor, by Dr. Hudson, without which he could not have prepared it.

period life, renounced non-conformity, and became a member of the Established Church, after, as her biographers tell us, she had read and mastered the whole controversy on the subject of separation; of which, however, great as were her natural and acquired talents, she must, at the age of thirteen years, have been a very imperfect judge. The advantage of such a parentage to the Wesleys was great. From their earliest years they had an example in their father of all that could render a clergyman respectable and influential; and, in the mother, there was a sanctified wisdom, a masculine understanding, and an acquired knowledge which they regarded with just deference after they became men and scholars. The influence of a piety so steadfast and uniform, joined to such qualities, and softened by maternal tenderness, could scarcely fail to produce effect. The firm and manly character, the practical sense, the active and unwearied habits of the father, with the calm, reflecting, and stable qualities of the mother, were in particular inherited by Mr. John Wesley, and in him were most happily blended. Mrs. Wesley was the instructress of her nineteen children (ten of these were raised to maturity) in their early years. "I can find," says Dr. Whitehead, "no evidence that the boys were ever put to any school in the country; their mother having a very bad opinion of the common methods of instructing and governing children."

On February 9, 1709, at midnight, when all the family were in bed, Samuel Wesley was awakened by a cry of fire, out-of-doors. His wife and her eldest daughters rose as quickly as possible. He then burst open the nursery door, where in their beds were sleeping five of his children and their nurse. The nurse seized Charles, the youngest, and bade the others follow. Three of the children did as they were bidden, but John (six years old) was left sleeping. Some of the children now escaped through the windows, and the rest, except John, through a little door into the garden. He was snatched from a window in the second story just as the roof fell in.

After this event, Mrs. Wesley said: "I intend to be more particularly careful of the soul of a child whom God has so mercifully provided for." The effect of this special care on the part of the mother was that, under the divine blessing, he became early serious; for at the age of eight years he was admitted by his father to partake of the sacrament.

In 1714, at the age of eleven years, he was placed at the Charterhouse school, "where he was noticed for his diligence and progress in learning." (Whitehead's Life.) "Here, for his quietness, regularity, and application, he became a favorite with the master, Dr. Walker, and through life he retained so great a predilection for the place that, on his annual visit to London, he made it a custom to walk through the scene of his boyhood." (Southey's Life.) When he had attained the age of seventeen, he was elected to Christ Church, Oxford, where he pursued his studies with great advantage. Mr. Wesley's natural temper in his youth was gay and sprightly, with a turn for wit and humor. When he was about twenty-one years of age, he "appeared," as Mr. Babcock has observed, "the very sensible and acute collegian; a young fellow of the finest classical taste, of the most liberal and manly sentiments."

John Wesley's father, the Rev. Samuel Wesley, Rector of Epworth, in Lincolnshire, was a man of extraordinary mird. He did a great deal of literary labor of vast magnitude. He wrote the Life of Christ in verse; the history of the Old and New Testaments, and "Dissertationes in Librum Jobi," a large folio book of six hundred pages. He was employed upon this remarkable production for more than twenty-five years, and death found him plodding away on the unfinished task.

John Wesley remained at Charterhouse six years, making such progress that, in 1720, he was elected on this foundation to Christ Church, Oxford, one of the noblest colleges in that illustrious seat of learning; here he continued until after his ordination in 1725. In reference to this period he writes: "I still said my prayers, both in public and private, and read with the scriptures several other books of religion, especially comments on the New Testament. Yet I had not all this while so much as a notion of inward holiness; nay, went on habitually and, for the most part, very contentedly in some or other known sins—though with some intermission and short struggles, especially before and after the holy communion, which I was obliged to receive thrice a year."

In 1726, he was elected Fellow of Lincoln College. He spent the summer, after he was elected, with his parents in Lincolnshire. In September he returned to Oxford and resumed his studies. His literary character was now established. He was acknowledged by all as a man of talent and an excellent critic in learned languages. On the seventh of November, 1727, when twenty-three years of age he was chosen Greek lecturer and moderator of the classes. The same year, in August, he became his father's curate. In 1728 he returned to Oxford to receive priest's orders, and paid another visit to Oxford in 1729. At this last visit, in 1729, he attended a small society, organized by his brother Charles, Mr. Morgan and some others, to assist each other in their studies, and to consult how to employ their time to the best of advantage. "The meeting with this small society," says Mr. Wesley, "gained for me the harmless name of Methodist."

The little society of Methodists, as they were called, began now to extend their operations. When Mr. Wesley joined them, they committed its management to him, and he has himself stated its original members: "In November, 1729, four young gentlemen of Oxford, Mr. John Wesley, Fellow of Lincoln College, Mr. Charles Wesley, student of Christ Church, Mr. Morgan, commoner of Christ Church, and Mr. Kirkman, of Merton College, began to spend some evenings in a week together, in reading chiefly the Greek Testament. The next year, two or three of Mr. John Wesley's pupils desired the liberty of meeting with them; and afterward one of Mr. Charles Wesley's pupils. It was in 1732 that Mr. Ingham, of Queen's College, and Mr. Broughton, of Exeter, were added to their number. To these, in April, was joined Mr. Clayton, of Brazen-nose, with two or three of his pupils. About the same time, Mr. James Hervey, was permitted to meet with them, and afterward Mr. Whitefield." (Journal.)

John Wesley remained Fellow of Lincoln College until 1735, when he sailed to Georgia as a missionary, with twenty-six Moravians, one hundred other emigrants, and Charles Wesley. These devout Moravians made a profound impression upon the Wesleys. On February 14, 1736, Wesley landed in Georgia, and on Sunday, March 7th, he entered upon his ministry at Savannah by preaching from the thirteenth chapter of I Corinthians.

Before the close of this year, Oglethorpe (who had command of the settlements of Georgia) was on his way to England, having left John Wesley and his two associates, Ingham and Delamotte, at Savannah. In February, Ingham returned home, and his departure left Mr. Wesley more than ever under the influence of his Georgia friends. A few months later he made his long intended visit to Ebenezer, the Moravian settlement, in company with one of the pastors there, a Mr. Spangenberg, for whom he cherished a high respect. It was this same Spangenberg with whom he had a significant interview soon after landing at Tybee Island. Mr. Wesley, attracted by his appearance and conversation, had asked for his advice in beginning missionary work. "My brother," replied the straightforward German, "I must first ask you one or two questions. Have you the witness

within yourself? Does the Spirit of God bear witness
with your spirit that you are the child of God?''
Wesley was somewhat nonplussed. Spangenberg
pressed the matter: ''Do you know Jesus Christ?'' ''I
know He is the Savior of the world,'' was the reply.
''True,'' said the German; ''but do you know He has
saved you?'' ''I hope,'' answered Wesley somewhat
feebly, ''that He has died to save me.'' The words
of Spangenberg seem to have made a distinct impression upon his mind.

Wesley had but little visible results as a missionary
in Georgia, and he doubtless told the reason why
he did not have success when he said: ''I had even
then the faith of a *servant*, but not of a *son*.'' He
had a stormy voyage back to England, but during the
passage he devoted himself to administering to the
spiritual wants of the passengers and crew. ''With
John Wesley's return to his native land, his character
strengthened and deepened by the unpleasant experiences through which he had passed, begins the heroic
chapter of his life.''

''The solemn review that Mr. Wesley made of the
state of his religious experience, both on his voyage
home and soon after landing in England, deserves to
be particularly noticed both for general instruction
and because it stands in immediate connection with a
point which has especially perplexed those who have
attributed his charges against himself, as to the defici-
ency of his Christianity at this period, to a strange
and fanatical fancy.'' By the most infallible of proofs,
he tells us,—that of his feelings—he was convinced of

his having "no such faith in Christ" as prevented his heart from being troubled; and he earnestly prays to be "saved by such a faith as implies peace in life and death." "I went to America to convert the Indians; but, O! who shall convert me! Who is he that will deliver me from this evil heart of unbelief? I have a fair summer religion; I can talk well, nay, and believe myself, while no danger is present; but let death look me in the face, and my spirit is troubled, nor can I say, 'To die is gain.'

> 'I have a sin of fear that when I've spun
> My last thread, I shall perish on the shore.'"

He thought, therefore, that a faith was attainable, which should deliver him entirely from guilty dread, and fill him with peace; but of this faith itself his notions were still confused.

Wesley had been in the Christian ministry for thirteen years, and having tried legalism and ritualism to the utmost, he found no health in them. He is now ready to be "taught the way of the Lord more perfectly;" and the Lord has prepared a teacher. On the 7th of February, about two years after he returned from Georgia, he met with Peter Bohler in London, a minister of the Moravian Church. "By whom," he says, "in the hand of the great God, I was clearly convinced of unbelief, of the want of that faith whereby alone we are saved with the full Christian salvation." In the fourth conversation with Bohler, Wesley was confirmed in the view, "that faith is, to use the words of our church, a sure trust and confidence which a man has in God, that through the merits of Christ his sins are forgiven, and he is reconciled to the favor of God." On May 24, 1738, in the evening, he went very unwillingly to a society in Aldersgate street, where a layman was reading Luther's preface to the Epistle to the Romans, describing saving faith. Possessed of it, the heart is "cheered, elevated, and transported with sweet affections toward God." Receiving the Holy Ghost through faith, the man "is renewed and made spiritual," and he is impelled to fulfill the law "by the vital energy in himself." Wesley says, "About a quarter before nine, while he was describing the change which God works in the heart through faith in Christ, I felt my heart strangely warmed. I felt I did trust in Christ, Christ alone, for salvation; and an assurance was given me that he had taken away my sins, even mine, and saved me from the 'law of sin and death.' I began to pray with all my might for those who had in a more especial manner despitefully used me and persecuted me. I then testified openly to all there what I now felt in my heart. But it was not long before the enemy suggested, 'This can not be faith, for where is thy joy?' Then I was taught that peace and victory over sin are essential to faith in the Captain of our salvation; but that as to the transports of joy that usually attend the beginning of it, especi ally in those who have mourned deeply, God some- times giveth, sometimes withholdeth them, according to the counsel of his own will. After my return home I was much buffeted with temptations, but cried out, and they fled away. They returned again and again: I as often lifted up my eyes, and he sent me help from his holy place. And herein I found the difference between this and my former state chiefly consisted. I was striving—yea, fighting—with all my might, under the law as well as under grace. But then I was sometimes, if not often conquered; *now*, I was always conqueror.''

Wesley visited the Moravian settlement in Germany and was delighted with Count Zinzendorf and other brethren, but he did not even then indorse all their views. In September, 1738, he arrived in London, and even then his future course does not seem to have been marked out. But he had found Jesus as his pardoning Lord and the fire of God's love was in his bones, and he could not be still. When Wesley says, ''I felt my heart strangely warmed,'' Methodism was born; and where God's people get this same ''warming'' they will go and tell others about him ''who can save *all men from all sin* in this life.''

In December, 1736, for the first time he preached in the open air, on a hill near Bristol, to more than two thousand people. On this memorable spot begins his field preaching, which made the Wesleyan revival such a power among the poor colliers of England.

While Wesley was still at Bristol he had a painful interview with the Bishop of Canterbury. The Bishop took no exception to his doctrine but hinted at excommunicating him for his ''irregular proceedings.'' This gave Wesley great trouble, but Whitefield persuaded him to preach in the fields the next Sabbath, and he said, ''the Lord was with me, even me, the weakest of his messengers.''

"My load was gone, and all my doubts and scruples. God shone on my path, and I knew this was his will concerning me. I walked to Kennington Common, and cried to multitudes upon multitudes, 'Repent ye, and believe the gospel.' The Lord was my strength, and my mouth, and my wisdom. O that all would therefore praise the Lord for his goodness." Six months after his conversion, Mr. Wesley and his brother Charles waited upon Dr. Edmund Gibson, Bishop of London, to answer the complaints he had heard against them to the effect that they preached an absolute assurance of salvation. The two being introduced, Gibson said: "If by assurance you mean an inward persuasion, whereby a man is conscious in himself, after examining his life by the law of God, and weighing his own sincerity, that he is in a state of salvation, and acceptable to God, I don't see how any good Christian can be without such assurance." The Wesleys meant more by "assurance" than this; but this doctrine, so far as it went, was one which they preached. The next point was the charge that they were Antinomians, because they preached justification by faith only. To this they replied: "Can any one preach otherwise who agrees with our Church and the scriptures?"

Bishop McTyeire says: "The doctrine of conscious conversion, and of a direct witness of the Spirit testifying to the heart of the believer that he is a child of God, was the doctrine which exposed the founder of Methodism to the opposition of the formalists of the church and the ridicule of the philosophists of the world."

John Wesley, the Fellow of Oxford, has been regen erated, and this salvation he tells everywhere, and this leaven in the lump is destined to trouble all England, and by and by the whole world.   Let the reader bear in mind the fact that Wesley tells "*where*" and "*when*" he was regenerated.   God's Spirit testified with his that he was a child of God.

About this time lay preaching began.   Charles Wesley frowned upon it; but John was away from home at the beginning of these "irregular proceedings."   Upon his return, his mother charged him to be careful and hear the young man before he said anything against it.   Wesley heard and was convinced that it was of God, and soon the Lord had raised up a large army of lay preachers who were a power in exhortation, song, and prayer; and by their help Wesley soon awakened England from her sleep and soon the New World heard the cry, "Salvation for all men from all sin in this life."

May 12, 1739, a piece of ground was procured near St. James' Churchyard, Broadmead.   Wesley at first did not intend to assume the responsibility of the building, so he appointed trustees; but his friends suggested that he could not control the building with the trustees, so he dismissed them and took charge.   Methodism now had two churches and a school house, access to the little "rooms" of the religious societies, halls, and all outside as a preaching place.   A high authority in Wesleyan history fixes July, 1740, as "in strict propriety the real commencement of the Methodist Societies."

Watson says in his Life of Wesley, page 76: "**About** this time he stated his doctrinal views in perhaps as clear a manner, though in a summary form, as at any period subsequently: 'A serious clergyman desired to know in what points we differed from the Church of England. I answered, to the best of my knowledge, in none; the doctrines we preach are the doctrines of the Church of England, indeed, the fundamental doctrines of the Church clearly laid down, both in her Prayers, Articles and Homilies.' He asked, 'In what points then do you differ from the other clergy of the Church of England?' I answered, 'In none from that part of the clergy who adhere to the doctrines of the Church; but from that part of the clergy who dissent from the Church (though they own it not) I differ in the points following: First. They speak of justification, either as the same thing with sanctification, or as something consequent upon it. I believe justification to be wholly distinct from sanctification, and necessarily antecedent to it. Secondly. They speak of our own holiness or good works as the cause of our justification, or that for the sake of which, on account of which, we are justified before God. I believe neither our own holiness nor good works are any part of the cause of our justification: but that the death and righteousness of Christ are the whole and sole cause of it, or that for the sake of which, on account of which, we are justified before God. Thirdly. They speak of good works as a condition of justification, necessarily previous to it. I believe no good work can be previous to justification, nor consequently a condition of it; but that we are justified (being till that hour ungodly, and therefore incapable of doing any good work) by faith alone; faith, without works; faith, though producing all, yet including no good works. Fourthly. They speak of sanctification, or holiness, as if it were an outward thing; as if it consisted chiefly, if not wholly, in these two points: 1. The doing no harm. 2. The doing good as it is called; that is, the using the means of grace, and helping our neighbors. I believe it to be an inward thing, namely, a participation of the Divine nature; the mind that was in Christ; or 'the renewal of our heart after the image of Him that created us.' Lastly. They speak of the new birth as an outward thing; as if it were no more than baptism, or, at most, a change from outward wickedness to outward goodness, from a vicious to what is called a virtuous life. I believe it to be an inward thing; a change from inward wickedness to inward goodness; an entire change of our inmost nature from the image of the devil, wherein we are born, to the image of God; a change from the love of the creature to the love of the Creator, from earthly and sensual to heavenly and holy affection; in a word, a change from the tempers of the spirits of darkness to those of the angels of God in heaven. There is therefore a wide, essential, fundamental, irreconcilable difference between us; so that if they speak the truth as it is in Jesus, I am found a false witness before God. But if I teach the way of God in truth, they are blind leaders of the blind.' "

Mrs. Wesley, the mother of Methodism, passed

away, and at her request the children gathered around her bed and sang a Psalm. Dr. Adam Clark said in reference to her: "Many daughters have done excellently, but thou excellest them all."

Wesley parted with his Moravian friends because they differed in some points on regeneration, etc. Whitefield and Wesley disagreed because Whitefield taught the doctrine of Calvinism; but Whitefield in his will requested that Wesley preach his funeral sermon.

Wesley provided for Christian fellowship by organizing Love Feasts, Bands, and Class Meetings. In 1740 the watch night services began. The Kingswood colliers had been in the habit before their conversion of watching the old year out and the new year in with riot and revelings, and now they spent it in song and praise. He visited his old home and preached to thousands of people from his father's tombstone. He said: "I believe I did more good preaching the three days from my father's tombstone than the three years I preached in his pulpit."

Wesley now took another step forward—the first Annual Conference. "He had been pursuing his itinerant course for five years and now had in connection with him forty-five preachers, including a half dozen ministers of the Establishment who co-operated with him."

This first conference was a meeting of his lay "helpers," or associates, and the pious clergymen who had sympathized with him. He says: "In 1744 I wrote to several clergymen, and to all who then served me as sons in the gospel, desiring them to meet me in

London, and to give me their advice concerning the
best method of carrying on the work of God." This
original conference was held at "the Foundry" in
London, and began June 25th. Those present were
John Wesley, Charles Wesley, John Hodges, rector o.
Wenvo; Henry Piers, vicar of Bexley; Samuel Tayloi,
vicar of Quinton; and John Meriton, a clergyman from
the Isle of Man; Thomas Richards, Thomas Maxfield,
John Bennett, and John Downes were the helpers or
lay preachers present. On the day before the conference commenced, besides the ordinary preaching service, a Love Feast was held, and during the day the
Lord's Supper was administered to the whole London
Society, now numbering between two and three thousand members. The sessions were held by agreement
from Monday, June 25th, till the end of the week.
Great precaution was taken by Wesley in enacting
suitable rules for the discussions of the conference. It
was decided to check no one either by word or look,
even though he should say what is quite wrong; to
beware of making haste, of showing or indulging any
impatience, whether of delay or contradiction; that
every question proposed be fully debated and "bolted
to the bran." Preliminaries having been arranged
and earnest prayers offered, the design of the meeting
was proposed under three heads, namely, to consider:
1. What to teach. 2. How to teach. 3. What to do;
that is, how to regulate our doctrine, discipline, and
practice. Under the first head the conversation was
continued throughout this and the following day, and
embraced the leading doctrines of the gospel, such as

justification, saving faith, imputed righteousness, and sanctification.

They then took up discipline. The general rules were read, and by the time adjournment was reached they not only understood each other, but were of one mind and heart. The spirit and substance of the compact made between the founder of Methodism and his preachers are contained in the rule of Enlistment into the heroic order of itinerants, adopted at their first conference.

The next conference met at Bristol with fewer clergy and more preachers. "We had our second conference," says Wesley, "with as many of the preachers who labor in the word as could be present." On this occasion the theological doctrines mooted at the first conference were carefully reviewed, the opinions then given, and the forms of expression in which they were conveyed, were now very carefully scrutinized and in some cases modified.

In regard to the suggestion that the Methodists might ultimately become a distinct sect, Wesley said to Charles: "Church or no church, we must attend to the work of saving souls. I neither set it up nor pull it down, but lets you and I build the City of God."

At the third conference (1746) the call and the qualification to preach were carefully considered and defined; and this important item of Methodist economy was then determined as we now have it in answer to the question, "How shall we try those who think they are moved by the Holy Ghost and called of God to

2

preach?'' At this conference also the circuits were mapped out and first published, seven in number.

About this time Count Zinzendorf directed the publication of an advertisement, declaring that he and his people had no connection with John and Charles Wesley, and concluded with a prophecy, ''That they would soon run their heads against a wall.'' On this Mr. Wesley contents himself with only remarking: ''We will not if we can help it.'' This estrangement was caused in part by Wesley taking issue with Zinzendorf because he taught that a believer is not fully regenerated until he is ''holy in heart.''

Mr. Wesley had occasionally employed himself in writing and getting printed small religious tracts, many thousands of which were distributed. This was revived with vigor on his return to London this year; and he thus by his example was probably the first to apply, on any large scale, this important means of usefulness to the reformation of the people. Wesley's publications were small and cheap, but they had an immense circulation and left a profit; this brought into Wesley's hands a large amount of money. He says: ''If I leave behind me ten pounds (above my debts and my books, or what may happen to be due on the account of them), you and all mankind bear witness against me that I have died a thief and a robber.'' Bishop McTyeire adds: ''The state of his affairs at his death justified this pledge.''

''Charles Wesley's happy marriage,'' says Bishop McTyeire, ''appears to have been the means of deepening his brother's conviction that it was not good for man to be alone." The object of his choice was a widow, Grace Murray. Her ability to be useful recommended her to wider services. He proposed marriage to her and she declared her willingness to go with him to the ends of the earth. But friends objected to their marriage, and she married one of Wesley's preachers, a Mr. Bennett. This is said to have been Wesley's greatest sorrow. About two years after this he was married to Mrs. Vizelle, a rich widow, but she proved no help to Wesley.

In 1752 Philip Embury was converted under Wesley's ministry. In 1760 Philip and his family, two of his brothers and their families, Paul Heck and Barbara, his wife, with a goodly company of their countrymen, emigrated to New York. On John street, in 1768, the first Wesleyan Chapel was built.

It is maintained by some that Robert Strawbridge preached the first sermon, formed the first society, and built the first meeting house for Methodism in Maryland and in America, at least three years before Wesley Chapel in John street was erected. Doctor Buckley, in his History of Methodism, page 114, says: "Doctor George E. Crook, of Drew Theological Seminary, has a letter in which Bishop Asbury states that Methodism was established in this country about the year 1770."

At the conference held in London a new circuit appears on the list, "No. 50 America." Boardman and Pilmoore are the preachers. Wesley and other presbyters ordained Asbury and Coke as superintendents in America.

Bishop McTyeire says: "About the year 1763 a

deep wave of revival passed over the societies. The peculiar work of the Spirit seemed to be what St. Paul calls the 'Perfecting of the Saints.' Many were awakened and converted, but the work of sanctification engaged preachers and people in a special manner.''

Visiting Ireland in July, Wesley records: ''I found three or four and forty in Dublin who seemed to enjoy the pure love of God. At least forty of these had been set at liberty within four months. Some others who had received the same blessing had removed to other parts. A large number had found 'remission of sins.' ''

In September he was in the west of England, where he writes: ''The more I converse with the believers in Cornwall, the more I am convinced that they have sustained great loss for want of hearing the doctrine of Christian Perfection clearly and strongly enforced.'' The bare word perfection, produced criticism and jests on the part of some who should have known its Bible origin.

To a doubting, if not a backslidden preacher, Wesley wrote at a later day: ''Many think they are justified, and are not; but we can not infer that none are justified. So neither, if many think they are perfected in love, and are not, will it follow that none are so? Blessed be God, though we set a hundred enthusiasts aside, we are still 'encompassed' with a cloud of witnesses, who have testified, and do testify, in life and in death, that perfection which I have taught for these forty years.

"This perfection can not be a delusion, unless the Bible be a delusion, too; I mean loving God with all our hearts, and our neighbor as ourselves. I pin down all its opposers to this definition of it. No evasion! No shifting the question: Where is the delusion of this? Either you received this love or you did not. If you did, dare you call it a delusion? If you received anything else, it does not at all affect the question."

In 1759 Wesley published "Thoughts on Christian Perfection." His sermon eighteen years before on the same subject, thus opens: "There is scarce any expression in Holy Writ which has given more offense than this. The word 'perfect' is what many can not bear. The very sound of it is an abomination to them; and whoever preaches perfection (as the phrase is), that it is attainable in this life, runs great hazard of being accounted by them worse than a heathen and a Publican."

"Wesley's Christian Perfection seized him like some invisible power, and dominated his whole being; he would not be diverted therefrom; he wrote about it, he sang it, it was up for review at each yearly conference. His profession of it is clear and emphatic, as it is beautiful; he encouraged those who professed it." Some have questioned Wesley's professing the experience of "Entire Sanctification." The following testimony is enough to settle the question for all time:

"In 1729 my brother Charles and I, reading the Bible, saw we could not be saved without holiness, followed after it, and incited others to do so. In 1737, we saw that this holiness comes by faith.   In 1738 we saw likewise that men are justified before they are sanctified.

"You have over and over denied instantaneous sanctification, but I have known and taught it above these twenty years.   I have continually testified for these five and twenty years, in private and public that we are sanctified as well as justified by faith. . . . Within five weeks five in our band received the 'second blessing.'" . . . "This morning one found peace and one the 'second blessing.'" . . . "Insist everywhere on full salvation received now by faith.   Press the instantaneous blessing." . . . "Let all our preachers make a point of preaching perfection to believers, constantly, strongly, explicitly." . . . "If you speak only faintly and indirectly none will be offended and none profited; but if you speak out, although some will probably be angry, yet others will soon find the power of God unto salvation."

"Many years since I saw without holiness no man shall see the Lord.   I began by following after it, and inciting all with whom I had any intercourse to do the same.   Ten years after, God gave me a clearer view than I had before of the way how to attain it, namely, by faith in the Son of God. And immediately I declared to all, WE ARE SAVED FROM SIN, WE ARE MADE HOLY BY FAITH. This I testified in private, in public, in print, and God confirmed it by a thousand witnesses."   (Works, Vol. 7, page 38.)

"In the evening, while I was reading prayers at Snowfield, I found such light and strength as I never remember to have had before. I waked the next morning, by the grace of God, in the same spirit; and about 8 o'clock, being with two or three that believed in Jesus, I felt such an awe and tender sense of the presence of God as greatly confirmed me therein; so that God was with me all day long. I sought and found him in every place, and could truly say, when I lay down at night, now I have lived a day."—Journal, December 23, 1744.

John Wesley died the second day of March, 1791, exclaiming, "The best of all is, God is with us."

Southey said: "I consider him the most influential mind of the last century, the man who will have produced the greatest results a century hence."

Dean Stanley says; "No man has risen in the Methodist Societies equal to their founder John Wesley."

Said Dobbins, of the Church of England: "A greater poet may arise than Homer or Milton, a greater theologian than Calvin, a greater philosopher than Bacon, a greater dramatist than any of ancient or modern fame, *a greater revivalist of the churches than John Wesley—NEVER.*"

Doctor H. T. Hudson says: "Though not a century and a half have elapsed since the founder of the Methodist Church died, yet no less than '*fifteen millions*' of persons, including communicants and adherents to his system, are his followers."

The following is the inscription on the marble tab·
let erected to his memory in the City Road Chapel:

Sacred to the Memory
Of the REV. JOHN WESLEY, M. A.
Sometime Fellow of Lincoln College, Oxford:
A Man in Learning and Sincere Piety
Scarcely inferior to any;
In Zeal, Ministerial Labours, and Extensive Usefulness,
Superior, perhaps, to all Men,
Since the days of St. Paul.
Regardless of Fatigue, personal Danger, and Disgrace,
He went out into the highways and hedges
Calling Sinners to Repentance,
And Publishing the Gospel of Peace.
He was the Founder of the Methodist Societies,
And the chief Promoter and Patron
Of the Plan of Itinerant Preaching,
Which he extended through Great Britain and Ireland,
The West Indies, and America,
With unexampled Success.
He was born the 17th of June, 1703;
And died the 2d of March, 1791,
In sure and certain hope of Eternal Life,
Through the Atonement and Mediation of a Crucified Saviour.
He was sixty-five Years in the Ministry,
And fifty-two an Itinerant Preacher:
He lived to see, in these Kingdoms only,
About three hundred Itinerant,
And one thousand Local Preachers,
Raised up from the midst of his own People;
And eighty thousand Persons in the Societies under his care.
His Name will be ever had in grateful Remembrance
By all who rejoice in the universal Spread
Of the Gospel of Christ.
Soli Deo Gloria.
(Glory to God alone.)

CHAPTER II.

Wesley's Plain Account of Christian Perfection.

BY REV JOHN J. TIGERT, D. D.

Please allow a deeply interested reader of the controversies about Christian Perfection that are now filling some of our church papers, including the *Nashville Advocate*, to submit an analysis of Wesley's doctrine, with Mr. Wesley's own scriptural proofs of it. In so doing, he desires to avoid taking even the smallest part in the current controversies; and, as he proposes to confine himself to the statement of a single fact—namely, what Mr. Wesley actually taught in his "Plain Account"—no room for difference of opinion will be made, unless the accuracy of the analysis herewith submitted is called in question. The writer will use all the caution at his command in avoiding error, and, should he fall into any grievous mistake, will gratefully acknowledge it when it is pointed out. Before proceeding to the analysis, it is necessary to state that the dissection of Mr. Wesley's luminous little work herewith presented follows very closely a similar analysis which appeared in the department of the *Methodist Review* (New York) entitled the "Itinerant's Club," in July last. Now for the analysis:

I. What Christian Perfection is not—and what it is.

1. It is not perfection of knowledge; nor is it freedom from mistakes, infirmities and temptations; nor

is it a perfection that is incapable of further increase. It is not a state in which the atonement is no longer needed: nor is it an experience which, once professed, can never be lost.

2. It is more than freedom from the commission of actual sin. Even babes in Christ are perfect in this sense. It is freedom from evil desires and tempers, from fear, pride, self-will, and anger. It involves the renewal of the soul in the image of God and the purification of the heart by faith. The Bible expressions descriptive of it are such as these: "walking in the light;" "abiding in Christ;" "rejoicing evermore·" "loving God with all the heart, mind, soul and strength;" and "perfect love."

II. Do the scriptures teach that this is an experience designed for all the children of God?

Yes: (1) by promises; (2) by prayer; (3) by commands; and (4) by example.

1. Psa. 130:8; Ezek. 36:25, 29; Deut. 30:6; II Cor. 7:1; I John 3:8; Eph. 5:15-27; Rom. 8:3,4.

2. John 17:20-23; Eph. 3:14-19; I Thess. 5:23.

3. Matt. 5:48; 22:37.

4. I John 4:17.

III. (1) When and (2) How may we obtain the blessing of Christian Perfection?

1. Not so early as justification (Heb. 6:1); but not necessarily so late as at death (Phil. 3:15). This follows, too, from the nature of commands, which are given not to the dead but to the living. Compare also these passages: Titus 2:11-14; Luke 1:69-75; I John 1:7, 9; 4:17. These passages teach complete deliver-

ance from sin in this world and in this life. Sanctification begins at justification. It proceeds by a gradual work of mortification of sin in the members, which is often of long duration; but this may be cut short in an instantaneous death to sin.

2. Not by careless indifference nor indolent inactivity; but by universal, zealous, watchful self-denial and obedience; more especially by prayer, fasting, and the constant use of all the means of grace; finally, the blessing is received instantaneously and by simple faith.

IV. How may one know that he has obtained the blessing?

1. When he has had a deep and clear conviction of inbred sin, followed by a consciousness of total death to sin and of renewal in the Divine image.

2. By the direct witness of the Spirit to his sanctification: I John 3:24; 5:19; I Cor. 2:12; Rom. 8:16. By the fruits of the Spirit—love, joy, peace, patience, fidelity, temperance, etc.

V. Is it the duty of a possessor of the experience also to be a professor of it?

At first he could hardly refrain. Later he could refrain.

1. It is advisable not to speak of it to them who know not God, nor to others without a special reason.

2. It should be professed cautiously, reverently, and with the deepest humility, lest one appear to boast.

3. By entire silence, crosses might be avoided, but this could not be done with a good conscience.

VI. May one in the enjoyment of Christian Perfection enjoy also the pleasures of sense?

1. Yes, but he needs them not to make him happy.

2. While he uses them, he does not seek them.

3. He is sparing in their use, and never for the sake of pleasure itself.

VII. Can we recognize this grace in another?

Not infallibly; but reasonable proofs must satisfy, *e. g.*, a previous exemplary life and truthful character, a straight-forward account of the experience, and a holy and unblamable life.

VIII. How shall the preacher treat professors of Christian Perfection?

1. He should talk with them freely and examine them carefully about their experience, avoiding all harshness, sternness, and contempt. He must not make himself an inquisitor-general or peremptory judge of the deep things of God.

2. He must labor to prevent the unjust or unkind treatment of those who profess it.

3. He must exhort them to pray fervently that God would show them all that is in their heart.

IX. What advice may be given professors of Christian Perfection?

1. Watch against spiritual pride.

2. Beware of enthusiasm, fanaticism and schism.

3. Beware of making void the law through faith.

4. Beware of bigotry, self-indulgence, and of sins of omission.

5. Be exemplary in all things, especially the little things, for in these lie both dangers and blessings.

CHAPTER III.

Mr. Wesley's Journal on Entire Sanctification.

BY REV B. F. GASSAWAY.

Mr. Wesley began his Journal October 14, 1735. The closing date is October 24, 1790. Thus we see that the Journal covers a space of fifty-five years, and the last entry was made only a few months before Mr. Wesley's death.

It has been frequently asserted that Mr. Wesley changed his views on the doctrine of sanctification before his death. I put in evidence his Journal, and will give extracts, in his own words, in chronological order, to show that he did not change his views.

September 13, 1739.—Noting the difference between his views and those of some others, he says "They speak of justification, either as the same thing with sanctification, or as something consequent upon it. I believe justification to be wholly distinct from sanctification and necessarily antecedent to it. * * *

"They speak of sanctification (or holiness) as if it were an outward thing, as if it consisted chiefly, if not wholly, in those two points, 1. The doing no harm; 2. The doing good, (as it is called) that is, the using the means of grace, and helping our neighbor.

"I believe it to be an inward thing, namely, the life of God in the soul of man; a participation of the Divine nature; the mind that was in Christ; or the renewal of our heart, after the image of Him that created us.''

Every succeeding entry in his Journal is in harmony with this statement.

''May 5, 1740.—I expounded those words, 'I write unto you, little children, because your sins are forgiven you:' and described the state of those who have forgiveness of sins, but have not yet a clean heart.''

Mr. Wesley makes the clear distinction between ''forgiveness of sins'' and ''a clean heart.''

''June 24, 1740.—* * * Your finding sin remaining in you still, is no proof that you are not a believer. Sin does remain in one that is justified, though it has not dominion over him. For he has not a clean heart at first, neither are 'all things' as yet 'become new.' But fear not, though you have an evil heart. Yet a little while, and you shall be endued with power from on high, whereby you may 'purify yourselves, even as He is pure;' and be 'holy, as He which hath called you is holy'.''

Here Mr. Wesley asserts that ''sin does remain in one that is justified,'' and gives holiness or entire sanctification, as a subsequent or second blessing, for a remedy.

August 10, 1740.—''From Gal. 6:3, I earnestly warned all who had tasted of the grace of God, 1. Not to think they were justified, before they had a clear assurance that God had forgiven their sins; bringing in a calm peace, the love of God, and dominion over all sin. 2. Not to think themselves anything after they had this; but to press forward for the prize of

their high calling, even a clean heart, throughly renewed after the image of God, in righteousness and
true holiness.''

Can language be plainer than this? From this
position Mr. Wesley never varied.

Under date of March 6, 1760, Mr. Wesley gives the
experiences of two of his members. 1st. They were
justified clearly. 2nd. They were sanctified wholly.
3rd. Their lives were in harmony with their professions. Mr. Wesley adds: "I observe the spirit and
experience of these two run exactly parallel. Constant communion with God the Father and the Son
fills their hearts with humble love. Now this is what
I always did, and do now, mean by perfection. And
this I believe many have attained, on the same evidence that I believe many are justified. May God
increase their number a thousand fold!''

Mr. Wesley prayed God to increase the number of
such professions. It is fashionable now to discourage
such professions, and in many places to discountenance
them altogether, and that, too, in the church which,
under God, Mr. Wesley founded.

"March 12, 1760.—Having desired that as many as
could of the neighboring towns, who believed they
were saved from sin, would meet me, I spent the greatest
part of this day in examining them one by one. The
testimony of some I could not receive; but concerning
the far greatest part, it is plain, (unless they could be
supposed to tell willful and deliberate lies,) 1. That
they feel no inward sin; and, to the best of their
knowledge, commit no outward sin. 2. That they see

and love God every moment, and pray, rejoice, give thanks evermore. 3. That they have constantly as clear a witness from God of sanctification as they have of justification. Now in this I do rejoice, and will rejoice, call it what you please; and I would to God thousands had experienced this much; let them afterward experience as much more as God pleases.''

See how Mr Wesley fosters the experience, and rejoices in its spread! Is there no one to bear his mantle now?

' May 21, 1761.—Among the believers, who met in the evening. God had kindled a vehement desire of His full salvation. Inquiring how it was that, in all these parts, we have scarce one living witness of this, I constantly received, from every person, one and the same answer:—'We see now, we sought it by works; we thought it was to come gradually; we never expected to receive it in a moment, by faith, as we did justification.' What wonder is it, then, that you have been fighting all these years as one that beateth the air?''

Notice that Mr. Wesley declares that those who seek sanctification by ''works,'' and expect to receive it ''gradually'' only ''beat the air.'' The ''air beating plan'' is quite fashionable at this age of the world, but, as in 1761, ''living witnesses'' to sanctification by this plan are conspicuously absent. ''Instantaneously by faith,'' is the Wesleyan doctrine.

''November 29, 1761 —We had a comfortable love-feast, at which several declared the blessings they had found lately. We need not be careful by what *name* to call them, while the *thing* is beyond dispute. Many have, and many do daily experience an unspeakable change. After being deeply convinced of *"inbred sin,"* particularly pride, anger, self-will, and unbelief, in a moment they feel all faith and love; no pride, no self-will, or anger; and from that moment they have continual fellowship with God, always rejoicing, praying, and giving thanks. Whoever ascribes such a change to the devil, I ascribe it to the Spirit of God: and I say, let whoever feels it wrought, cry to God that it may continue; which it will, if he walks closely with God; otherwise it will not.''

What a plain statement of the Wesleyan doctrine! From this I find no variation from beginning to ending of the Journal.

For lack of space I omit many entries, in harmony with those already given, and pass on to 1762.

"September 15.—* * * The more I converse with the believers in Cornwall, the more I am convinced that they have sustained great loss for want of hearing the doctrine of Christian perfection clearly and strongly enforced. I see wherever this is not done, the believers grow dead and cold. Nor can this be prevented, but by keeping up in them an hourly expectation of being perfected in love. I say an hourly expectation; for to expect it at death, or sometime hence, is much the same as not expecting it at all."

How exactly is this opposed to what our great men teach us now!

"October 28, 1762. — * * * Many years ago my brother frequently said, 'Your day of Pentecost is not

3

fully come; but I doubt not it will; and you will then hear of persons sanctified, as frequently as you do now of persons justified.' Any unprejudiced reader may observe, that it was now fully come. And accordingly we did hear of persons sanctified, in London, and most other parts of England, and in Dublin, and many other parts of Ireland, as frequently as of persons justified; although instances of the latter were far more frequent than they had been for twenty years before.''

That which Mr. Wesley denominated his "day of Pentecost" in 1762, has come to be regarded, by many in 1900, one hundred and thirty-eight years later, as a "day of calamity" to Methodism. Evidently *somebody* has changed "views;" but, as the reader can see, *not* Mr. Wesley—up to 1762.

October 29, 1762, Mr. Wesley wrote his celebrated letter to Maxfield. In it occurs this paragraph:—"I like your doctrine of Perfection, or pure love; love excluding sin; your insisting that it is merely by faith; that consequently it is instantaneous (though preceded and followed by a gradual work): and that it may be now, at this instant."

Thus Mr. Wesley stands by the truth, while he points out (in other paragraphs), and condemns the error. Many of our Methodist readers, in this day, condemn the statements of this paragraph of Mr. Wesley as untruth, and class those who teach doctrines in harmony with this Wesleyan statement with Maxfield, Bell and Company. These are the men who tell us that Mr Wesley "changed his views;" but they fail to give us the volume and page of his writings where the change is noted.

"March 28, 1763.—I retired to Lewisham, and wrote the sermon on 'Sin in Believers,' in order to re-move a mistake which some were laboring to propa-gate,—that there is no sin in any that are justified."

If Mr. Wesley could return to earth, and take a survey of Methodism at this time, he would find the great Southern Methodist Publishing House sending out to the church, Boland's "Problem of Methodism," in which this "mistake" of "No Sin in Believers," is laboriously propagated, and he would find hundreds of Methodist preachers (some in high positions), maintain-ing the same error. My! My! what a "shaking among the dry bones" if Mr. Wesley could come back and ex-ercise his old time power for a brief season! Many a preacher, now in high position, would be "out of a job."

"June 6, 1763.—* * * A little after preaching one came to me who believed God had just set her soul at full liberty. She had been clearly justified long before; but said, the change she now experienced was ex-tremely different from what she experienced then; as different as the noonday light from that of daybreak; that she now felt her soul all love, and quite swallowed up in God. Now suppose, ten weeks or ten months hence, this person should be cold or dead, shall I say, 'She *deceived* herself; this was merely the work of her own imagination?' Not at all. I have no right so to judge, nor authority so to speak. I will rather say, 'She was *unfaithful* to the grace of God, and so *cast away* what was *really given*.'"

Remember this was after the Maxfield trouble, and still Mr. Wesley maintains the doctrine of entire sanctification as a second work of grace.

"June 12, 1763. * * * At every place I endeavored to settle the minds of the poor people, who had been not a little harassed by a new doctrine which honest Jonathan C——— and his converts had industriously propagated among them,—that 'there is *no sin* in believers; but the moment we believe, sin is destroyed root and branch.' I trust this plague also is stayed." All the "honest (?) Jonathan C———'s" are not yet dead, and still near the twentieth century, they "industriously" propagate the heresy of "*no sin* in believers."

"November 15, 1763.—* * * Here I stood and looked back on the late occurrences. Before Thomas Welsh left England, God began that great work which has continued ever since without any considerable intermission. During the whole time, many have been convinced of sin, many justified, and many backsliders healed. But the peculiar work of this season has been, what St. Paul calls 'the perfecting of the saints.' Many persons in London, in Bristol, in York, and in various parts both of England and Ireland, have experienced so deep and universal a change, as it had not entered into their hearts to conceive. After a deep conviction of inbred sin, of their total fall from God, they have been so filled with faith and love (and generally in a moment), that sin vanished, and they found from that time, no pride, anger, desire, or unbelief. They could rejoice evermore, pray without ceasing and in every thing give thanks. Now, whether we call this the destruction or suspension of sin, it is a glorious work of God; such a work as, considering both the depth and extent of it, we never saw in these kingdoms before.''

No decrying the truth on account of Maxfield's defection, but a continued encouragement and commendation of the ''peculiar work'' of ''perfecting the saints.''

''April 4, 1764.—In the morning I explained at large the nature of Christian Perfection. Many who had doubted of it before were fully satisfied. It remains only to *experience* what we believe.'' No indication of ''change of views'' yet.

''April 21, 1764.—I visited one who was ill in bed; and, after having buried seven of her family in six months, had just heard that the eighth, her beloved husband, was cast away at sea. I asked, 'Do not you fret at any of those things?' She said, with a lovely smile upon her pale cheek, 'Oh, no! How can I fret at any thing which is the will of God? Let Him take all besides; He has given me Himself. I love, I praise Him every moment.' Let any that doubts of Christian Perfection look on such a spectacle as this! One in such circumstances rejoicing evermore, and continually giving thanks.'' Mr. Wesley certainly had not ''changed views'' when he wrote this entry.

''October 22, 1764.—I was much refreshed by hearing the experience of Mary G———, once a determined enemy to the doctrine of perfection, opposing it with great eagerness and many reasons; but now a happy witness of it." And this "refreshed" Mr. Wesley. There are many among us at this day who are not "refreshed" by such testimony.

In a letter to a friend dated May 14, 1765, Mr. Wesley writes:—" * * * January 1, 1733, I preached the sermon on the Circumcision of the Heart; which contains all that I now teach concerning salvation from all sin, and loving God with an undivided heart. * * * Now, whether you desire and expect this blessing or not, is it not an astonishing thing that you, or any man living, should be disgusted at me for expecting it; and that they should persuade one another that this hope is 'subversive of the very foundations of Christian experience?' Why then, whoever retains it cannot possibly have any Christian experience at all. Then, my brother, Mr. Fletcher, and I, and twenty thousand more, who seem both to fear and to love God, are, in reality, children of the devil, and in the road to eternal damnation!"

Mr. Wesley gives no sign of "change of views" to this date; but many alas! now hold with Mr. Wesley's "friend"—that the doctrine of sanctification is "subversive of the foundation of Christian experience."

"September 30, 1765.—Monday, and the two following days, I examined the society at Bristol, and was surprised to find fifty members fewer than I left in it last October. One reason is, Christian Perfection has been little insisted on; and wherever this is not done, be the preachers ever so eloquent, there is little increase, either in the number or the grace of the hearers."

Not much evidence of change in this.

"December 29, 1766.—At five in the morning I again began a course of sermons on Christian Perfection; if haply that thirst after it might return which was so general a few years ago."

Mr. Wesley wanted the "thirst after it" to "return."

In a letter to a friend dated August 27, 1768, Mr. Wesley says:—" * * * It is true still further, that many serious, humble, sober-minded believers, who do feel the love of God sometimes, and do then rejoice in God their Savior, cannot be content with this; but pray continually, that He would enable them to love and rejoice in the Lord always. And no fact under heaven is more undeniable, than that God does answer this prayer; that He does, for the sake of His Son, and through the power of His Spirit, enable one and another so to do. It is also a plain fact, that this power does commonly overshadow them in an instant; and that from that time they enjoy that inward and outward holiness, to which they were utter strangers before. * * * Blessed be God, though we set a hundred enthusiasts aside we are still 'encompassed with a cloud of witnesses,' who have testified and do testify, in life and in death, that perfection which I have taught these forty years!"

Those who think Mr. Wesley "changed his views," will find no comfort here.

"March 15, 1770.—I met the select society. How swiftly God has deepened His work in these! * * * The account all whom I had time to examine gave, was scriptural and rational; and, suppose they spoke true, they are witnesses to the Perfection which I preach."

"October 22, 1772. * * * A large congregation was present at five in the morning, many of whom were athirst for full salvation. I talked with twelve of them, who seemed to have experienced it. This is genuine Christianity!"

Mr. Wesley termed it "genuine Christianity." No "change of views" to this date.

"January 28, 1774.—I buried the remains of that venerable mother in Israel, Bilhah Aspernell. She found peace with God in 1738; and soon after, purity of heart. From that time she walked in the light of God's countenance, day and night, without the least intermission."

What a good place for Mr. Wesley to have mentioned any "change" in his "views" on the second blessing!

October 24, 1774.—Mr. Wesley gives the experience of Susannah Spencer. I give a short extract: "From the very time of her justification, she clearly saw the necessity of being wholly sanctified; and found an unspeakable hunger and thirst after the full image of God; and in the year 1772, God answered her desire. The second change was wrought in as strong and distinct a manner as the first had been."

Mr. Wesley still writes it "first" and "second."

"August 4, 1775.—I preached at Bradford, where the people are all alive. Many here have lately experienced the great salvation, and their zeal has been a general blessing. Indeed, this I always observe, wherever a work of sanctification breaks out, the whole work of God prospers. Some are convinced of sin, others justified, and all stirred up to greater earnestness for salvation."

No comfort here for the "change in view" brethren.

"April 26, 1776.—I preached in the new chapel at Eccleshall, to a people just sprung out of the dust, exceeding artless, and exceeding earnest; many of whom seemed to be already saved from sin. Oh, why do we not encourage all to expect this blessing every hour, from the moment they are justified!"

No change of view yet, and the date is 1776.

"August 15, 1776.—Here I found the plain reason why the work of God had gained no ground in this circuit all the year. The preachers had given up the Methodist testimony. Either they did not speak of perfection at all (the peculiar doctrine committed to our trust), or they spoke of it in general terms, without urging the believers to 'go on unto perfection' and to expect it every moment. And wherever this is not earnestly done, the work of God does not prosper."

What an impeachment of numbers of the leading men in Methodism at this time! If Mr. Wesley did *not* change, they are fighting against the "peculiar doctrine committed to our trust," and are engaged in an effort to tear down that which they vowed to defend.

"June 17, 1779.—I examined the society. In five years I found five members had been gained! * * * What then have our preachers been doing all this time? * * * When Mr. Brackenburg preached the old Methodist doctrine, one of them said, 'You must not preach such doctrine here. The doctrine of perfection is not calculated for the meridian of Edinburgh.' Waiving, then, all other hindrances, is it any wonder that the work of God has not prospered here?"

One thing is evident, if Mr. Wesley *did not* change his views from those expressed in his Journal, and if these "views" are to be considered as orthodox Wesleyan Methodist doctrine, then numbers of modern Methodists are not "Methodistic" in the Wesleyan meaning of the word.

"May 20, 1781. * * * In the afternoon I preached a funeral sermon for Mary Charlton, an Israelite indeed. From the hour that she first knew the pardoning love of God, she never lost sight of it for a moment. Eleven years ago she believed that God had cleansed her from all sin, and she showed that she had not believed in vain, by her holy and unblamable conversation."

Mr. Wesley still endorses the "second blessing" as late as 1781.

"April 3, 1786. * * * It is chiefly among these enormous mountains that so many have been awakened, justified, and soon after perfected in love."

The "first" and "second" are plain to be seen here.

"February 6, 1786.—Being the quarterly day for meeting the local preachers, between twenty and thirty of them met at West street, and opened their hearts to each other. Taking the opportunity of having them all together, at the watch-night, I strongly insisted on St. Paul's advice to Timothy, 'Keep that which is committed to thy trust;' particularly the doctrine of Christian Perfection, which God has peculiarly entrusted to the Methodists."

The same story, without "variableness, neither shadow of turning."

"March 13, 1790.—This week I visited the classes in Bristol. I wonder we do not increase in numbers, although many are convinced, many justified, and a few perfected in love."

Within one year of Mr. Wesley's death, and yet the distinction is noted between the "justified," and those "perfected in love."

"September 9, 1790 —I read over the experience of Joseph Humphreys, the first lay preacher that assisted me in England, in 1738. From his own mouth I learn that he was perfected in love, and so continued for at least a twelvemonth. Afterward he turned Calvinist, and joined Mr. Whitefield. * * * In a while he renounced Mr. Whitefield, and was ordained a Presbyterian minister. At last he received Episcopal ordination. He then scoffed at inward religion; and when reminded of his own experience, replied, 'That was one of the foolish things which I wrote in the time of my madness!'"

While Mr. Wesley was entering in his Journal this account of his first lay preacher, in which is showed his defection from the doctrine of sanctification, how appropriate to have mentioned his own "change of views," *provided* there had been any change.

The first quotation from Mr. Wesley's Journal bears date September 13, 1739, and the last September 9, 1790, covering an interval of fifty-one years, and bringing us within a few months of the death of Mr. Wesley. Not a shadow of contradiction on the subject of sanctification occurs; on the contrary, consistency flows from beginning to end. If Mr. Wesley were alive now, with the same views he maintained when on earth, it is evident that numbers of Methodists would have to change *their* "views" in order to be in harmony with their founder; and it is equally evident that those who preach, teach, experience, and exemplify the doctrine of entire sanctification would hear from John Wesley, the father and founder of Methodism, "well done good and faithful servants."

CHAPTER IV.

John Wesley on Holiness.*

BY REV. H. C. MORRISON,
Editor Pentecostal Herald.

"But we do not know a single instance, in any place, of a person's receiving in one and the same moment remission of sins, the abiding witness of the Spirit, and a new and clean heart."

"We may learn the mischievousness of that opinion, that we are wholly sanctified when we are justified; that our hearts are then cleansed from all sin."

"I can not, therefore, by any means receive this assertion, that there is no sin in a believer from the moment he is justified:

1. Because it is contrary to the whole tenor of scripture.

2. Because it is contrary to the experience of the children of God.

3. Because it is absolutely new, never heard of in the world till yesterday."

"I have been lately thinking a good deal on one point, wherein, perhaps, we have all been wanting. We have not made it a RULE, AS SOON AS EVER PERSONS ARE JUSTIFIED, to remind them of 'going on unto perfection.' WHEREAS THIS IS THE VERY TIME PREFERABLE TO ALL OTHERS. They have then the simplicity of little children; and they are fervent in

*This is a collocation of extracts from Mr. Wesley's writings. The quotations can be relied upon, though the references are omitted. This chapter was published in the "Pentecostal Herald" several years ago.— EDITOR. (45)

spirit, **ready to** cut off a right hand or pluck out the right eye. But if we once suffer this fervor to subside, **we shall find** it hard enough to bring them again even **to this** point.''

''Everyone, though born of God in an instant, aye, and SANCTIFIED IN AN INSTANT, yet undoubtedly grows by slow degrees, both after the former and latter change: But it does not follow from thence that there may not be a considerable tract of time between the one and the other. A year or a month is the same with God as a thousand. It is therefore our duty to pray and look for this full salvation every day, every hour, every moment, without waiting until we have either done or suffered more.''

''Both my brother and I maintain that Christian perfection is that love of God and our neighbor which implies deliverance from all sin.''

''One perfected in love may grow in grace far swifter than he did before.''

''Though we watch and pray ever so much, we can not wholly cleanse either our hearts or hands. Most sure we can not, till it please our God to speak to our hearts again—to speak the SECOND time, 'Be clean;' and THEN ONLY THE LEPROSY IS CLEANSED. Then only the evil ROOT, the CARNAL MIND is destroyed; INBRED SIN subsists no more.''

''Inquiring (in 1761) how it was that in all these parts we had so few witnesses of full salvation, I constantly received one and the same answer: 'We see now we sought it by our WORKS; we thought it was to come GRADUALLY; we never expected it to come in a MO-

MENT, by simple faith, in the very same manner as we received justification.' What wonder is it then, that you have been fighting all these years as one that beateth the air?''

''You may obtain a growing victory over sin from the moment you are justified. But this is not enough. The body of sin, the carnal mind, must be destroyed; the old man must be slain, or we can not put on the new man, which is created after God (or which is the image of God) in righteousness and true holiness; and this is done in a moment. To talk of this work as being gradual, would be nonsense, as much as if we talked of gradual justification.''

''As to the manner, I believe this perfection is ALWAYS wrought in the soul by a simple act of faith; consequently in an instant. * * * Look for it every day, every hour, every moment. Why not this hour —this moment? Certainly you may look for it now, if you believe it is by faith. And by this token you may surely know whether you seek it by faith or by works. If by works, you want something to be done first before you are sanctified. You think, I must be or do thus and thus. Then you are seeking it by works unto this day. If you seek it by faith, you expect it as you are; and if as you are, then expect it now. It is important to observe that there is an inseparable connection between these three points—expect it by faith, expect it as you are, and expect it now. To deny one is to deny them all.''

''In London alone I found six hundred and fifty-two members of our Society, who were exceeding clear in their experience, and of whose testimony I could see no reason to doubt. * * * And every one of these (after the most careful inquiry, I have not found one exception either in Great Britain or Ireland, has declared that this deliverance from sin was instantaneous; that all the change was wrought in a moment. Had half of these, or one-third, or one in twenty, declared it was gradually wrought within, I should have believed this in regard to them, and thought some were gradually sanctified, and some instantaneously. But as I have not found, in so long a space of time (more than thirty years) a single person speaking thus; as all, who believe they are sanctified, declare with one voice, that the change was wrought in a moment; I can not but believe that sanctification is commonly, if not always, an instantaneous work."

"The voice of God to your soul is, Believe and be saved. Faith is the condition, and the only condition of sanctification, exactly as it is in justification. No man is sanctified till he believes; every man when he believes is sanctified."

"But what is that faith whereby we are sanctified, saved from sin and perfected in love? This faith is a divine evidence or conviction,—

1. That God hath promised this sanctification in the Holy Scriptures.

2. It is a divine evidence or conviction that what God hath promised he is able to perform.

3. It is a divine evidence or conviction that he is able and willing to do it NOW.

4. To this confidence that God is able and willing to

sanctify us now, there needs to be added one thing more—a divine evidence or conviction that he doth do it now."

"The repentance consequent upon justification is widely different from that which is antecedent to it. This implies no guilt, no sense of condemnation, no consciousness of the wrath of God, or any fear that hath torment. It is properly a conviction, wrought by the Holy Ghost, of the sin which still remains in our heart; of the carnal mind, which 'does still remain (as our church speaks) even in them that are regenerate,' although it does no longer reign; it has not now dominion over them."

"But how do you know that you are sanctified, saved from your inbred corruption? I can know it no otherwise than I know that I am justified. 'Hereby know we that we are of God,' in either sense, 'by the Spirit he hath given us.' We know it by the witness and by the fruit of the Spirit."

"None, therefore, ought to believe that the work is done till there is added the testimony of the Spirit witnessing his entire sanctification AS CLEARLY AS HIS JUSTIFICATION."

."Some have the testimony both of their sanctification and justification, without any intermission at all, which, I presume, more might have, did they walk humbly and closely with God."

"The mind itself may be perplexed, and pressed down by heaviness and anguish, even to agony, while the heart cleaves to God by perfect love, and the will is wholly resigned to him. Was it not so with the Son of God himself?"

4

"One reason why those who are saved from sin should freely DECLARE IT to believers is, because nothing is a stronger incitement for them to seek after the same blessing. And we ought, by EVERY POSSIBLE MEANS, TO PRESS EVERY SERIOUS believer to forget the things which are behind, and with all earnestness go on to perfection."

"You can never speak too strongly or explicitly upon the head of Christian perfection. If you speak only faintly and indirectly, none will be offended and none profited. But if you speak out, although some will probably be angry, yet others will soon find the power of God unto salvation."

"It requires a great degree of watchfulness to retain the perfect love of God; and one great means of retaining it, is frankly to declare what God has given you, and earnestly to exhort all the believers you meet with to follow after full salvation."

"But is there no way to prevent these crosses which usually fall on those who speak of being thus saved? It seems they can not be prevented altogether while so much of nature remains even in believers. But something might be done if the preacher in every place would: (1) Talk freely with all who speak thus; and, (2) Labor to prevent the unjust or unkind treatment of those in favor of whom there is reasonable proof."

"I am afraid Christian perfection will be forgotten. Encourage Richmond Blackwell and Mr. Colley to speak plainly. A general faintness in this respect has fallen on the whole Kingdom. Sometimes I seem almost weary of striving against the stream of both preachers and people.''

''I hope he is not ashamed to preach full salvation, receivable now, by faith. This is the word which God will always bless and which the devil peculiarly hates; therefore, he is constantly stirring up both his own children, and the weak children of God, against it.''

''All our preachers should make a point of preaching perfection to believers, CONSTANTLY, STRONGLY, and EXPLICITLY; and ALL believers should mind this one thing, and continually agonize for it.''

''Those who love God with all their heart must expect much opposition from professors who have gone on for twenty years in an old beaten track, and fancy they are wiser than all the world. These always oppose the work of sanctification.''

''I preached at Bradford, where the people are all alive. Many here have lately experienced the great salvation, and their zeal has been a general blessing. Indeed, this I always observe, wherever a work of sanctification breaks out, the whole work of God prospers. Some are convinced of sin, others are justified, and all are stirred up to greater earnestness for salvation.''

But why multiply further quotations? Are not these enough? A thousand more which might be gleaned from Wesley's works could not make his views stronger than expressed herein. These extracts are taken from his Sermons, Journal, and Letters, and a few from other reliable sources.

In the face of all this, who will dare to rise up and say we teach a new doctrine, a modern heresy?

Let truth and honesty compel all to acknowledge that the teachings of the great holiness movement are at least Methodistic and Wesleyan, and then it remains to be proven that the position of Wesley and of Methodism is unscriptural.

Who will overthrow this grand doctrine of **Holiness** which God has so peculiarly and wonderfully **blessed?**

Brethren, we are founded on a rock: the wind can't wreck it, and the waves can't destroy the foundation. God is with us; He is in the great truth of holiness, and it shall prevail; yea, is prevailing.

Let holiness unto the Lord be the pass-word, and on with the revival.

The crown of life is almost in sight. PRESS ON WE ARE RIGHT.

CHAPTER V.

John Fletcher on Holiness.

BY REV. II. C. MORRISON,
Editor Pentecostal Herald.

"We do not deny that the remains of the CARNAL MIND still cleave to imperfect Christians." "This fault, corruption or infection, doth remain in them who are regenerated."

"It is the PURE love of God and man shed abroad in a faithful believer's heart by the Holy Ghost given unto him, to CLEANSE him, and to KEEP HIM CLEAN, 'from all the filthiness of the flesh and spirit,' and to enable him to 'fulfill the law of Christ,' according to the talents he is intrusted with, and the circumstances in which he is placed in this world."

"To say that the doctrine of Christian perfection supercedes the need of Christ's blood is not less absurd than to assert that the perfection of navigation renders the great deep a useless reservoir of waters."

"A perfect Christian grows far more than a feeble believer, whose growth is still OBSTRUCTED by the shady thorns of sin, and by the DRAWING SUCKERS OF INIQUITY."—Last Check, p. 499.

"It is, I think, allowed on all sides that 'we are saved,' that is sanctified, as well as justified, 'by faith.' Now, that particular height of sanctification, that full circumcision of the heart,' which certainly PURIFIES

the soul, springs from a peculiar DEGREE of saving
faith, and from a particular operation of the 'spirit of
burning;' a QUICK OPERATION THIS, which is compared to a baptism of fire, and proves sometimes so
sharp and searching, that it is as much as a healthy,
strong man can bear up under it.''—Last Check, p. 566.

"As when you reckon with your creditor or with
your host, and as, when you have paid all, you make
yourselves free, so now reckon with God.   Jesus has
paid all; and he hath paid for thee—hath purchased
thy pardon and holiness.   Therefore it is now God's
command, 'Reckon thyself dead unto sin;' and thou
art alive unto God from this hour.   Oh, begin, begin
to reckon now; fear not; believe, BELIEVE, BELIEVE,
and continue to BELIEVE every moment.   So shalt
thou continue free; for it is RETAINED as it is RE-
CEIVED, by faith alone.''—Journal of Mrs. H. A. Rogers, p, 137.

"Beware of looking for any peace or joy PREVIOUS
to your believing; and let this be uppermost in your
mind.''

A few brief extracts from Fletcher's testimony:

"I received this blessing (sanctification) four or five
times before, but I lost it by not observing the order
of God, who has told us, 'With the heart man believeth unto righteousness, and with the mouth confession
is made unto salvation.'   But the enemy offered his
bait under various colors, to keep me from a PUBLIC
DECLARATION of what my Lord had wrought.

"When I first received this grace, Satan bid me wait
a while, till I saw more of the fruits.   I resolved to do

so; but I soon began to doubt of the witness which before I had felt in my heart, and was in a little time sensible I had lost both.

"At another time I was prevailed upon to hide it by reasoning: 'How few even of the children of God will receive this testimony! many of them supposing even transgression of the Adamic law is sin; and therefore if I profess myself to be free from sin, all these will give my profession the lie, because I am not free in their sense; I am not free from ignorance, mistakes and various infirmities. I will therefore enjoy what God hath wrought in me, but I will not say I am perfect in love.' Alas, I soon found again, 'He that hideth his Lord's talent, and improveth it not, from that unprofitable servant shall be taken away even what he hath.'

"Now, my brethren, you see my folly; I have confessed it in your presence; and now I resolve before you all to confess my Master; I will confess him to all the world, and I will declare unto you, in the presence of the Holy Trinity, I am now 'dead indeed unto sin.'"

So much for his testimony.

"So long as a Christian believer SINCERELY PRESSES AFTER Christian perfection, HE IS SAFE, because he is in the WAY OF DUTY; and were he to die at midnight, before midnight God would certainly bring him to Christian perfection, or bring Christian perfection to him."—Last Check, p. 622.

CHAPTER VI.

Wesley's Letter to Maxfield.

Without any preface or ceremony, which is useless between you and me, I will simply and plainly tell you what I dislike in your doctrine, spirit, or outward behavior.

1. I like your doctrine of perfection, or pure love; love excluding sin; your insisting that it is merely by faith; that consequently it is instantaneous (though preceded and followed by a gradual work), and that it may be now, at this instant. But I dislike your supposing man may be as perfect as an angel, that he can be absolutely perfect; that he can be infallible, or above being tempted, or that the moment he is pure in heart he can not fall from it. I dislike the saying, this was not known or taught among us till within two or three years. I grant you did not know it. You have over and over denied instantaneous sanctification to me; but I have known and taught it (and so has my brother, as our writings show) above these twenty years. I dislike your directly or indirectly depreciating justification—saying a justified person is not in Christ, is not born of God, is not a new creature, has not a new heart, *is not sanctified*, not a temple of the Holy Ghost; or hat he can not please God, or can not grow in grace.

I dislike your saying that one saved from sin needs

nothing more than looking to Jesus; needs not to hear or think of anything else; believe, believe, is enough; that he needs no self-examination; no times of private prayer; needs not mind little or outward things; and that he can not be taught by any person who is not in the same state.

I dislike your affirming that justified persons in general persecute them that are saved from sin; that they have persecuted you on this account; and that for two years past you have been more persecuted by the two brothers, than ever you was by the world in all your life.

2. As to your spirit I like your confidence in God, and your zeal for the salvation of souls.

But I dislike something which has the appearance of pride, of overvaluing yourselves and undervaluing others; particularly the preachers; thinking not only that they are blind, and that they are not sent of God, but even that they are dead—dead to God, and walking in the way of hell; that they are going one way, you another; that they have no life in them; your speaking of yourselves as though you were the only men who knew and taught the gospel; and as if not only all the clergy, but all the Methodists besides, were in utter darkness.

I dislike something that has the appearance of enthusiasm; overvaluing feelings and inward impressions; mistaking the mere work of imagination for the voice of the Spirit; expecting the end without the means, and undervaluing reason, knowledge, and wisdom in general.

I dislike something that has the appearance of anti-nomianism; not magnifying the law and making it honorable; not enough valuing tenderness of conscience and exact watchfulness in order thereto; using faith rather as contradistinguished from holiness than as productive of it.

But what I most of all dislike is your littleness of love to your brethren, to your own society; your want of union of heart with them, and bowels of mercy toward them; your want of meekness, gentleness, long-suffering; your impatience of contradiction; your counting every man your enemy that reproves or admonishes you in love; your bigotry and narrowness of spirit, loving in a manner, only those that love you; your sensoriousness, proneness to think hardly of all who do not exactly agree with you; in one word, your divisive spirit. Indeed, I do not believe that any of you either design or desire a separation. But you do not enough fear, abhor, and detest it, shuddering at the very thought; and all the preceding tempers tend to it, and gradually prepare you for it. Observe, I tell you before. God grant you may immediately and affectionately take the warning!

3. As to your outward behavior, I like the general tenor of your life, devoted to God and spent in doing good. But I dislike your slighting any, the very least rules of the bands or society; and your doing anything that tends to hinder others from exactly observing them. Therefore, I dislike your appointing such meetings as hinder others from attending either the public preaching, or their class or band; or any other meeting, which

the rules of the society, or their office requires them to attend. I dislike your spending so much time in several meetings, as many that attend can ill spare from the other duties of their calling, unless they omit either the preaching or their class or band. This naturally tends to dissolve our society by cutting the sinews of it. As to your more public meetings, I like the praying fervently, and largely for all the blessings of God; and I know much good has been done hereby, and I hope much more will be done. But I dislike several things therein: 1. The singing, or speaking, or praying of several at once: 2. The praying to the Son of God only, or more than to the Father: 3. The using improper expressions in prayer—sometimes too bold, if not irreverent; sometimes too pompous and magnificent, extolling yourselves rather than God, and telling him what you are, not what you want: 4. Using poor, flat, bald hymns: 5. The never kneeling at prayer: 6. Your using postures or gestures highly indecent: 7. Your screaming, even so as to make the words unintelligible: 8. Your affirming people will be justified or sanctified just now: 9. The affirming they are, when they are not: 10. The bidding them say, I believe: 11. The bitterly condemning any that oppose, calling them wolves, etc., and pronouncing them hypocrites, or not justified.

Read this calmly and impartially before the Lord, in prayer: so shall the evil cease, and the good remain; and then you will be more than ever united to

Your affectionate brother,

Canterbury, Nov. 2, 1762.   JOHN WESLEY.

CHAPTER VII.

The Difference Between the Present Holiness Movement and the "Bell-Maxfield Movement," in Mr. Wesley's Day.

BY REV. CLEMENT C. CARY.

Those who confound what is commonly called the "holiness movement" of this day with the "Bell-Maxfield" movement in the days of John Wesley, which gave that good man so much trouble, must certainly know as little of the one as of the other movement. He has read Methodist history to little purpose. He who can confound the two movements possesses very shallow and limited information. There is but one point of similarity between these mistaken men and the leaders of the present-day movement, viz: Both are and were advocates and professors of entire sanctification as a distinct experience received subsequent to regeneration. But this no more confounds that movement with the present "holiness movement," than any other two distinct movements, differing in character, can be confounded, simply because the several agents made the same profession of religion or belonged to the same church.

Let us look at the facts in what is known as the "Bell and Maxfield" movement. We condense from Steven's History of Methodism.

The year 1760 was signalized in England by a more

extraordinary religious interest than had hitherto prevailed among Methodist "Societies." "Here began," says Wesley, "that glorious work of sanctification which had been nearly at a stand for twenty years. From time to time it spread; and wherever the work of sanctification increased, the whole work of God increased in all its branches."

In 1762, he states that his brother, Charles Wesley, had some years before said to him that "the day of the Methodist Pentecost" had not fully come; but he doubted not it would come; and that then they would hear of people sanctified as frequently as they had heard of them justified.

"It was now fully come," said Wesley, and his "Journal" for successive years records the spread of this higher Christian experience. Wherever he went he found this work of God was spreading. In 1762, he discovered there were about four hundred witnesses to this experience in the London "Societies." In 1763 in looking back over this wonderful revival of the doctrine and experience of entire sanctification, he says, "the peculiar work of this season has been what Paul calls *the perfecting of the saints.*"

Many persons, he goes on to say, in various parts of England and Ireland experienced such a change as they had never anticipated. We quote his own words: "After a deep conviction of inbred sin, they were so filled with faith and love that sin vanished; and they found from that time no pride, anger or unbelief."

"Now," he adds, "whether we call this the destruction or suspension of sin, it is a glorious work of

God, such as we never saw in these kingdoms before."

Some, he admits, had lost the blessing. A very few compared to the whole number of witnesses had given way to "enthusiasm," and separated from the brethren. But though these errors were a hindrance. still the work went on, and these were the parties who belonged to the "Bell-Maxfield movement," which gave Mr. Wesley so much trouble.

As late as 1768, he writes, blessing God that if a hundred "enthusiasts" were set aside, they were still encompassed with a cloud of witnesses, who testify to the *perfection* he had taught for forty years.

The "enthusiasm" to which Wesley alludes, which marred this special revival of the work of entire sanctification, was mostly limited to London, where George Bell, one of his local preachers, lived. Bell supposed he had effected a miraculous cure, and attempted another cure upon a blind man, but utterly failed. His language became fanatical, and he asserted that his "perfection" rendered him infallible, that he was above temptation, and claimed to be superior to the instructions of all persons who were not perfect in love, as well as superior to the "Rules" of the "Bands" and of the "United Societies"—things, let it be said, which have no place whatever either in the teachings or professions of "holiness teachers" of the present day.

The fanaticism of Bell became infectious, and spread rapidly. So much so, that Maxfield, another one of Wesley's preachers, became involved, and allied himself with these "enthusiasts." It is difficult to ascer-

tain how far Maxfield shared the fanaticism of Bell
and his associates. He seems unconsciously to have
been inclined to side with them more from discontent
with Wesley's authority than from sympathy with
their errors. Whatever was Maxfield's motive, he
took sides with these enthusiasts, and really became
their head, though Bell continued to afford, by his
extreme ravings, the chief stimulus of their extravagances.

After bearing with him for some time, Wesley was
compelled to expel Bell from his "Societies," and to
publicly disclaim in the newspapers a prophecy which
Bell had circulated that the world would end on a certain day, which prophecy was doing hurt to the cause.

In time, Bell lost his religious ardor, became a
skeptic, and then a politician. Maxfield gathered
around him the alienated members of the London
"Society," and opened an independent chapel, where
he labored for twenty years. He became a Calvinist,
and published a severe pamphlet against Mr. Wesley.
Some of the Methodists who seceded with him continued with him to the last, but the larger number
returned to Wesley's "Society."

These then were the facts in the case which called
forth the now famous letter of Mr. Wesley to these
men and their followers, who had become fanatical,
and had gone into grave errors, which any honest,
unprejudiced seeker after truth can perceive, if he will
but read Mr. Wesley's "Journals," bear no resemblance whatever to the "holiness movement" of the
present day. In that letter, and in Mr. Wesley's writ-

ings of that day, there is not a sentence which in any·
wise contravenes the doctrine of entire sanctification as
an experience receivable after regeneration.   The principal fault Mr. Wesley finds with these men is because
of their extravagances, fanaticism, and grave errors.
Bell so distorted the doctrine of Christian perfection
that it became a great hindrance to the work.   And
that man is wofully ignorant who seeks to confound
the "holiness people" of this day, as a class, with Bell
and Maxfield and their fanatical followers in their
absurd positions assumed.

A careful and critical study of the "Bell-Maxfield"
letter and Mr. Wesley's writings—which letter the
opponents of the doctrine of entire sanctification are
so ready to print on every occasion, as if it applied to
the present-day "holiness movement," will reveal the
fact that he *commends* much in these men, while there
are other things which he *condemns*.   And it will be
clearly seen that no word escapes his lips which cen-
sures any effort which looks to getting believers into
the experience of sanctification by faith; nor does he
oppose the specific preaching of perfect love as a distinct second blessing.   Neither does he say anything
against the profession of this experience.   He only
condemns their fatal extravagances and serious errors,
which were but excrescences, hurtful to them and damaging to a doctrine which he says he had preached for
forty years.   If any such like errors or extravagances
were to occur in this day in connection with this remarkable revival of entire sanctification, there is not
an intelligent advocate of this second blessing doc-

trine who would not be ready to correct and oppose them. The leaders of the present holiness movement endorse the sentiment of Mr. Wesley concerning these mistaken men.

Now, note in detail and analyze the errors of Bell and Maxfield and their followers which are censurable. Then examine the teachings of the leaders of the present day "holiness movement." Then tell us where is there any resemblance between the two. Here and there, there may be an occasional professor of sanctification who runs off into some minor error, but these are the exceptions and not the rule. By no sort of means can such glaring errors and outrageous extravagances of Bell and his co-partners be coupled on to the holiness movement of this day, nor can any likeness be seen in them to the present holiness teachers.

Passing by the less important errors with which Mr. Wesley finds fault in Bell and Maxfield, such as many of them praying at once, praying to Jesus Christ only, never kneeling in prayer, using postures or gestures highly indecent, screaming so as to make words unintelligible, and other things objectionable, note those errors more serious, which strike directly at a sound and Scriptural interpretation of Christian perfection. Then inquire where are similar errors now held or taught by the leaders of the present-day "holiness movement?"

Notice what Mr. Wesley says *he likes* in these men:

"1. I like your doctrine of perfection or pure love; love excluding sin; your insisting that it is merely by faith; that consequently it is instantaneous (though

5

preceded and followed by a gradual work), and that it may be now, at this instant."

The same things are taught by the leaders of the present holiness movement. Will others who oppose this movement be as frank and go as far as Mr. Wesley in saying they like these things as taught?

"2. As to your spirit, I like your confidence in God and your zeal for the salvation of souls."

Here are two commendable things found in "holiness" workers in these times, things for which they are conspicuous.

"3. As to your outward behavior, I like the general tenor of your life, devoted to God, and spent in doing good."

Mark: This may be largely said of the "holiness people" now.

Now note some of the important errors complained of by Mr. Wesley in these fanatical men, and ask where the same errors now exist in the leaders of the present "holiness movement."

"1. I dislike your supposing man may be as perfect as an angel; that he can be absolutely perfect; that he can be infallible, or above being tempted; or, that the moment he is pure in heart, he cannot fall from it."

So far from any such teaching being now found in the present "holiness movement," the leaders make prominent Mr. Wesley's teachings upon these points named, and use as a text-book his "Plain Account of Christian Perfection," which affirms perfection is neither Adamic nor angelic perfection; that it is not a state where there are no temptations, where one can not fall, or that frees a believer from mistakes and infirmities. Point out any reliable teacher connected with the present "holiness movement" who makes any such declaration as is implied in the things named which Mr. Wesley disliked.

"2. You have over and over denied *instantaneous* sanctification to me; but I have known and taught it (and so has my brother, as our writings show) above these twenty years."

But who denies *instantaneous* sanctification now? Not those who are in the "holiness movement," but those opposed to it, who use Mr. Wesley's letter to Bell and Maxfield as a stick to crack the heads of the present-day "holiness" teachers. The letter therefore at this point lies against the anti-second blessing brethren.

"3. I dislike your directly or indirectly depreciating justification; saying, a justified person is not in Christ; is not born of God, is not a new creature, has not a new heart, is not sanctified, not a temple of the Holy Ghost; or that he can not please God, or can not grow in grace."

Where is any such error found in the present "holiness movement?" If there is any depreciation of justification or minifying of regeneration, it is not found among the ranks of "holiness teachers." The standard of the new birth is placed much higher in their teaching than in that of those who oppose this Wesleyan doctrine.

"4. I dislike your saying one saved from sin needs nothing more than looking to Jesus; needs not to hear or think of anything else; believe, believe, is enough;

that he needs no self-examination, no times of private prayer; needs not mind little or outward things; and that he can not be taught by any person who is not in the same state."

Who says and does these things among holiness people? Where are the holiness teachers who affirm any such errors? Who is it that encourages people to believe they "can not be taught by any person who is not in the same state" of perfect love? Do not hundreds who enjoy this experience, all over this broad land, sit weekly under the ministrations of men who are strangers to this blessing? Yea, more; they often sit under a ministry, not only where they find no food for their souls, but where said ministry feels called upon to make war upon this same Wesleyan doctrine and Scriptural experience, professed and enjoyed by these "holiness" people.

It is not necessary to notice everything in connection with these enthusiasts which Mr. Wesley censured. But one other matter needs to be mentioned which shows conclusively the dissimilarity between the "Bell-Maxfield movement" and the present-day "holiness movement."

That movement was one which resulted in "come-out-ism." These men withdrew from Mr. Wesley's "Societies" and set up an independent organization. Some of these said Mr. Wesley "was a hypocrite," therefore they could have no fellowship with him; and when several left the "Society," they said (one of whom was Bell), "Blind John Wesley is not capable of teaching us; we will keep to Mr. Maxfield."

Who is it in these latter days who says "John Wesley is not capable of teaching us?" Certainly not the "holiness people." Rather they are to be found among the unbelievers in this second-blessing doctrine and the opposers of this modern "holiness movement."

Again; Where is any "come-out-ism," that is naturally connected with or which inseparably grows out of the present "holiness movement?" Here is one thing Mr. Wesley feared and disliked in Bell, Maxfield & Co. But is there anything in this present-day "holiness movement" which bears any resemblance to this objectionable and hurtful thing of "come-out-ism?" If anybody points to one here and there who has withdrawn from the church, let it be remembered these are only sporadic or exceptional cases, and do not belong to the movement as such. If it should be said the tendency of the present movement is toward separation from the church, the reply is, that the "movement" has been started long enough to show what it is, and to develop any latent tendencies in that direction if any ever existed. For about fifteen years this thing has been growing in the South; and although fearful ones have often looked with forebodings upon the evils which they thought would soon show themselves (which evils only existed in their imagination), the "holiness movement" has neither "split the church" nor developed any race of "come-outers." Surely by this time, if there had been any of the Bell and Maxfield spirit in it, we would have ere this seen the "split" which was prophecied, and have discovered the "come-out-ism" which superficial readers of

Methodist history have confounded with the present
"holiness movement." But where are these things
seen? Point them out, and we will ask for another
Wesley to arise, to write to and correct the errors of
the leaders of this dreadful "holiness movement."

Consult the "holiness" literature of the present day.
Listen to the preaching of those men connected with
and prominent in this "holiness movement." Hear
the general run of the experiences of these same people, and nowhere will be found these grave errors and
sad extravagances of Bell, Maxfield & Co.

On the other hand, their teaching and experiences
will all be found to harmonize with Mr. Wesley's
teachings on sanctification, and all of it tending to
promote love for and loyalty to the church.

There is this material difference between Mr. Wesley
in his motives and aims in his opposition to Bell and
Maxfield, and those opposed to the present "holiness
movement," and who use Mr. Wesley's letter to these
men as against the present movement, viz:

Mr. Wesley encouraged and was a direct party to
the wonderful revival of the experience of sanctification in his day; was in full sympathy with sanctification as a second blessing, and co-operated with all who
were seeking to bring believers into this gracious experience. He wrote what he did only to correct errors
into which some advocates of the second-blessing doctrine had fallen.

Those who use that "Bell-Maxfield" letter now, do
so largely to oppose the whole "holiness movement"
as a movement. They confound the "holiness move-

ment'' people with errors and extravagances not necessarily connected with either the doctrine or the movement. And, unlike Mr. Wesley, they are not in harmony with the doctrine of sanctification as taught by Mr. Wesley, nor are they in sympathy with a movement whose leading object is to lead believers into this gracious and happy experience.

Another marked difference between Mr. Wesley in his dislike to the "Bell and Maxfield" movement and those who confound that movement with the present holiness movement, is in the spirit and aim of the two.

Mr. Wesley bore in great patience with Bell and his followers, and, while finding no fault with the doctrine of sanctification as held and taught by them, or the effort to lead believers into the experience, sought only to correct the errors of these people which were hindering the "holiness movement" at that day.

But, "tell it not in Gath," nor publish it in the journals of Methodism, the lack of love and patience is conspicuously absent in many of those who are so swift to confound these two movements, so unlike in their character and fruits. Moreover, their design seems not to correct any errors into which the "holiness people" have fallen, while bidding them God-speed in their main object of leading the church up to this high and holy state. But it seems to be their aim to break down this "holiness movement," while at the same time they have no sympathy whatever for the movement.

At no time nor place—either in Mr. Wesley's writings, nor in any communication to Bell and Maxfield–

did he ever intimate, much less say, he "disliked" the doctrine of sin in believers, or of sanctification as a second blessing. Nor did he ever seek to hinder or discourage those who were urging and teaching these twin doctrines. The things he "disliked" so much in those men were not inseparably connected with sanctification, but the abuses of the doctrine.

Here then is the marked difference between the "Bell and Maxfield movement" and the "holiness movement" of the present day.

The former was an excresence upon the "holiness movement" of that day, which carried its leaders far away from sound doctrine and good sense, and led them into fanaticism, and brought forth secession and "come-out-ism."

The latter has alone for its aim the "perfecting of the saints," and is free as a movement from the fanaticism, extravagances, and errors of the "Bell-Maxfield" movement.

CHAPTER VIII.

Did Mr. Wesley Change His Views on Sanctification?

BY REV. CLEMENT C. CARY.

We think not, the opinion of some leading men in the Methodist Church to the contrary notwithstanding.

Three things on this doctrine were believed in and advocated by Mr. Wesley until his death:

1. Inbred sin remains in regenerated believers.

2. Entire sanctification is a "second blessing, properly so-called," which cleanses the hearts of the regenerate of all remaining carnality, and is to be received before death.

3. The experience was to be obtained here and now by faith.

This covers the material points of the doctrine as taught by Mr. Wesley without change till his death. Yet, ever and anon some writer makes bold to declare that in his later years this man radically changed his views on this doctrine, and rejected "sin in believers" and the "second blessing" doctrines. Such writers concede that in his earlier years Mr. Wesley advocated the "second blessing," but say that he rejected it before he died.

But did he change his convictions of many years on the points above named? We think not. There is not only no grounds for believing such a change of mind took place, but every reason to believe otherwise.

Those who charge that he changed his views base their declaration upon two things.

1. His statement in later years that there are some things in his writings which needed to be corrected; but that he would leave this to those who would come after him.   But this assumes the very point at issue; for by itself it could be as easily used to show that he changed his mind upon any other doctrine which he held.   This by itself proves nothing or proves too much.

2. His act in eliminating from the Ninth Article of Religion of the Church of England, in preparing Articles of Religion for the Methodists in America, that part which teaches that this "infection of our nature" remains in the regenerated.

What was the moving cause in his mind for this elimination does not appear from any record.   But if any one thing is clear, it is that it was not because of any radical change in Mr. Wesley's mind, such as would involve the rejection of the "second blessing" doctrine.

The following are reasons for believing Mr. Wesley never changed his mind in the last years of his life on "sin in believers," and the twin doctrine of the "second blessing:"

1. There are frequent statements in his writings from the year 1784 (the year when he is reported to have altered the Ninth Article of Religion) till his death, which go to show that he never entertained a thought of giving up the views on sanctification which he had so long taught, and of renouncing what he so earn-

estly, frequently and clearly insisted upon for so many years. To quote all these statements would take up too much space. Let any one interested read up on this point, and he will readily see that there is not the least break nor change in Mr. Wesley's mind on the point named.

We give, however, a few of the many quotations. Mark you, all of these extracts were written after 1784, the year Mr. Wesley prepared the Articles of Religion for the American Methodists. Hear how he talks on this doctrine.

To Mr. John Kings, in 1787, he writes:

"It requires a great deal of watchfulness to retain the perfect love of God; and one great means of retaining it is frankly to declare what God has given you, and earnestly to exhort all the believers you meet with to follow after full salvation."

To Rev. Adam Clarke, in 1786:

"You do well insisting upon full and present salvation, whether men will hear or forbear."

In 1790, two years before he died, he wrote to Robert Carr Brackenburg, Esq.:

"I am glad Brother D—— has more light with regard to full sanctification. This doctrine is the grand depositum which God has lodged with the people called Methodists; and for the sake of propagating this chiefly, He appears to have raised us up."

To Rev. John Booth, in 1791, some months before Mr. Wesley's death, he writes:

"Wherever you have opportunity of speaking to believers, urge them to go on to perfection. Spare no pains and God, our own God, still give you His bless-ing.''

To Rev. John Ogilvie, in 1785, he says:

"As long as you are yourself aspiring after full deliverance from all sin, and a renewal in the whole image of God, He will prosper you in your labor; especially if you constantly and strongly exhort all believers to expect full sanctification now by simple faith.''

To Rev. Freeborn Garretson, in 1785:

"It will be well, as soon as any of them find peace with God, to exhort them to go on to perfection. The more explicitly and strongly you press all believers to aspire after entire sanctification, as attainable now by simple faith, the more the whole work of God will prosper.''

To Mr. E. Lewby (some years after the so-called change in Mr. Wesley's mind) he says:

"A man that is not a thorough friend to Christian perfection will easily puzzle others, and thereby weaken if not destroy, any select society.''

To Dr. Adam Clarke, in 1790, he writes:

"To retain the grace of God is much more than to gain it. Hardly one in three does this. And this should be strongly and explicitly urged on all who have tasted of perfect love. If we can prove that any of our local preachers or leaders, either directly or indirectly, speak against it, let him be a local preacher or leader no longer. I doubt whether he should con-tinue in the Society; because he that could speak thus in our congregations can not be an honest man. Last week I had an excellent letter from Mrs. Pawson (a glorious witness of full salvation), showing how impossible it is to retain true love without growing therein.''

In his Journal in March, 1790, five years after he altered the Ninth Article of Religion, he makes a clear distinction between regenerated persons and those who have been made perfect in love. "This week I visited the classes in Bristol. I wonder we do not increase in number, although many are convinced, many justified, and a few perfected in love.''

In May, 1789, in his Journal, the same distinction is made: "Many in every place have been deeply convinced, many converted to God, and some perfected in love.''

After reading these many quotations, can any reasonable man for one moment believe Mr. Wesley changed his views on this doctrine he loved so well, and which he so strongly advocated?

What will our modern brethren who are so swift to charge Mr. Wesley with rejecting the doctrine of the "second blessing," do with these oft-repeated statements of the founder of Methodism, made after 1784, in which he continually reiterates his devotion to this doctrine and urges it upon others? The very same terms are employed without qualification to express his views which he so long held unchanged. Is it possible that in their great zeal to overturn this great doctrine as taught by Mr. Wesley and as found in the Standards of Methodism, they have failed to read what this great and good man said in his later years? Why so swift to charge him with changing his mind and rejecting a doctrine so explicitly taught and so long held by him if his Journal had been read carefully?

Not only are his writings strangely silent upon a change of mind, which change of mind would imply almost a mental revolution, but he writes and talks just as he always did upon entire sanctification. That man must be very credulous, with Mr. Wesley's writings before him, who can assert that his mind underwent such a radical change on this doctrine as to reject it entirely.

2. On the assumption that Mr. Wesley radically changed his views upon this question, after having taught it for so many years, is it not passing strange that he left no clear written or verbal statement to that effect for the benefit of his followers? Strange that on a question in which he was so vitally interested and so firmly grounded—a doctrine he had urged so persistently and so zealously upon his preachers and people —a doctrine with which his name had been so directly connected wherever he had gone or was known— strange that he would have failed to inform the Methodists in England and America of such a radical change in his mind. The plea that he lacked the time will not stand, for it would have taken only a short while to have penned a few lines to that effect and sent it broadcast throughout Methodism. He had the time to write and continue to urge the doctrine as will be seen by the extracts above quoted. If he had rejected this doctrine he would have been silent then and there, and could have used the same time and effort in informing his people that he had changed his mind on the

doctrine and cautioned them against his former error.

His people had a right to know if such a great change in his views had taken place; and in keeping them in ignorance he would have done them a great wrong.

If the "second blessing" be so serious an error, as some of our brethren would lead us to believe—if it be so very unscriptural and unreasonable—and Mr. Wesley discovered this several years before he died—at least as early as 1784, he was in duty bound to publicly recant his views, and in such a way as could not be misunderstood, and thus set himself right before his people, who had such confidence in him, and save them from the like error. Not to have done so would have put himself in a very questionable attitude. He would have laid himself liable to the charge of duplicity, insincerity and double-facedness, evils from which he was as free as it was possible for man to be.

In making, therefore, the charge that Mr. Wesley rejected this much disputed doctrine of sanctification as a second work of grace, our brethren reflect very seriously upon his sincerity, which charge, if sustained, would convict him of something much more serious than an honest change of opinion, viz., that which strikes at the very integrity of his character. After writing and speaking so much in favor of this doctrine, he would stand charged with and convicted of covering up and failing openly to acknowledge a grievous error into which he had fallen, and which he had discovered in his later years, when as a leader and prominent preacher he had led thousands to embrace that same error. Such a charge, if sustained, would affect our confidence not alone in his judgment, but in his integrity as a Christian man.

If entire sanctification is not a "second blessing," received by faith subsequently to regeneration, which he had for many years taught and believed, then the Methodists in both countries should have known it; and should have known, too, that Mr. Wesley had been holding and teaching a serious and damaging doctrine, and now had the manhood to publicly recant and acknowledge his error. His utter silence upon any such change of view proves one of two things: either he never changed his views upon the "second blessing," or, if he did, he purposely concealed it from his followers and was double-faced.

Not only, therefore, is there no proof to be found in the records that Mr. Wesley's mind underwent such a radical change as to cause him to give up his long cherished views on sanctification, but on the contrary the records show clearly that he held fast to, and uniformly taught to the close of his life that entire sanctification was subsequent to regeneration, and necessarily a second blessing, properly so-called.

SECTION II.

DISTINCTIVE METHODIST TEACHING.

CHAPTER I.

Our Standards.

BY REV. W. J. SNIVELY.

The legally authorized "Standards of Doctrine" of the M. E. Church, South, are the first fifty-two of Mr. Wesley's Sermons in our series, and his "Notes on the New Testament." From this fact we are not apprised of a dissenting voice for about a hundred years.

I. In support of the above proposition we shall offer some historical facts as presumptive proof.

1. From the first Methodist preaching in this country by Philip Embury, in 1766, to the organization of the M. E. Church, in 1784, a period of eighteen years, Wesley's Sermons and Notes above named, were the only theological text-books used by the preachers. They were strictly loyal to Wesley as their chosen leader, and cheerfully bore the name applied to him and his followers in England—"Methodists."

2. "The title of the Minutes of the first formal conference ever held by Methodist preachers on the continent of America is, 'Minutes of some Conversations Between the Preachers in Connection with the Rever-

end Mr. John Wesley.' And this continued to be the official heading of the proceedings of the American Conference down to and including the Conference which sat in April and May, 1784. * * * Its legislation was of two general descriptions; (1) Declared agreement with, and subordination to, Mr. Wesley and the British Conference in the fundamentals of doctrine and polity," etc. (Tigert's Constitutional History, pp. 58, 59.)

At this Conference two queries were "proposed to every preacher."

"The first was, 'Ought not the authority of Mr. Wesley and that Conference to extend to the preachers and people of America? * * * The answer was, 'Yes.'

"The second was like unto the first, 'Ought not the doctrine and discipline of the Methodists, as contained in the [English] Minutes to be sole rule of our conduct, who labor in the connection with Mr. Wesley in America?' A similar answer was given, 'Yes.' (*Idem* pp. 60, 61.)

"On Christmas eve, 1783, Asbury reached the home of Mr. Pettigrew, * * * North Carolina, and makes this important minute: 'Here I received a letter from Mr. Wesley in which he directs me to act as general assistant, and to receive no preachers from Europe that are not recommended by him; nor any in America who will not submit to me and to the Minutes of the Conference." (*Idem* p. 134.)

It will be noted that this letter from Wesley was received by Asbury just one year before the organization of the M. E. Church. The American Conference

met in the spring of 1784, in the Minutes of which the
the following question and answer occur:

"Question. How shall we conduct ourselves toward
European preachers?"

"Answer. If they are recommended by Mr. Wesley,
will be subject to the American Conference, preach the
doctrine taught in the four volumes and Notes on the
New Testament, * * * we shall receive them," etc.
(*Idem* p. 136.)

All Methodist bodies have the same standards of
doctrine, but only the Canadians named them in their
Discipline. (*Idem* p. 139.)

"American Methodism (1781) vowed to preach the
old Methodist doctrine of Wesley's 'Notes and Sermons.' May, 1784, 'the doctrine taught in the four
volumes of sermons [the first fifty-two of our edition]
and Notes on the New Testament was affirmed.'"
(*Idem* p. 141, from McTyeire's "Manual of the Discipline.")

3. The chapels and other society property being
deemed insecure to the societies after his death, "Wesley, after legal advice, prepared a 'Deed of Declaration,' constituting one hundred preachers whom he
named therein, the Conference of the people called
Methodists, * * * so as to secure the occupancy of the
meeting houses, and other society property to the
Methodists, according to the original design. This
Deed being recorded in the High Court of Chancery,
the questions of identity, doctrine, and government
were settled." (McTyeire's History, p. 140.)

"At the British Conference of 1784, the 'Deed of

Declaration,' which gave consistency and permanence to Methodism at home, was announced as enrolled and in operation; and at the same Conference was announced the carrying out of another measure of equal importance to America." (McTyeire's History, pp. 340, 341.)

The thing here alluded to as announced was the previous determination to send Dr. Coke to America to organize a Methodist Church there. This step had frequently been urged upon Mr. Wesley by Mr. Asbury as the only thing that could save the societies from a schism.

Dr. Coke reached Baltimore in time to hold the Christmas Conference, which convened there in December, 1784, with full power from Mr. Wesley to organize a church, ordain deacons, elders, and overseers, and put in order all things neccessary to a church to make it effective in soul saving.

4. The Articles of Religion as a declaration of faith are defective. They are silent on the doctrine of the Witness of the Spirit and Christian Perfection, either of which may be opposed, together with the possibility of apostacy, baptism by immersion or affusion, without violating the Articles of Religion!

Such are some of the presumptive proofs that Episcopal Methodism continued to accept those Standards held sacred by Wesley, and the Colonial Conference to *complete* their declaration of faith; and that they are the Standards referred to in the *first* Restrictive Rule.

II. Now let us take some positive proof to the same effect. Bishop McTyeire, in his History of Method-

ism, says: "The Articles of Religion prepared by
Wesley are an abridgement of the thirty-nine Articles
of the Church of England. * * * These being for the
first time proposed in form were unanimously adopted.
* * * The standards of doctrine received by British
Methodism, and in the late 'Deed of Declaration'
named, were Wesley's four volumes of Sermons (com-
prising from one to fifty-three, in our current series)
and 'Notes on the New Testament.' These had also
been received. and the preachers in conference assembled had more than once pledged themselves to 'preach
the doctrines taught in the four volumes of Sermons'
and the 'Notes on the New Testament.' They had
also resolved by way of guarding against unsound
European preachers who might come over, to hold them
to that doctrinal test. The 'Articles' are a terse and
strong setting forth of Christian dogma, so far as they
go; and they could not have been left out of any
abridgement of the 'Book of Common Prayer,' by
Wesley,. without an improper inference; but there are
essential Wesleyan doctrines not named in them, as
the Witness of the Spirit, and Christian Perfection.
*The 'Articles of Religion,' together with the 'established
standards' of doctrine, make a system as complete as it is
orthodox; and Episcopal Methodism has not only been
faithful to these Articles and standards, but has thrown
around them the strongest constitutional safeguards.*"
(p. 350.)

This ought to be conclusive proof that the above
named Sermons and Notes are our legally authorized
standards of doctrine. Dr. Coke, who was sent to or-

ganize the church, was Wesley's most trusted friend and in full sympathy with him, as was also Mr. Asbury, which is ample reason for believing that Mr. Wesley's doctrines and Discipline were faithfully guarded in the organization of the church.

But that organization proved inadequate in its *organic law* to meet the growing demands of the church. Accordingly the General Conference of 1808 completed its organization and protected its most vital interests from abuse. Joshua Soule (afterward Bishop Soule) was a member of that General Conference, and wrote the six Restrictive Rules, which are the "constitutional safeguards" thrown around the "Articles of Religion and Standards" spoken of above by Bishop McTyeire.

Now let us make a brief summary of the foregoing historic facts.

1. Wesley's first fifty-two sermons, and his "Notes on the New Testament," constituted the doctrinal standards of the people called Methodists in America from their first existence in 1766 to the adoption of the Episcopal form in 1784.

2. The Colonial Conference, at its first session in 1773, headed their Minutes with a declaration that they were preachers in connection with Wesley, which they continued to do annually down to and including the conference in May, 1784.

3. That in the Conference in May, 1773, they affirmed the doctrines taught in those Notes and Sermons.

4. That in the session of the Conference held in

May, 1784, only about seven months before they were organized into Episcopal Methodism, they reaffirmed the same standards of doctrine.

5. That the Articles of Religion are incomplete as a declaration of the faith of Methodists.

6. That all bodies of Methodists have the same "Articles of Religion and standards of doctrine," which unifies them in the faith the world over.

7. The General Conference of 1808, by constitional limitation — as will be shown hereafter — threw the strongest protection around these standards of doctrine.

Where, then, is the room for denying that the Sermons and Notes above named, are our legally ordained standards of doctrine? Sure "the *wish* is the father of the thought!"

WHAT THE STANDARDS TEACH.

As the first fifty-two of Wesley's sermons and his Notes on the New Testament are our authorized standards; and as our church was founded upon the doctrines they teach, it is necessary to know what those doctrines are in order to know whether they are orthodox, and whether we have a right to exist.

No person or persons have a right to organize a *new* church unless there is (1) something in their *doctrine* or polity they deem necessary to church life and work that is not in any other church; or (2) that they are so environed by circumstances over which they have no control as to deprive them of church privileges. To organize a church under any other circumstances would be schism.

Waiving the question of polity, we propose a brief inquiry into our *distinctive* doctrines which give us right of existence, especially such as are *now* in dispute—that of "sin in believers" and the "entire sanctification" of believers *by faith* subsequent to regeneration, as a second work of grace.

The first—sin in believers—is taught in our standards, not as a doctrine peculiar to Methodism, but in common with all orthodox churches of all time. The difference between Methodism and other churches on that subject is, others hold that the sin left in the heart after justification (I use the terms the justified, regenerate, and believer interchangeably) must remain there until in the article of death, when it is removed, and is then called "*dying grace*," while our standards teach that it is the privilege of all God's children to be saved from all sin, inward and outward, actual and original, by faith, in the moment they *believe* for it, and this perfect cleansing is called *entire sanctification*.

I. Our standards teach that regeneration does not cleanse the heart from all sin.

Count Zinzendorf taught that regeneration cleanses from all sin, inward and outward, original and actual. To counteract that heresy as far as possible, Mr. Wesley wrote his *thirteenth* sermon on "SIN IN BELIEVERS," which he followed with his fourteenth, on "THE REPENTANCE OF BELIEVERS." He opens the first one as follows:

"1. 1. Is there then sin in him that he is in Christ? Does sin remain in one that believes in Him? Is there

any sin in them that are born of God, or are they
wholly delivered from it? Let no one imagine this t ʾ
be a question of mere curiosity; or that it is of little
importance whether it be determined one way or the
other. Rather it is a point of the utmost moment to
every serious Christian; the resolving of which very
nearly concerns both his present and eternal happiness." (p. 183.)

But, how does Mr. Wesley resolve it? Hear him:

"2. By sin I here understand inward sin; any sinful temper, passion, or affection, such as pride, self-
will, love of the world, in any kind or degree; such as
lust, anger, peevishness; any disposition contrary to
the mind which was in Christ." (p. 185.)

And then, after describing the state of the justified
as "inexpressibly great and glorious," he adds:

"III. 1. 'But was he not then freed from all sin, so
that there is no sin in his heart?' I can not say this;
I can not believe it; because St. Paul says the contrary.
He is speaking to believers, and describing the state of
believers in general, when he says: 'The flesh lusteth
against the spirit, and the spirit against the flesh: these
are contrary the one to the other.'" (p. 186.)

"I can not, therefore, by any means receive this
assertion, that there is no sin in a believer from the
moment he is justified; first, because it is contrary to
to the whole tenor of Scripture; secondly, because it is
contrary to the experience of the children of God;
thirdly, because it is absolutely new, never heard of in
the world till yesterday; and, lastly, because it is naturally attended with the most fatal consequences; not

only grieving those whom God has not grieved, but perhaps dragging them into everlasting perdition." (p. 189.)

Nothing can be more express than the foregoing. Our "standards" speak out on the doctrine of sin in the justified with no uncertain sound.

II. Our "Standards" teach that entire sanctification cleanses from all the remains of sin after regeneration, which is sanctification begun; that it is by faith, and therefore is necessarily as instantaneous in its accomplishment as is justification.

In his forty-third sermon Mr. Wesley says:

"3. But we at present are concerned only with that salvation which the apostle is speaking of. And this consists of two general parts: justification and sanctification." (Vol. II, p. 236.)

"4. And, at the same time that we are justified, yea, at that very moment, sanctification begins." (*Idem* p. 237.)

"8. From the time of our being born again, the gradual work of sanctification takes place." (*Idem*, p. 238.)

"11. Hence may be seen the extreme mischievousness of that seemingly innocent opinion that there is no sin in a believer; that all sin is destroyed, root and branch, the moment a man is justified. By totally preventing that repentance, it quite blocks up the way to sanctification. There is no place for repentance in him who believes there is no sin either in his life or heart; consequently, there is no place for his being perfected in love [entirely sanctified] to which that repentance is necessary." (Vol. II, pp. 244, 246.)

"18. But does God work this great work in the soul gradually or instantaneously?" And after showing that, in a certain sense, it may be either, he continues as follows: "If you seek it by faith, you may expect it as *you are;* and if as you are, then expect it now. It is of importance to observe that there is an inseparable connection between these three points—accept it *by faith*, accept it *as you are*, and accept it *now*." (*Idem*, p. 247.)

We introduce one passage more from his fourteenth sermon, on "*The Repentance of Believers*," to show that entire sanctification is taught as a *second* work of grace in purifying the heart from the remains of carnality or inbred sin. After showing the utter impossibility of the "justified cleansing their own hearts and lips from improper affections and works," and challenging a fair trial several times repeated, he continues as follows:

"20. Indeed this is so evident a truth, that well nigh all the children of God scattered abroad, however they differ in other points, yet generally agree in this, that although we may, by the Spirit, mortify the deeds of the body; resist and conquer both outward and inward sin; although we may *weaken* our enemies day by day; yet we can not drive them out. By all the grace which is given in justification we can not extirpate them. Though we watch and pray ever so much, we can not wholly cleanse our hearts or hands. Most sure we can not, till it shall please our Lord to speak to our hearts again, to speak the second time, 'Be clean,' and then only the leprosy is cleansed. Then only the evil root, the carnal mind is destroyed; and inbred sin subsists no more." (Vol. I, p. 208.)

Such are the teachings of our standards.

OUR CHURCH ACCEPTS THEM.

We shall now show that our church has ever accepted and taught the doctrines contained in our standards, namely, that regeneration leaves more or less of original, or inbred sin in the heart which must be cleansed away by entire sanctification. To do this we shall draw upon other authors than Mr. Wesley—our book of Discipline, our Hymn Book, and our recognized Catechism, all of which ought to be good current with Methodists.

1. Corroborating Authorities.

Let us first hear the learned Richard Watson, who reduced our theology to a system. His "Institutes" have always occupied a place in our Course of Study. Mr. Watson says:

"We have already spoken of *justification*, *adoption*, *regeneration*, and *the witness of the Spirit*, and we proceed to another AS DISTINCTLY MARKED, AND AS GRACIOUSLY PROMISED IN THE HOLY SCRIPTURES: THIS IS THE ENTIRE SANCTIFICATION, OR THE PERFECTED HOLINESS OF BELIEVERS: and as this doctrine, in some respects, has been the subject of controversy, the scriptural evidence of it must be appealed to and examined. Happily for us, a subject of so great importance, is not involved in obscurity.

"That a distinction exists between a regenerate state and a state of entire and perfect holiness, will be

generally allowed. Regeneration, we have seen, is concomitant with justification; but the apostles, in addressing the body of believers in the churches to whom
they wrote their epistles, set before them, both in the
prayers they offer in their behalf, and in the exhortations they administer, a still higher degree of deliverance from sin, as well as a higher growth in Christian
virtues. Two passages only need be quoted to prove this:
I Thess. 5:23. 'And the very God of peace sanctify you
wholly; and I pray God your whole spirit and soul and
body be preserved blameless unto the coming of our Lord
Jesus Christ.' II Cor. 7:1. 'Having therefore these
promises, dearly beloved, let us cleanse ourselves from
all filthiness of the flesh and spirit, perfecting holiness
in the fear of God.' In both these passages deliverance from sin is the subject spoken of; and the prayer
in one instance, and the exhortation in the other, goes
to the extent of the entire sanctification of the 'soul'
and 'spirit,' as well as of the 'flesh' or 'body,' from all
sin; by which can only be meant our complete deliverance from all pollution, all inward depravity of
the heart, as well as that which, expressing itself
outwardly by the indulgence of the senses, is called
'filthiness of the flesh.'" (Theological Institutes,
Vol. II, p. 450.)

The temptation to quote more from this great and
good man is strong, but space forbids. This is enough,
however, to show that he—our favorite author—is in
perfect harmony with our standards on the subjects
under consideration.

We shall have to be content with citing a few out

of many scores of names who have given testimony to the truth of our standards. They embrace such men as Bishops Asbury, Whatcoat, George, McKendree and Soule—to mention no more—and Drs. Bangs, Bond, Olin, Trimble, Durbin, Lovick Pierce (whose ministry dates back to 1804, and who bore his last testimony to its truth as late as 1878, including a ministry of seventy-four years), Summers, and who wrote a book on holiness in 1851 and dedicated it to Bishop Soule, who was then living and a zealous defender of the doctrine of our standards. These, besides Jesse Lee, Finley. Strawbridge, Valentine Cook, Martin Ruter, and—well, there is no end to them!

2. *Our book of Discipline.*

Candidates for deacons' orders are asked the followlowing questions, in open Conference by the Bishop: "Have you faith in Christ? Are you going on to perfection? Do you expect to be made perfect in love in this life? Are you groaning after it?" These questions must be answered in the affirmative before any Bishop can legally lay hands upon them.

Now turn to the ritual:

(1) In the baptism of infants, inbred sin is recognized in this prayer: "O merciful God, grant that the old Adam in *this* child may be so buried, that the new man may be raised up in *him*.

"Grant that all carnal affections may die in him," etc. This latter passage occurs also in the formula for adult baptism.

(2) In the administration of the Lord's Supper perfect love is thus taught: "Cleanse the thoughts of our

hearts by the inspiration of thy Holy Spirit, that we may perfectly love Thee,'' etc.

(3) In the ordination of elders these words occur in a prayer:

> "Come Holy Ghost our hearts inspire,
> And lighten with celestial fire,
> Thy blessed unction from above,
> Is comfort, life, and fire of love," etc.

3. Our Hymn Book.

From the earliest copy of our Hymn Book the writer remembers to have seen, down to the edition next to the last, the following order—in part—was never changed, to wit: "The Gospel Call," "Penitential Exercises," "Justification," "Entire Sanctification." The last revision which came out about 1890, retains the same order of headings intact, except the word *"entire"* before "sanctification." The hymns are adapted as nearly as possible to the ideas expressed in the headings. Those under *entire sanctification* recognize the remains of sin in the heart and pray for its extermination, as Hymn 444, "Let us find that second rest," "Take away our bent to sinning," etc.

> "Prone to wander, Lord, I feel it,
> Prone to leave the God I love,"

is also a recognition of indwelling sin in the heart of justified believers.

4. Our Catechism.

Our church has always been so well satisfied with the Wesleyan Catechism that it never did provide one of its own. The one I quote from is No. 2—"for chil-

dren of seven years of age and upward," "revised by
Thomas O. Summers," printed in our "Publishing
House" by Barbee and Smith, Agents, 1897. Pretty
good authority, isn't it? Then hear it:

"Q. What is regeneration or the new birth?"

"A. It is that great change which God works in
the soul, when he raises it from the death of sin to the
life of righteousness. It is the change wrought in the
whole soul by the Almighty, when it is created anew
in Christ Jesus, when it is renewed after the image of
God, in righteousness and true holiness."

"Q. What follows from our regeneration, or being
born again?"

"A. Then our sanctification being begun, we receive power to grow in grace and in the knowledge of
Christ, and to live in the exercise of inward and outward holiness."

"Q. What is entire sanctification?"

"A. The state of being entirely cleansed from sin,
so as to love God with all our heart, and mind, and
soul, and strength, and our neighbor as ourselves."

"Q. What offices does the Holy Ghost perform for
those who believe in Christ?"

"A. * * * sanctifies them from all sin, inward and
outward, fills their hearts with perfect love to God and
to all mankind," etc.

This doctrine runs through our church like the
warp through the web.

We have now proven, we think, beyond cavil, (1)
that our standards teach the doctrine of sin remaining
in the heart after justification, and that entire sancti-

fication is a subsequent cleansing from all sin and the implantation of perfect love in the heart. (2) That our church was founded upon that faith, and no General Conference from that time to this has dared to lay its hand on that sacred ark. (3) That every ordained minister in our church, from Deacon to Bishop, has given his pledge of *sacred honor* on the church's altar —which is God's altar—to *preach* and *defend* those doctrines against all "strange doctrines" contrary to them.

Such being the legal and moral state of our church, the attitude of any man, of whatever ministerial grade, in our church, who lives upon the church's money while he tramples those doctrines under his feet, places himself in no enviable position. It does not require a philosopher to see that he is subsisting off of the church while he is seeking its overthrow. Grant for argument's sake, that our doctrines are wrong, does that justify treason to the church? Are we ready to take up the Papal dogma that "the end justifies the means?" But our doctrines are scriptural, and if they are, the crime of opposition to them from their morally sworn supporters is the more criminal.

THEY CAN NOT BE CHANGED.

Having shown what our standards *teach*, and that our church has ever taught in harmony with them, we now propose to show that they—like the laws of the Medes and Persians—can not be changed. And let it be distinctly understood in the outset that we are not inquiring into the *propriety* of our fathers having

7

bound those standards upon the church for all time, but as to the *fact* that they did so. Let us again hear Bishop McTyeire on this point. He says:

"The Articles of Religion, together with the established Standards of Doctrine, make a system as complete as it is orthodox; and Episcopal Methodism has not only been faithful to these Articles and standards, but has thrown around them the strongest constitutional guards." (History of Methodism, p. 350.)

Now let us look into the Discipline for those "constitutional guards." They are found in the "*Restrictive Rules,*" which provide as follows?

"(1) The General Conference shall not revoke, alter or change our Articles of Religion, or establish any new standards or rules of doctrine contrary to our present existing and established Standards of Doctrine."

(2) The second fixes the ratio of representation in the General Conference.

(3) The third prohibits the General Conference doing away Episcopacy, or destroying the plan of our itinerant general superintendency.

(4) They shall not revoke or change the General Rules of the United Societies.

(5) The fifth secures to both the ministry and laity the right of trial by a committee, and of appeal.

(6) The sixth prohibits the diversion of the produce of the Publishing House from certain of the traveling preachers, "their wives, widows, and children."

These rules are followed with a proviso, namely:

"*Provided, nevertheless,* that upon the concurrent ecommendation of three-fourths of all the member of the several Annual Conferences, who shall be present and vote on such recommendation, then a majority of two-thirds of the General Conference succeeding shall suffice to alter any of the above restrictions, *except the first article,*" etc.

Is not that plain? Are not these the "constitutional guards" spoken of by Bishop McTyeire? Can any one doubt that the Bishop honestly believed--when he wrote the above words for his History—that the Notes and Sermons he named as completing a system of orthodox theology and receiving the strongest constitutional guards were, the legally authorized standards of our church? To do so would be to question his good sense or his honesty. Those words were not the product of heated discourse, but were written after consulting all Methodist history, tradition, usage, and faith at his command.

On the assumption that we have no standards of doctrine but the Articles of Religion, who can explain the wonderful fact that the whole church—down to Bishop McTyeire, and including him—was kept in profound ignorance on the subject for over a hundred years; and that since its discovery only a few years ago, it has become so *very visible* that a mere tyro in such matters can see it! Surely "the world do move!"

Now let us note what the church with the constitutional majority in the Annual and General Conferences can and can *not* do.

First, then, what it *can* do: (1) It can change the ratio of representation in the General Conference. (2) It can do away with the Episcopacy. (3) It can do away with a general itinerant superintendency. (4) It can change or revoke the General Rules. (5) It can deny the right of trial to ministers or members by a committee of their peers. (6) It can deny to them the right of appeal. (7) It can divert the "proceeds of the Publishing House to any church enterprise it pleases."

So much for protected interests; but what of the rest? Without such majorities it can, (8) abolish the presiding eldership. (9) It can remove all restriction, regulating the time a preacher may be appointed to one charge. (10) It can revoke the appointing power and the itineracy altogether, and other nameless changes too numerous to mention.

Ques. What, then, can *it not* do?

Ans. It can not change its "*Articles of Religion,*" nor its "*Standards of Doctrine;*" and we think it can be safely affirmed that—to the doctrine they teach every dollar's worth of real estate held by the M. E. Church, South, is anchored by deed. Every church going into court—like every person— must have an *identity;* and its doctrine forms an indispensable, if not the chief, part of its identity. The M. E. Church, South, went into court with the M. E. Church, for her *pro rata* part of the property held by the M. E. Church, according to the Plan of Separation, and won her suit. Now can any one believe that had she, in her organization, adopted the Calvinistic or Unitarian faith, the verdict of the court would have been the same? The M. E. Church tried hard to prove us seceders, and had they been successful; who can doubt but the verdict would have been reversed? And had we changed our doctrine contrary to the provision of the first restrictive rule, who can doubt that we would have forfeited both our church identity and property?

Now if it be true that our doctrine as taught in our Articles of Religion and Standards has any thing to do in establishing our church identity, as long as there is a people bearing the name and preaching those doctrines they can go into the United States Court with our History, Discipline and Hymn Book, and come out with a *decree* giving *them* the entire property of the Church against any and all claimants who not only fail to drive away strange doctrines from our Church, but who are actively engaged in disseminating them among us. Nor would the court's decree depend upon majorities nor the official standing of the litigants. And that is not all. Any minority in our church who can't enforce its Discipline on account of those in authority over them, opposing them to the overthrowing of the doctrines of the Church, may enjoin such persons in the United States courts, to cease their opposition to the established doctrines of the Church as taught in the Standards, and to preach them or vacate our pulpits, and the court will sustain the injunction.

As our doctrines can not be changed without violence both to the Church and to the consciences of those who pledged their sacred honor upon her altars to preach and defend her doctrines, it is both honorable and manly for all who can not conscientiously accept and preach her doctrines in good faith, to quietly withdraw from her and seek a communion more compatible with their views, and they will win the confidence of all good men. But not so when they eat the bread of the church while they strive and plan to render her doctrines contemptible before the public. It will do no good—but much harm—to deny the standards on the one hand, or what they teach, on the other, for two reasons: 1. Just as talented, just as cultured, just as holy men as yourselves, have seen and still see quite the contrary. 2. When the church fails to agree, the courts are open to settle the question for us. But may our heavenly Father prevent this last disgrace!

CHAPTER II.

Our Book of Discipline and Entire Sanctification

REV. LEWIS POWELL.

As the Holy Bible is a treatise on holiness, so our book of Discipline commits us as a church formally to the doctrine and experience of holiness.

There is a philosophic basis for this Scriptural doctrine of entire sanctification, and the church declares the philosophy of it in the Seventh Article of our Confession.

OF ORIGINAL OR BIRTH SIN."

"Original sin standeth not in the following of Adam (as the Pelagians do vainly talk), but it is the corruption of the nature of every man, that naturally is engendered of the offspring of Adam, whereby man is very far gone from original righteousness, and of his own nature inclined to evil, and that continually."

It is not my province to prove the truth of this Article of our Confession. If it were, proof is abundant, not only from the Holy Scriptures, but from human experience and observation. But it is my business simply to call attention to this Article as an expression of our theological teaching at this point. We teach here that man has a corrupt and fallen nature. We teach that he has inherited a carnal mind, "and of his own nature" is "inclined to evil, and that continually."

In the Ritual of our church, found in this same **Book** of Discipline, there are prayers for the destruction of this same evil nature.

In the ritual for the Baptism of Infants we have the following significant and pertinent prayers:—

"O merciful God, grant that the old Adam in *this child* may be so buried, that the new man may be raised up in him.   Amen.

"Grant that all carnal affections may die in *him*, and that all things belonging to the Spirit may live and grow in *him*.   Amen."

These prayers are consistent with the teaching of our Seventh Article, and also with the uniform teaching of the Word of God that "man is conceived in sin and born in iniquity."   And in those petitions we are praying for the sanctification of the child's moral nature.   They are not prayers for the justification of the child.   He is born in a justified state, but they are prayers for his sanctification.

Again, in "The Ministration of Baptism to Such as are of Riper Years," we pray:

"O merciful God, grant that the old Adam in *these persons* may be so buried, that the new man may be raised up in *them*.   Amen.

"Grant that all carnal affections may die in *them*, and that all things belonging to the Spirit may live and grow in *them*.   Amen."

Here also in these forms we are praying for the sanctification of believers.   These persons have been converted, so it is not their justification we are taught to pray for in this ritual, but their sanctification.

And every intelligent Methodist preacher and layman knows this to be true.

Again in the "Form of the Reception and Recognition of Members," after praying for their sanctification and administering baptism to them, we commend them to the church in these words:—

"Brethren, I commend to your love and care these *persons* whom we this day recognize as *members* of the Church of Christ. Do all in your power to increase *their* faith, confirm *their* hope, and *perfect them in love.*"

In other words, do your duty to get them sanctified. "Perfect love" is interchangeable with, and convertible to sanctification. Every intelligent Methodist knows this is true—these words have no other meaning.

In "The Collect" in the order for the Administration of the Lord's Supper, the elder prays for the sanctification of himself and the communicants in these words:

"Almighty God, unto whom all hearts be open, all desires known, and from whom no secrets are hid; cleanse the thoughts of our hearts, by the inspiration of thy Holy Spirit, that we may perfectly love thee, and worthily magnify thy holy name through Christ our Lord. Amen."

It does not require much sense or learning to see that the burden of the prayer is for a sanctified heart and a holy life. And this Collect is used in all of our congregations whenever the sacrament of the Lord's Supper is properly administered. At paragraph 146, and on page 69 in answer to the question, "What method do we use in admitting a preacher into full connection at the conference?"

"Answer. After solemn fasting and prayer, every person proposed shall then be asked, before the conference, the following questions, (with any others that may be thought necessary) namely: Have you faith in Christ? Are you going on to perfection? Do you expect to be made perfect in love in this life? Are you groaning after it?"

And I have yet to meet the first intelligent Methodist who does not say that these questions commit every preacher in the traveling connection to the experience of entire sanctification. Honest men know that these questions commit every man at the bar of the conference, formally, and doctrinally, and experimentally to the second blessing, which is the Methodist statement of entire sanctification. And unless the preacher who answers all of these questions with an audible *yes* is a stark fool, he knows it, too! And the laymen all over the church are coming to know that these questions are formally asked every preacher before he is admitted into full connection, and they, too, understand the import of these questions, and from their standpoint the matter is becoming more and more grave. The only remaining question is, How can men who have been thus formally committed to the doctrine and experience of entire sanctification, and who thereafter live on the bread of the Church and jingle her hard-earned money in their pockets, and oppose the holiness movement, and fight the second blessing, how can such men be honest men? That is the question that tens of thousands of honest yeomanry all over Methodism are asking. John Wesley makes answer to this question in a letter to Dr. Adam

Clarke in 1790, of those who oppose this very doctrine, and concludes—"He that could speak thus in our congregations can not be an honest man."

Under the head of "The Form of Consecrating a Bishop," at the proper time two elders present the bishop-elect to the Bishop for ordination, saying, "We present unto you this holy man to be ordained a Bishop." So every man ordained a bishop in our church professes to be a holy man. This is not ceremonial or fictitious holiness that is attributed to him, and which he claims, or is claimed for him, and by his not denying it, he professes it. If he is not a holy man; if he is not holy in heart as well as in life, he should disclaim it when the two elders formally present him and declare him to be a holy man. According to our nomenclature and Methodist terminology, we call a man or woman holy who has the experience of entire sanctification, and so when a bishop claims to be a holy man we naturally expect him to be in the experience of holiness, which, according to the Methodist statement, is a second blessing. And it was true of our early bishops. They sought and obtained as an experience this precious truth. They kept inviolate this "Grand Deposition of Methodism." It was held by them as the palladium of our rights and the seal of our mission as a Church in the world. Read the Journal of Bishop Asbury and the Life of Bishop McKendree, by Bishop Paine, and see how those grand and busy and useful men fasted and prayed and struggled for this blessing which sets men free, and see how they preached it and emphasized it. And so all the early

Methodist preachers were in this glorious experience; and Dr. Pierce said that ninety-five per cent of all our members were either in the experience or seeking it less than one hundred years ago.

This doctrine is in Methodism to-day. For fifty or seventy-five years the Church well nigh lost the experience, but it can never lose the doctrine. As much as some men would like to do so, they have no power to dispose of the doctrine. It has its place in the very heart of Methodism, and there is no hope of displacing it. See paragraph 42 and page 29: "The General Conference shall have full power to make rules and regulations for our Church; under the following limitations and restrictions, viz.: (1) "The General Conference shall not revoke, alter, or change our Articles of Religion, or establish any new standards or rule of doctrine contrary to our present existing and established standards of doctrine." And among the other doctrines of our glorious system is that of entire sanctification which is thus guarded and protected by this Restrictive Rule.

In the Discipline of 1790 we find over the signatures of Bishops Coke and Asbury, the following: "In 1729 two young men in England, reading the Bible, saw they could not be saved without holiness, followed after it, and incited others to do so. In 1737 they saw likewise that men are justified before they are sanctified. But still holiness was their object, and God then thrust them out to raise up a holy people."

They continue:

"We humbly believe that God's design in raising

up the people called Methodists in America, was to reform the continent and to spread scriptural holiness over these lands.''

Here is the section as it appeared in the Discipline of 1790:

"Let us strongly and explicitly exhort all believers to go on to perfection. That we all may speak the same thing, we ask once for all, Shall we defend this perfection or give it up? We all agree to defend it, meaning thereby (as we did from the beginning), salvation from all sin, by the love of God and man filling our hearts. The Papists say, 'This can not be attained till we have been refined by the fires of purgatory.' Some professors say, 'Nay, it will be attained as soon as the soul and body part.' Others say, 'It may be attained before we die; a moment after is too late.' Is it so or not? We are all agreed we may be saved from all sin before death, properly so-called sinful tempers, but we can not always speak or think or act aright as dwelling in houses of clay. The substance, then, is settled. But as to the circumstances, is the change gradual or instantaneous? It is both the one and the other. But should we in preaching insist on both one and the other? Certainly we should insist on the gradual change, and that earnestly and continually. And are there not reasons why we should insist on the instantaneous change? If there be such a blessed change before death, should we not encourage all believers to expect it? And then, rather, because constant experience shows the more earnestly they expect this, the more swiftly and steadily does the gradual

work of God go on in their souls; the more careful
are they to grow in grace; the more zealous of good
works, and the more punctual in their attendance on
all the ordinances of God (whereas just the contrary
effects are observed whenever this expectation ceases.)
They are saved by hope, by this hope of a total change,
with a gradually increasing salvation. Destroy this
hope and that salvation stands still, or rather decreases
daily. Therefore whoever would advance the gradual
change in believers should strongly insist on the instantaneous.''

Let us be careful to observe that in this statement
Bishops Coke and Asbury did not say that sanctification was either gradual or instantaneous, but that it
was both gradual and instantaneous. There is a vast
difference between the statements *either* and *both.*

In the quadrennial address to the General Confer-
ference of 1824, the Bishops said: ''Do we come to the
people in the fullness of the blessing of the Gospel of
peace? Do we insist on the witness of the Spirit and
entire sanctification through faith in Christ? Are we
contented to have the doctrine of Christian holiness
an article of our faith only, without becoming experimentally acquainted with it; or are we pressing after
it as 'the prize of our high calling in Christ Jesus?'
If Methodists give up the doctrine of entire sanctification, or suffer it to become a dead letter, we are a
fallen people. It is this that lays the axe at the root
of the Antinomian tree in all its forms and degrees
of growth. It is this that inflames and diffuses
life, arouses to action, prompts to perseverance, and

urges the soul forward in every holy exercise and useful work. If the Methodists lose sight of this doctrine, they fall by their own weight. Their success in gaining numbers will be the cause of their dissolution. Holiness is the main cord that binds us together—relax this, and you loose the whole system. This will appear the more evident if we call to mind the original design of Methodism. It was to raise up and preserve a holy people. This is the principal object which Mr. Wesley, who, under God, was the great founder of our order, had in view. To this all the doctrines believed and preached by Methodists tend."

The pastoral address of the General Conference of 1832 is also very strong:

"When we speak of holiness we mean that state in which God is loved with all the heart and served with all the power. This, as Methodists, we have said, is the privilege of the Christian in this life. And we have further said that this privilege may be secured instantaneously by an act of faith, as in justification. Why, then, have we so few living witnesses that the blood of Jesus Christ cleanseth? Among primitive Methodists the experience of this high attainment in religion may justly be said to have been common. Now a profession of it is rarely to be met with among us. Is it not time to return to first principles? Is it not time to throw off the inconsistency with which we are charged in this matter? Only let all who have been born of the Spirit seek with the same ardor to be made perfect in love as they sought for the pardon of their sins, and soon will our class-meetings and love-feasts be cheered by the relation of experiences of this character, as they now are with those which tell of justification and the new birth."

In 1840 the Pastoral Address says:

"The doctrine of entire sanctification constitutes the leading feature of original Methodism. But let us not suppose it enough to have it in our standards; let us labor to have the experience, and the power of it in our lives. Be assured, brethren, that if our influence and usefulness as a religious community depends upon one thing more than any other, it is upon our carrying out the great doctrine of sanctification in our life and conversation. When we fail to do this, then shall we lose our pre-eminence; and the halo of glory which surrounded the head and lit up the path of our sainted fathers, will have departed from their unworthy sons. O, brethren, let our motto be, 'Holiness to the Lord.'"

In 1874 the bishops give a very clear paragraph in their pastoral:

"Extensive revivals of religion have crowned the labors of our preachers; and the life-giving energy of the gospel in the conversion of sinners and the sanctification of believers, has been seldom more apparent among us. The boon of Wesleyan Methodism, as we received it from our fathers, has not been forfeited in our hands."

Our present College of Bishops, with the exception of Bishops Candler and Morrison, who were elevated to the bench in May, 1898, in their Quadrennial Address in 1894, said on this subject:

"The privilege of believers to attain unto the state of entire sanctification, or perfect love, and to abide herein, is a well-known teaching of Methodism. Witnesses to this experience have never been wanting in our church, though few in comparison with the whole membership. Among them have been men and women of beautiful consistency and seraphic ardor, jewels of the Church. Let the doctrine still be proclaimed, and the experience still be testified.''

This is the last official deliverance that our Church has made on the subject, but this was only six years ago. In this address the M. E. Church, South, speaks officially through her bishops, and in this paragraph they give no uncertain sound. This address, at this point, is consistent with the whole tenor of Disciplinary and Pastoral Addresses from Coke and Asbury down to the present. And our present College of Bishops conclude their address at this point by saying: "Let the doctrine still be proclaimed, and the experience still be testified." And, by the grace of God, that is what a great many of us are doing. Our Bishops have put their official endorsement upon this doctrine and experience, and in preaching it and testifying to it we are simply obeying our chief shepherds in the Lord.

Don't let our Bishops, therefore, be slandered any more by any one saying that they do not believe in the Second Blessing. It is clear from the Book of Discipline, and from the first to the last Pastoral Address on this subject, that our Bishops all believe in the Second Blessing, which is the Methodist statement of the doctrine of entire sanctification.

8

CHAPTER III.

Methodist Hymns and Entire Sanctification.

BY REV. L. L. PICKETT.

The religion of Christ is a holy religion, and it is consequently a singing religion. Infidelity has no songs; it has nothing over which to sing. It has the low, ribald jest, and the impure, lustful ditty. But it can never beget an exalting, inspiring song. Hell has no songs; only weeping, wailing, gnashing of teeth; no hope, no faith, no love, no song. But heaven is all aglow with holy, undying, uplifting music. The sweetest strains of holy melody, the purest, richest, grandest of harmonies pour forth from the God-built organ of the skies, accompanied by the tuneful voices of the vast multitude, which no man can number, of those who sing: "Unto Him that loved us and washed us from our sins in His own blood," with the chorus, as the sound of many waters, which is a ringing "Halleluiah."

Our holy religion is the song producer of the world. Just as infidelity is tuneless, so false religions and heathen systems are songless. True, some of them have a monotonous sing-sing, a gutteral wail, like the dirge of the lost, but these lack inspiration and are unworthy the name of songs.

As with heathenism, so with the cold formalism, the lifeless Pharisaism of many so-called Christian churches. When a church congregation of a hundred, or five hundred members, has to hire its singing, it is because God has departed from them. Lifeless religionists can not sing. When ungodly choirs sing over and for the spiritual corpses of our churches at so much per month, it is a sign of death. Resurrection power must be had, or an early funeral becomes a necessity.

Genuine revivals are essential to the prosperity of Zion, and so the spirit of song will freeze where the revival fires are allowed to go out.

The doctrine of sanctification is an uncompromising foe of dead formalism. It is a fiery, sin-consuming, revival-kindling doctrine. As it spreads, the spirit of holy song rises. When full salvation is preached and realized, unsaved choirs fade away, either by fleeing as from judgment, or by their conversion into spiritual singers in Zion. Then the congregations enter the realm and catch the spirit of song and begin making melody in their hearts to the Lord.

Good, spiritual singing comes only from hearts overflowing with joyful praises and heaven-born gladness. "The joy of the Lord is your strength" (Neh. 8:10), and we may add, the fountain of holy song. "Serve the Lord with gladness; come before His presence with singing" (Psa. 100:2.)

Sanctification, being the most joyful religion, is the greatest inspiration for song known. Wholly sanctified people are so joyous they can not keep from singing; they are full of melody. It is in them "as a well of water springing up."

Methodism was named in her cradle "The Holy Club," and, true to her name, she sprang forth from her cradle with songs that astonished the world, and doubtless caught the ears of angels. She has been singing from her birth, and her songs, being God's gospel truth set on fire, have burnt like lightning into the benumbed consciences of sinners lost; while they have fallen like gentle showers of life from clouds of mercy upon the aching hearts of pleading penitents. Again, they have distilled like dews of glory upon hearts struggling with self and carnal propensities until perfect liberty was gained and the soul, with the new strength of perfect love, rose as on wings of fire upward, heavenward, Godward.

Methodism was the first organized religious movement since the apostolic days to preach definitely and aggressively this great Bible doctrine; hence she had to create her own hymnology in the main—especially on this line. And well did she do her work. Her hymns have girdled the globe and set all Christendom to singing with more or less energy and devotion her divinely-inspired hymns.

John Wesley preached full salvation to Europe. Charles Wesley sang it to the world. John preached that the blood of Jesus Christ "cleanseth us from all sin." Charles sang of "A heart from sin set free," and set the Methodist world, and through them all Christendom, to singing on the key-note of full salvation. He wrote many songs on entire sanctification as any Methodist Hymnal will show. We give a few verses as samples of many any reader who desires to investigate further can easily find. Holiness for this life is expressed in the following:

> "O joyful sound of gospel grace!
>   Christ shall in me appear;
> I, even I, shall see His face,
>   I shall be holy here."

Yet again he sings of the rest of faith's victory:

> "A rest where all our soul's desire
>   Is fixed on things above;
> Where fear, and sin, and grief expire,
>   Cast out by perfect love."

In the verse following he treats of this rest as a present experience, a remedy for sin. His prayer-songs for this gracious experience cover every phase of it. As if struggling with the bondage of the carnal nature, he cries out:

> "Break off the yoke of inbred sin,
>   And fully set my spirit free;
> I can not rest till pure within,
>   Till I am wholly lost in Thee."

Notice (1) "Inbred sin," not actual; (2) it is a galling "yoke" which must be broken; (3) God must break this yoke, man can not; (4) the spirit is then (*a*) "free;" (*b*) "pure;" (*c*) "wholly lost" in God.

Again he pleads:

> "Refining fire, go through my heart;
>   Illuminate my soul;
> Scatter thy life through every part,
>   And sanctify the whole."

(1) This is a refining process; (2) by fire; (3) it illuminates; (4) brings in fulness of divine life; (5) sanctifies the whole being.

These words were on the lips of the great class-leader, Carvosso, when he was sanctified.

Thus we might fill pages with these prayers for the experience, or shouts of praise over its prospective hope or joyous realization.

But at this day the manner of obtaining this rich experience is much debated and war rages around the questions: Is sanctification obtained with conversion? Is it a growth? Is it an experience obtained from on high by faith and after conversion? Charles Wesley, being the associate of his brother John in founding Methodism, and being himself the father of our hymnology, shall answer the question for us.

> "Breathe, O breathe Thy loving Spirit
>   Into every troubled breast !
> Let us all in Thee inherit,
>   Let us find that second rest.
> Take away our bent to sinning;
>   Alpha and omega be;
> End of faith, as its beginning,
>   Set our hearts at liberty."

And yet again we hear him pray:

> "Speak the second time, 'Be clean!'
> Take away my inbred sin;
> Every stumbling-block remove;
> Cast it out by perfect love."

(1) It is the voice of God that says, "Be clean;" (2) it is a "second" blessing; (3) this takes away, not

actual, but "inbred sin;" (4) it removes the "stumbling blocks;" (5) and brings in "perfect love."

But not only has the gifted Wesley sung of this "glorious hope of perfect love." Many others have done lasting work on this line. Who that has sung the lovely hymns of the sweet-spirited Fanny Crosby, or the pious Mary D. James, or the seraphic Phœbe Palmer, or the glowing, thrilling songs of the many Spirit-anointed poets whose gifts have been set on fire by the present "holiness movement" which is sweeping through the land, but must admit that Methodism has set fire to the world's songs by restating and emphasizing so powerfully the great Bible doctrine of entire sanctification?

But the end is not yet. Wesley's parish was the world, the spread of scriptural holiness his aim. Methodism is his successor, and she must work her parish on this line. Entire sanctification gives power for service, and marshals the armies of the living God with the bugle blast of "the world for Jesus." When the hosts of Methodism are fully sanctified they will preach and pray and sing and shout their way around the world beneath the all-conquering banner whose folds bear the inscription of "Holiness to the Lord."

CHAPTER IV.

Entire Sanctification in the Course of Study for Undergraduates.

REV. W. E. ARNOLD.

According to the law of the Methodist Episcopal Church, South, every traveling preacher, before he is admitted to elder's orders, must pass an approved examination on a Course of Study covering a period of four years. This Course of Study is arranged by the Bishops of the church, and the books thereof are (presumably) selected with reference to the needs of the preacher in order to fit him for the duties of the Methodist ministry. No special training in a theological seminary is required in order to admission into the traveling connection. But those who preach among us must needs have some knowledge of the doctrines, discipline and history of the church which sends them forth. To secure this knowledge, the church has wisely adopted the plan of requiring its ministers, during the first four years of their connection with the the Conference, to take up and pass examination on a course of study covering the points upon which information is most needed.

It is to be taken for granted that our Bishops know what Methodist doctrine is, and that in selecting a Course of Study for undergraduates, they have selected those books which give the truest and best expression

(120)

to the teachings of our church. If, therefore, a ques tion be raised as to what we, as a church, believe, 't is reasonable to suppose that a satisfactory answer can be obtained by consulting the books of the Course of Study prescribed by the Bishops for our undergraduates.

On the doctrine of Entire Sanctification this Course of Study is not silent. At lease five of the books prescribed treat the subject specifically, or touch it in such a manner as to give it a doctrinal expression; and certainly these ought to have some weight in determining the teachings of the Methodist Episcopal Church, South, on this vital doctrine.

The books of the Course of Study which treat of this doctrine, are these: Wesley's "Explanatory Notes on the New Testament," Wesley's "Sermons" (I and LII, inclusive.), Watson's "Theological Institutes," Pope's "Higher Catechism of Theology," and Mc-Tyeire's "History of Methodism." An examination of these books discovers the following teachings:

1. A clear distinction between the *guilt, power* and *being* of sin. "The *guilt* is one thing, the *power* another, and the *being* yet another." (Wesley.)

2. That *justification* is "pardon, the forgiveness of sins," by which we are delivered from the "consequences of our guilt;" that *regeneration* "is that renewal of our nature which gives us dominion over sin, and enables us to serve God from love, and not merely from fear." (Watson.)—"The one is the taking away the guilt, the other the taking away the power, of sin" (Wesley); and that *entire sanctification* is "a still higher deliverance from sin" (Watson) by

which the "being," or "body" of sin is destroyed. "That believers" (i. e. the justified and regenerated) "are delivered from the *guilt* and *power* of sin, we allow; that they are delivered from the *being* of it, we deny." (Wesley.)

3. While *justification* is a relative change affecting our legal standing before God, *sanctification* is an actual change wrought in the soul by the Holy Spirit in delivering it from sin and renewing it in the image of God. It is a comprehensive term, covering the whole process of the soul's deliverance, and includes all there is in regeneration, dying to sin, mortification of our members, etc.

4. They constantly distinguish between "*sanctification*," (the process) and "*entire sanctification*" (the completion of the process). While "sanctification" *begins* in regeneration and is concomitant with justification, it is not *complete* until the "root," or "body," or "being" of sin is destroyed. It then becomes *entire* sanctification.

5. That *entire* sanctification is not identical with regeneration, but is subsequent to it; that it is attainable in this life; that it is not gradual and by growth, though it may be preceded by a gradual dying to sin, and be followed by a subsequent growth in grace; but entire sanctification is "instantaneous" and "by faith."

That the above propositions furnish a true and faithful exposition of the teachings of these books, we shall now proceed to show by quotations from each. We take up the authors in the order given above.

I AND II, WESLEY: NOTES AND SERMONS.

Inasmuch as the works of Mr. Wesley are included
in our doctrinal standards and are fully considered in
another part of this book, we shall be content with a
few quotations from the Sermons, and refer the reader
to the chapter on "Our Doctrinal Standards" for a
further exposition of their teachings.

In the sermon on "Sin in Believers" (No. XIII) Mr.
Wesley says: "I use indifferently the words *regenerate,
justified,* or *believers,* since, though they have not precisely the same meaning (the first implying an inward,
actual change, the second a relative one, and the third the
means whereby both the one and the other are wrought),
yet they come to one and the same thing, as everyone
that believes is both justified and born of God." He
goes at once to the heart of the issue by propounding
the following question: "Is there any sin in them that
are born of God, or are they wholly delivered from it?"
That there may be no misunderstanding as to his
meaning, he adds: "By sin, I here understand inward
sin; any sinful temper, passion, or affection, such as
pride, self-will, love of the world, in any kind or
degree; such as lust, anger, peevishness; any disposition contrary to the mind which was in Christ.

"The question is not concerning *outward sin;*
whether a child of God *commit sin,* * * * but simply
this: Is a justified or regenerate man free from *all sin*
as soon as he is justified? Is there then no sin in his
heart?—nor ever after, unless he fall from grace?"
Having thus made the issue plain, he proceeds to a

statement of his views as follows: "We allow that the state of a justified person is inexpressibly great and glorious. He is born again. * * * He is a child of God, a member of Christ, an heir of the Kingdom. * * * His very body is the 'temple of the Holy Ghost.' * * * He is 'created anew in Christ Jesus'; he is *washed*, he is *sanctified* * * * and he has power both over inward and outward. sin, even from the moment he is justified.

"'But was he not then freed from all sin, so that there is no sin in his heart? I can not say this; I can not believe it; because St. Paul says the contrary."

In the sermon on "The Repentance of Believers," he says: "We allow, that at the very moment of justification we are *born again;* in that instant we experience that inward change from 'darkness into marvelous light'; from the image of the brute and the devil into the image of God; from the earthly, sensual, devilish mind, to the mind which was in Christ Jesus. But are we then *entirely* changed? Are we *wholly* transformed into the image of him that created us? Far from it; we still retain a depth of sin; and it is the consciousness of this which constrains us to groan, for a full deliverance, to Him that is mighty to save." In this same sermon he says: "From what has been said we may easily learn the mischievousness of that opinion—that we are *wholly* sanctified when we are justified; that our hearts are then cleansed from all sin. It is true, we are then delivered, as was observed before, from the dominion of outward sin; and at the same time, the power of inward sin is so broken that we need no longer follow, or be led by, it; but it is by no means true, that inward sin is then totally destroyed; that the root of pride, self-will, anger, love of the world, is then taken out of the heart; or that the carnal mind, and the heart bent to backsliding, are entirely extirpated."

Nor does Mr. Wesley leave us in doubt as to *how* and *when* deliverance from this remaining sin may be had.   It is *by faith*, and *instantaneous*.   You are to believe (1) that "he is able to save you from all the sin that still remains in your heart;" (2) that he is not only *able*, but *willing* to do this.   "He has promised it over and over in the strongest terms."   "You have therefore good reason to believe, he is not only able, but willing to do this, to cleanse you from all your filthiness of flesh and spirit; to 'save you from all your uncleanness.'   This is the thing you now long for; this is the faith which you now particularly need, namely, that the Great Physician, the lover of my soul, is willing to make me clean.   But is he willing to do this to-morrow, or to-day?   Let him answer for himself.   'To-day if ye will hear' my 'voice, harden not your hearts.'   If you put it off till to-morrow, you harden your hearts; you refuse to hear his voice.   Believe, therefore, that he is willing to save you *to-day*. He is willing to save you *now*.   'Behold, now is the accepted time.'   He now saith, 'Be thou clean!' Only believe, and you also will immediately find 'all things are possible to him that believeth.' ''

Words could not be plainer than these.   How fully they confirm the propositions laid down above, the reader will at once perceive. With these Sermons in the hands of every itinerant preacher, it is astounding that there should ever be, among Methodist people, any question as to the teachings of our Standards upon the doctrine of entire sanctification.

III. WATSON'S INSTITUTES.

Since the days of Wesley, no mind has appeared among the people called Methodists greater than that of Richard Watson; and no book has been of greater authority among us than his "Theological Institutes." This monumental work has done more to determine Methodist theology, and to secure unity of doctrine among the various branches of Methodism than any other book ever written. If the opinions of any man should have weight among us, certainly the opinions of Richard Watson are entitled to respect. His Institutes are divided into four books, and run through the entire Course of Study, a year being given to each book. The following quotations will show how fully this great theologian agrees with Mr. Wesley upon the doctrine of entire sanctification.

In discussing the subject of Regeneration, Mr. Watson says of this great blessing (Institutes, vol. 2, page 267): "It is that mighty change in man, wrought by the Holy Spirit, by which the dominion which sin has over him in his natural state, and which he deplores and struggles against in his penitent state, is broken and abolished, so that with full choice of will and the energy of right affections, he serves God freely, and 'runs in the way of His commandments.'" Again, on page 268, he says; "Regeneration is that renewal of our nature which gives us dominion over sin and enables us to serve God from love, and not merely from fear." Observe, that according to Mr. Watson, regeneration is, (1) a "mighty change in man, wrought by the Holy Spirit;" (2) this change is a renewal of our nature; and (3) that it is such a renewal as "gives us *dominion* over sin and enables us to serve God." "Deliverance from the bondage of sin, and the power and the will to do all things which are pleasing to God, both as to inward habits and outward acts, are, therefore, the distinguishing characteristics of this state." (Page 267.)

But while Mr. Watson so clearly teaches that regeneration gives dominion over sin, yet he does not teach that there is in regeneration a complete deliverance from sin, or that this blessing destroys the "body" or "being" of sin. On page 269, he says: "The regenerate state is, also, called in scripture, sanctification; though a distinction is made by the Apostle Paul between that and being 'sanctified *wholly;*' a doctrine to be afterward considered. In this regenerate, or sanctified state, *the former corruptions of the heart may remain and strive for the mastery*" (emphasis mine); "but that which characterizes and distinguishes it from the state of a penitent before justification, before he is in Christ, is, that they are not even his inward *habit;* and that they have no *dominion*."

Here it will be seen that Mr. Watson clearly distinguishes between "sanctification" and "ENTIRE sanctification." He tells us that the regenerate state

is sometimes spoken of in scripture as sanctification;
and, on page 251, he tells us this sanctification is "concomitant with justification." But in this state of sanctification, "the former corruptions of the heart may
remain and strive for the mastery," though they do not
reign; the extermination of these corruptions being
reserved for a subsequent work, in which "entire deliverance from inward sin" (page 455) is effected.

On page 450, in the chapter on "*Redemption—
Further Benefits*," he says: "**We have already**
spoken *of justification, adoption, regeneration,* and *the
witness of the Holy Spirit,* and we proceed to another
as distinctly marked and as graciously promised in the
holy scriptures; this is the *entire sanctification,* or the
perfected *holiness* of believers." He then proceeds:
"That a distinction exists between a regenerate state
and a state of entire and perfect holiness will be generally allowed." Nor is this distinction between the
two states, according to Mr. Watson, merely a matter
of growth—merely the difference between *a babe* and
a man. "Regeneration, we have seen, is concomitant
with justification; but the apostles, in addressing the
body of believers in the churches to whom they wrote
their epistles, set before them, both in the prayers they
offer in their behalf, and in the exhortations they
administer, *a still higher degree of deliverance from sin,*
as well as a higher growth in Christian virtues." Not
only is there in entire sanctification "a higher growth
in Christian virtues," but also "a higher degree of
deliverance from sin." It is not merely a question of
growth in grace, but a question of cleansing, likewise.

But *how*, and *when* is this "higher degree of deliv-erance from sin" to be obtained?

Everyone who is at all familiar with the history of this doctrine knows that the point of contention, in Mr. Watson's day, was not whether a complete deliv-erance from all sin is effected in regeneration; few, if any, believed this. This "Devil's great gun" (Bramwell) was reserved for a later period in the his-tory of Methodism. But the question was whether such a deliverance is attainable in this life. After a lengthy discussion of this point, in which he clearly demonstrates both from reason and Scripture that "the old man" may be "crucified," that "the body of sin" may be "destroyed," and that "deliverance from all inward and outward sin" "can neither be referred to the hour of death, nor placed subsequently to this present life," our author concludes: "Not only the time, but the *manner* also of our sanctification has been matter of controversy; some contending that all attainable degrees of it are acquired by the process of gradual mortification, and the acquisition of holy habits; others alleging it to be instantaneous and the fruit of an act of faith in the divine promises.

"That the regeneration which accompanies justifi-cation is a large approach to this state of perfect holi-ness; and that all dying to sin, and all growth in grace, advances us nearer to this point of *entire* sanc-tity, is so obvious that on these points there can be no reasonable dispute. But they are not at all incon-sistent with a more instantaneous work, when, the depth of our natural depravity being more painfully

9

felt, we plead in faith the accomplishment of the promises of God. The great question to be settled is, whether the deliverance sighed after be held out to us in these promises as a present blessing! And, from what has already been said, there appears no ground to doubt this; since no small violence would be offered to the passages already quoted, as well as to many others, by the opposite opinion. All these promises of God which are not expressly, or from their order, referred to future time, are objects of *present trust;* and their fulfillment *now* is conditional *only* upon our faith. They can not, therefore, be pleaded in our prayer with an entire reliance upon the truth of God, in vain. The general promises that we shall inherit all things whatsoever we ask in prayer, believing, comprehends, of course, all things suited to our case which God has engaged to bestow; and if the entire renewal of our nature be included in the number, without any limitations in time except that in which we ask it in faith, *then to this faith shall the promise of entire sanctification be given; which, in the nature of the case, supposes an instantaneous work, immediately following upon our entire and unwavering faith."*

Thus clearly does Mr. Watson set forth this great blessing as a work subsequent to regeneration, attainable now, in an instant, by faith.

IV. POPE'S HIGHER CATECHISM OF THEOLOGY.

William Burt Pope is one of the later writers of English Methodism. His "Higher Catechism," and his larger treatise on Systematic Theology have received very general endorsement, and have been adopted as text-books among the various branches of Methodism throughout the world. Profound, metaphysical, abounding in subtle distinctions, largely devoted to the discussion of incidental questions and side issues, and withal, cast in an abbreviated and catechetical form, it is not an easy matter to exhibit the teachings of the book now under review. The entire volume must be closely studied before it can be fully appreciated. While differing from every other writer in his analysis and method of treatment, we find him in substantial agreement with Wesley and Watson on the doctrines of Regeneration and Entire Sanctification. In discussing the doctrine of regeneration he gives the following definition:

"What is the grace of regeneration?"

(Ans.) "The divine act which imparts to the penitent believer the new and higher life in personal union with Christ." Pg. 24. Further on (page 245) he says "As to original sin, regeneration brings entire freedom from its power." But let no one suppose that by this he means that regeneration brings entire deliverance from sin. In noting certain errors that have been held, he asks (pg. 248): "Is there no other error akin to these?" and answers: "That of those who suppose the Holy Spirit to give such an ascendency to the renewed spirit that no sin remains in the regenerate, supposed to preserve his union with Christ." On page 136 he asks: "What is the character of sin in the regenerate?"

(Ans.) "Strictly speaking it is reduced to original

sin," etc.   He also says, "in the regenerate life the old man has yet to be mortified" (put to death).

Thus it will be seen that Dr. Pope is strictly Wesleyan on these points.   Regeneration imparts new life to the penitent believer; it brings freedom from the power of original sin; yet sin remains in the regenerate. We pass now to his discussion of the doctrine of sanctification.

"What do we mean by Christian sanctification?"

(Ans.) "The whole estate of believers as they are made partakers of divine holiness, and consecrated to the fellowship and service of God through the Mediator."—Page 250.

"It follows then that all who are regenerated and justified are sanctified also?"

(Ans.) "Most assuredly   They have, through that common grace, acceptance as pardon at the bar; acceptance as the adoption of sons, and acceptance on the altar as the consecrated property and servants of God; in all these senses they have that GRACE WHICH HE BESTOWS ON US IN THE BELOVED."—Page 252.

"What is meant by ENTIRE sanctification?"

(Ans.) "This is the work of the Holy Spirit alone, applying the virtue of the atonement in the removal of the last trace of the indwelling or pollution of sin, and consecrating the entire nature of the believer to God in perfected love."—Page 256.   "It may be added that there is danger also of forgetting the distinction between sanctification and entire sanctification; as if holiness or consecration to God" (i. e., sanctification) "were a second blessing bestowed at some interval after believing. Its entireness'' (i. e., entire sanctification) "may be called a second blessing, but holiness itself begins the life of acceptance."—Page 262.

"What is the relation of repentance and faith to entire sanctification?"

(Ans.) "Repentance is, in the consecrated soul, an habitual loathing of sin as remaining defilement; faith is the conviction that it may be entirely removed, and the instrument in man that obtains its removal; actively laying hold of the promise and passively receiving its fulfillment."

"Does any promise encourage this faith?"

(Ans.) "(1) When under the influence of the Spirit, faith beholds Christ as having in himself NO SIN, and as MANIFESTED TO TAKE AWAY SINS (I John 3:5), it has promise enough for its encouragement.

"(2). 'BY GRACE ARE YE SAVED THROUGH FAITH' (Eph. 2:8); salvation is redemption from all sin in this world, since there is no purgatorial purification after death.

"Faith, therefore, WORKING THROUGH LOVE as a condition is the final and only instrument in man for the attainment of the Spirit's grace in the utter destruction of evil as defilement, and all that is called sin."—Page 258.

"Has the present privilege of deliverance from the last taint or spot of sin been ever taught in the Christian church?"

(Ans.) "Not explicitly by any branch of it until the Methodist theology made this entire sanctification prominent."

"How does Methodist theology deal with this?"

(Ans.) "(1) By insisting that the perfect love of God is shed abroad in the heart, and that this must needs extinguish the very principle of self which is the true defilement of original sin; (2) by its doctrine of Christian Perfection generally."—Page 261.

"What, more particularly, are the main elements of the Methodist teaching on Christian perfection?"

(Ans.) "They may be best stated in the words of John Wesley." (Here follows a lengthy quotation from Wesley's works.)

"What is the cardinal principle in the teaching as a whole?"

(Ans.) "(1) 'Pure love reigning alone in the heart and life; this is the whole of Scriptural perfection.' But love is invariably exhibited as the unwearied energy of all good works.

"(2) That perfection is solely the Spirit's work in the believer, but implies his most strenuous co-operation; as to the former," (i. e., the Spirit's work) "it is received merely by faith; and hence may be given instantaneously, 'in a moment;' as to the latter" (i.e., the believer's co-operation) "there is a gradual work both preceding and following this instant."—Pages 273-4.

Thus we see the substantial agreement between the teachings of this great writer of later English Methodism and the teachings of Wesley and Watson. Sin remains in the regenerate; but "faith is the conviction that it may be entirely removed, and the instrument in man that obtains its removal." Entire sanctification is "the work of the Holy Spirit alone, applying the virtue of the atonement in the removal of the last trace of the indwelling or pollution of sin;" and this "work of the Spirit" is received "merely by faith, and hence may be given instantaneously; in a moment."

V. McTyeire's History of Methodism.

A writer in a recent number of the *Methodist Review* says that the doctrine of entire sanctification "runs through this book like a red thread." Without attempting to follow our author in all he says upon this subject, we will give only a few quotations that will exhibit the Methodist teachings and experiences during the decades of the past.

Speaking of the death of Bishop Whatcoat, McTyeire quotes from the funeral sermon of Bishop Asbury as follows: "The brief record, is born in 1736; converted September 3, 1758; sanctified March 28, 1761."—Page 510.

Recording the religious experiences of Bishop McKendree, he relates (pages 482–3) that after a severe and protracted struggle with his convictions, he was powerfully converted under the ministry of Rev. John Easter. He then proceeds: "The same preacher by whom he had believed, followed 'not long after,' with a sermon on sanctification. McKendree examined the doctrine and found it true; examined himself, and found 'remaining corruption, and diligently sought the blessing held forth.' In its pursuit he says, 'My soul grew in grace and in the faith that overcomes the world;' and he thus concludes the description of this phase of his experience: 'One morning I walked into the field, and while I was musing, such an overwhelming power of the Divine Being overshadowed me as I had never experienced before. Unable to stand, I sunk down to the ground, more than filled with transport. My cup ran over and I shouted aloud'."

Ever after this Bishop McKendree was an ardent advocate of this doctrine. One of the latest sermons preached by him in the city of Nashville, and very probably in the old McKendree church, elaborated the doctrine of entire sanctification as a second work of grace, subsequent to regeneration, as clearly as any holiness evangelist would do at the present day. See Paine's Life of Bishop McKendree.

Of Wilbur Fisk it is said (page 433): "He lived for many years in the enjoyment of 'perfect love;' exemplifying a Wesleyan doctrine in experience." These are the words of Bishop McTyeire.

Philip Bruce was one of the committee of fourteen appointed to draft a plan for a delegated General Conference, and, with Ezekiel Cooper and Joshua Soule, drew up the constitution under which that body is organized. McTyeire says that "Philip Bruce professed, preached and exemplified sanctification."— Page 312.

William Watters and Philip Gatch were the first native preachers reported in the minutes of American Methodism. Watters was an earnest and successful preacher, and speaking of him, McTyeire says: "He was not a great preacher, but, closing up a happy and prosperous year, he gives *the key to his success:* 'The most glorious work that I ever beheld was in this circuit amongst believers. Scores professed to be sanctified unto the Lord. I could not be satisfied without pressing on Christians their privilege; and indeed I could not but remark that however able the speakers, if nothing of the sanctification of the Spirit was dwelt on, believers appeared not to be satisfied; and that however weak, if they, from the fullness of their hearts, and in faith, exhorted believers to go on to perfection, the Word was blessed.'" McTyeire calls this "The key to his success." Have not some of his successors lost the key?

"The first itinerant preacher who came over to the help of our cause in the New World was Robert Williams." Of him Deveraux Jarratt, an evangelical clergyman of the Church of England, writes: "He was a plain, active, indefatigable preacher of the gospel. He was greatly blessed in detecting the hypocrite, razing false foundations, and *stirring up believers to press after present salvation from the remains of sin.*" —Page 267.

We shall close this paper with an extract from a letter written by Deveraux Jarratt to Mr. Wesley, and quoted in McTyeire's History, pages 303-5. George Shadford had been sent over from England in 1773. He soon fell in with Jarratt, the evangelical clergyman, and, upon invitation, spent some time assisting him in his work. Describing the revival that attended their labors, Jarratt says: "Many sinners were profoundly convinced, and 'Mercy!' 'Mercy!' was their cry. In January the news of convictions and conversions was common; and the people of God were inspired with new life and vigor by the happiness of others. But in a little time they were made thoroughly sensible that they themselves stood in need of a deeper work in their own hearts than they had yet experienced. And while those were panting and groaning for pardon, these were entreating God, with strong cries and tears, to save them from the ramains of inbred sin, to 'sanctify them throughout in spirit, soul and body;' so 'to circumcise their hearts' that they might 'love God with all their hearts' and serve him with all their strength.

"One of the doctrines, as you know, which we particularly insist upon, is that of a present salvation; a salvation not only from the guilt and power, but also from the root of sin; a cleansing from all filthiness of the flesh and spirit, that we may perfect holiness in the fear of God; a going on to perfection, which we sometimes define by loving God with all our hearts. Several who had believed were deeply sensible of their want of this. I have seen both men and women, who had long been happy in a sense of God's pardoning love, as much convicted on account of the remains of sin in their hearts, and as much distressed for a total deliverance from them as ever I saw any for justification. Their whole cry was:

> 'O that I now the rest might know,
>   Believe and enter in!
> Now, Savior, now the power bestow
>   And let me cease from sin"

"And I have been present when they believed that

God answered this prayer and bestowed this blessing upon them. I have conversed with them several times since, and find them thoroughly devoted to God. They all testify that they have received the gift, instantaneously, and by simple faith. We have sundry witnesses of this perfect love who are above all suspicion."

Bishop McTyeire significantly adds: THIS READS AS IF A METHODIST HAD WRITTEN IT!"

CHAPTER V.

The Place and Work of Sanctification in Methodist Theology.

REV. T. H. B. ANDERSON, D. D.

1. *Justification* is something "done *for* us." It means, when done, pardon of sin, "reconciliation," "righteousness," or, that right relations have been established with God. Chronologically, it is first in the Divine order. But it is also true that no man can be justified and at the same time not regenerated. Therefore,

2. *Regeneration* is, according to Methodist theology, a concomitant of justification, its invariable accompaniment. Were it otherwise, the singular spectacle of a pardoned man, but not made a new creature, would be before us. Regeneration is a *divine act* whereby the Holy Ghost re creates the pardoned sinner. In this act he not only finds himself sustaining the relation of an enemy reconciled, but in possession of a new nature. "He is born *of* the Spirit;" "born *from* above;" "born *of* incorruptible seed." This is as distinctly an act of creation as that of the heavens and earth in the beginning. All terms employed in scripture to express it convey the idea that it is a supernatural work.

3. Both justification and regeneration are perfect works—divine acts; something done *for* and *in* us.

They do all that God intended they should; they are the "principles" of the divine life in the soul. Paul called them, with other things, "the principles of the doctrine of Christ."

4. The doctrine of assurance, the witness of the Spirit, must not be overlooked at this point. Men thus "reconciled" and "born of the Spirit" were to have a knowledge of their sonship. "God sending forth the Spirit of his Son into their hearts, crying, Abba, Father."—Gal. 4:6.

Justification and the new birth introduce the individual into the kingdom of God. In the language of Jesus, he "enters" and "sees" the kingdom. These terms mean that he stands on the shore and sees, for the first time, the kingdom of peace, of righteousness, and of joy. Standing thus, his only "guide" through it is the Spirit. (John 3; *ibid* 15.)

Wesleyan theology teaches that sanctification *begins* in the pardon of sins and the regeneration of our nature. This is important; indeed the key which unlocks the mysteries of Methodism. Sanctification *begins* the moment of our espousal to Christ. PARDON: "Thy sins which are many are *all* forgiven thee." NEW NATURE: "Made *partakers* of the *divine nature.*" In these there is at least one element of sanctification — *separation.* It is called by St. Paul, "Translation into the kingdom of God's dear Son." Keep the thought steadily in mind: Sanctification begins in justification; also that whatever the degree of this sanctification it is an invariable concomitant of it. Pardon and the new birth, both divine acts, take us

out of the world and put us *into Christ*.   Here is separation.

But is this all?   Are sanctification and *entire* sanctification the same?   They are as to quality, but not
as to quantity.   Methodist theology and hymnology
have kept the distinction plainly and palpably before
the church every hour since the days of Wesley.   He
distinguished between them; so did Fletcher, Clarke,
Watson, *et al*.   Space forbids us giving excerpts from
their writings.

If we have read aright, our theology teaches that
justification is a sentence from God, by which we are
transferred relatively to Him, which gives us peace
with Him, displacing in our minds the fear of wrath.
We shall therefore use the term justification as inclusive of the new birth.

The foundation, to use an architectural figure, is
laid in this work; and on that we must stand.   Moreover, it being the first work, the initial of the life of
God, by the Spirit, in the human soul, there is no
such thing as reaching entire sanctification independent of it.   There we must stand, and, by the new life
it furnishes, make the consecration and exercise the
faith so necessary to the obtainment of the richer and
fuller experience promised in his word.   The continuity of Christian experience must be maintained.

Beginning in justification, the Wesleys taught (and
so did the fathers of American Methodism), that
entire sanctification might be reached gradually or
intantaneously; the latter he believed to be the scriptural method.   For the proofs we must depend upon

two things: 1. "God's Word written;" 2. That Word turned into flesh and blood in men's lives, or what we call Christian experience.

The disputed ground seems to be this: That sanctification is not a subsequent work wrought in us by the Holy Spirit; that in justification we come in possession of all—pardon, regeneration, and *entire* sanctification; that after these are bestowed, it only remains for us to *grow*, and GROW, and GROW; that the realm of sanctification, where it does its work, is not inherited depravity, or as it has been called, "original sin." There is wide divergence of opinion here. How there could be, we confess that we do not understand. The first view is not entertained by any considerable number, but its advocacy served a purpose—confused the minds of good people, and obscured the doctrine. As a thoughtful man said: "I wish, in my heart, I knew what the Methodist Church taught. The doctors say—some of them—that sanctification comes *before* either repentance or faith; others by growth; others still by growth and faith after pardon. I wish I knew. I am a good subject for the first, as I have neither repented nor believed." The utter untenableness of such a theory relegates it at once to the theological curio-shop, where so many opinions are laid away in state. Let the theory rest; it became a source of "revenue only."

The second view has a larger following; cultured, thoughtful men entertain it; but it lacks the essential element—truth. It is neither the New Testament nor the Methodistic view. It crept into the church just as, in many places, aversion to confession of sin and the mourner's bench came—stealthily, silently. It is here, and by its presence is dropping us to the level of an ecclesiasticism. Neither Mr. Wesley, nor his co-laborers, knew anything about such a doctrine. He said sanctification *began* in justification: that was all.

The third view—growth, pure and simple, has an element of truth in it, but bating that, it is a most dangerous doctrine, because of its apparent fairness. Who could object to *growth?* The "mustard seed;" the "seed," the "blade," and the "full corn;" "babes in Christ," and many other parables and subjects are referred to as proof. Mr. Wesley and his orthodox followers have affirmed, over and over again, that, in the justified, there must be growth; but always in the *direction* of *entire* sanctification. Nor did he and his immediate successors teach that *justification* grew. That, as all Arminians affirm, was an accomplished fact—complete in itself. It was neither justification nor regeneration that increased, but the *individual* who was saved. With the pardon of sin and a new nature; with a strength and life he had not possessed before; conscious of what Christ had done *for* and *in* him, could he not grasp—not "principles," these he already had—the higher and deeper experiences promised by our Lord? "*Leaving* the principles of the doctrine of Christ," said Paul, "let us *go* on unto perfection." The figure here is not that of growth, but of walking—going somewhere, and the objective point, or thing to be reached—"perfection."

The last proposition, that in the realm of inherited

depravity, sanctification does its work, was the doctrine of Mr. Wesley and his coadjutors. His sermon on "Sin in Believers," or on "The Wilderness State," or on "Christian Perfection" furnishes abundant proof. Nor can it be shown that he changed his views. We have seen it stated that he did; but Dr. Harrison, once our Book Editor, put those sermons in the volumes published by the M. E. Church, South, and labeled them—"Standards." After reading Wesley's Sermons, "Journals," and many "Lives" of the great founder — Watson, Tyerman, and others — we now declare that, anxious as we were to discover the change, we failed to find it.

We are face to face with the problem, Did Mr. Wesley attempt to support his views by an appeal to the scriptures? Read his sermons, note carefully the passages quoted, and as an honest exegete, can you put upon them any other construction? Again: Could Methodists everywhere realize in their hearts the necessity of what Mr. Wesley said they should have, and go in quest of it, would it be a crime? or, in other words, against the doctrinal and spiritual integrity of the Church? This question we put to a rank Zinzendorfian a few years ago and he called for a stay of proceedings. Again: How comes it to pass that seekers of the experience are often ridiculed? That men and women who have it, and base their claims to it on the very passages Mr. Wesley believed taught it, are regarded as "unsafe," etc.? But do the scriptures teach it, as Mr. Wesley repeatedly affirmed? We now declare that we can take the commentaries and writ-

10

ings of Presbyterian, Baptist, Dutch Reformed, Evangelical and Church of England divines and scholars of the last forty years and prove that Mr. Wesley's view of sanctification filtered itself through them and changed, in a wonderful way, their statement of the doctrine.   Lange's Commentary on Acts; Stier's "Words of the Lord Jesus"; Jukes' "New Man"; Godet on Romans; A. J. Gordon's Works; D. L. Moody, and scores of others are full of what Wesley taught.   But they do not call it a "second blessing"; nor did Mr. Wesley in the sense that other terms should not be used to designate it.   "It was a second blessing," he said, "properly so-called."   By reading his works you will find him using scriptural terms almost invariably: "Sanctification," "*entire* sanctification" (I Thess. 5:23), "perfection," "perfect love." He is not to be set at naught by the builders for coining this formula, nor his followers discounted should they use it.   When Adam Clarke, Richard Watson, Joseph Benson, John Fletcher, Nathan Bangs, Wilbur Fisk, Lovick Pierce, Joshua Soule, Thos. O. Summers, W. F. Tillet (he concedes that Wesley taught it as a "second blessing"), J. J. Tigert, fourteen of the bishops of the M. E. Church, Bishop J. S. Key, of the M. E. Church, South, held, and do now hold it, it looks as if there might be something in it.

We shall confine ourself to the lives and training of the Holy Twelve and one hundred and eight besides in the Upper Room for proof.

1. Of growth, but in the direction of entire sanctification.

2. Of the *entire sanctification* of their natures, *instantaneously and by faith*.

Take the twelve, the men whom He called. At first view their faith seemed unnaturally sudden and mature. That it was *sudden*, we do not doubt; "they forsook all and followed Him." That it was *mature*, we are equally certain it was not. Their faith was what we might expect in beginners.

For three years and a half they went in and out before Him. They were daily seeing and hearing "greater things;" truth after truth came and took its place in their hearts, like stars "in the sky as daylight fades away."

During these years, they gave expression to doubt, fear, anger, ambition, and cupidity. This is, in brief, a history of their lives. Every point stated is susceptible of proof. At no time, during our Lord's personal ministry, were they prepared to leave Him; to go out as apostles, and to confront the world and its powers. He had them in *training*. He first called them "servants;" then "friends;" lastly, "apostles." But as He trained them, He more than once hinted that a richer experience awaited them; and as he approached the time his interest in them became more and more intense. In the twelve, we see an upward movement, particularly during the "Forty Days." The hearts of two, as they walked to Emmaus, "burned within them"—a prelude of Pentecost. To another company He appeared, "the door being shut," and said: "Peace be unto you." After a few gracious words, "He breathed upon them and said: Receive ye the

Holy Ghost." This passage has been misunderstood—made a stumbling block to thousands. The question is asked, "Did not the disciples receive the Holy Ghost ten, twenty or more days *before* Pentecost?" Certainly; even before that. Did not Jesus say: "My words are spirit and life" before he entered into the shadows of the crucifixion? Every "sermon," "parable," "saying" and "miracle" He spake and wrought came out of the fires of the Holy Ghost, and conveyed to the twelve "spirit and life." They were being constantly lifted from lower to higher levels; Jesus being the reservoir of the Spirit, He communicated of that "fullness" to them as they were able to receive it. Jesus was always in advance spiritually of the twelve. He was always moving the disciples to the level of the stage his kingdom and its manifestations had reached.

This will enable us to understand the remarkable saying: "*Receive ye the Holy Ghost.*"

1. Jesus had risen from the dead. He had thrown off, as it were, restrictions and limitations. His kingly manifestations were palpable. His kingdom, like himself, was assuming a new and startling aspect as a kingdom of power and glory. As had been his custom, He now brought his disciples to the level of that manifestation. He breathed, therefore, his resurrection life into them. The climax, however, had not been reached—Jesus had not ascended. In a sense He was still local; but when he ascends, He will begin "*filling* all things" with himself.

2. This reception of the Spirit was also a *prepara*

tion for Pentecost; the day Jesus had repeatedly promised his disciples that He would return to them. After that day He would be no longer the *objective* Christ, but WITHIN them, and they *in* Him. These were only heavy drops before the storm.

3. There had been miniature Pentecosts before the advent: (1) The day itself; (2) The Lord had once taken the spirit of Moses, a type of Christ, and put it upon the seventy Elders of Israel, without diminishing it in the least in the great lawgiver. The Holy Spirit was now the "Spirit of Christ," and his coming on the day of Pentecost was Christ's return *de facto* to his temple—the Church.

4. Will my readers now pause a moment and review the road along which we have traveled. They will see the call of the twelve; they will hear the Sermon on the Mount, his parables and sayings; they will witness his miracles, those shining points where He celebrated his grandest festivals; they will enter with the disciples into the fourteenth, fifteenth, sixteenth and seventeenth chapters of John; thence into Gethsemane, Pilate's "Judgment Hall," and the scenes of the crucifixion and burial. They will be impressed with a few things:

(1.) That there was *growth* in the disciples.

(2.) That *gradually* they became more and more attached to Christ.

(3.) That the moods and tenses of His life were reflected in them; that is to say, when He was depressed, when shadows fell thick and fast about Him, they were almost ready to give up the work. (*Vide* Peter, *et al.*)

(4.) When **He died** they all forsook him, except the women, Joseph of Aramathea and Nicodemus.

(5.) That during His interment in the tomb, hope died; indeed, *it was in the grave!* (*Vide* Luke 24:13-22.) They all *doubted.* (Luke 24:11.)

(6.) That with the assurance of His resurrection, there was a *revival* of hope and of joy. The twelve, in a far deeper sense than many are wont to believe, when Jesus entered the grave went in with him; when He revived, they were "raised with Him."

(7.) That the "Forty Days," so full of interest to all believers, were employed by the risen Lord in imparting to his disciples his *resurrection* life, and preparing them for the scenes of the "Upper Room"—the time and place they should receive his *glorified life.* When that day came, Jesus had been glorified ten days. This, and nothing more, was what He gave the one hundred and twenty; and this was imported into them by the Holy Ghost. This day there was a full realization, by Peter, James, John, and the entire company, "that the final Adam," the Man from Heaven, "had been made a *quickening spirit.*" (I Cor. 15:45.) This is what Paul also realized: "I *was* crucified *with* Christ; nevertheless, I live; yet not I, *but Christ liveth in me.*"

Now, a few facts:

1. We see growth, increase, development in the eleven; and no doubt there was a corresponding increase of faith, humility, purpose and of love in others. This had been going on in the eleven for three and a half years; in others, not so long, perhaps. Mary, the mother of our Lord, with other women, had

followed Him from the beginning. Who could say that they were not *converted?* They had been *called* by Him; they had been his only *friends;* they had gone in and out with Him. Before they went into the "Upper Room," they were a company of justified people. They were there ten days, deporting themselves as "becometh godly men and women." "They all," without an exception, "continued with one accord in prayer and supplication." (Acts 1:14.)

2. Jesus himself had moved them, for three years and a half, along the line of his own life. Jesus had been tempted, tried, persecuted, cast down; they had in a sense entered into these things. But in the midst of all, He kept this fact radiantly before them: "You lack equipment; you know not what manner of spirit ye are of; you *need* something I shall be able to do *in* you; but not now. I must go away and be *glorified;* then I will come to you, and I and my Father will take up our abode *in* you. This can not be until I have died, risen, and ascended. The thing I promise you is the *complete* restoration of the "image of God." I have seen it only outlined, veiled; but what I purpose, after I have returned to the Father, is to give you *myself* full-orbed. Instead of being the *objective* Christ, walking *with* you, I shall become *subjective* and live *in* you."

3. He called their attention to the *place* where this mighty work would be wrought—Jerusalem. He also gave the *time*—beyond the ascension. He told them what to do—"tarry"—sit down, wait. To *strengthen* their faith He assured them it was the "*promise* of his

Father." Why did He make so much of the day and so steadily turn the hearts of his disciples toward it, if it were not in some way to deeply affect them *personally?*

(1.) *Personally.* There were in them trends, inclinations, and "wild shoots," which called for purging; they could not bear full, perfect fruit as long as these remained. (John 15;2.) The fires of Pentecost were to be *purgative.* Who doubts that?

(2) These disciples, antecedently to the death of their Lord, were *ambitious* and worldly. Pentecost was to destroy utterly the desire to be the "greatest in the Kingdom of God." Thereafter they were a company of men who "in honor preferred one another."

(3) When the shepherd was smitten, the sheep were *scattered.* Notwithstanding Christ's presence, teaching and training, He had not secured perfect unity among his followers. Pentecost was to be *unitive.*

(4.) Before that day, the disciples were *cowardly*— afraid of the powers of the world, whether Jewish or Roman. Pentecost was to give them *boldness.*

(5.) Before, they were only *partially* filled. Pentecost was to cut the last tie that bound them to the world—eliminate the last element of weakness. "They were all filled with the Holy Ghost." The Greek word, *pletho,* translated "filled," means "to make full, to fill." Some part of them—let the opponents of Wesleyanism say—was a void—unfilled; but now filled.

(6.) This experience—such it was—came to them "*suddenly.*" Processes which led to it had gone on for years as ante-Pentecostal preparation. The new nature imparted in pardon and regeneration, the "prayer and supplication" Luke mentions, were the foundation and condition upon which they "received" the Holy Ghost, and therefore "power." Justification the word being inclusive of the new birth, was the basal fact; and sanctification having already begun, they sprang, by the power of the believer's faith, *suddenly* into the marvelous light and liberty of the Pentecostal experiences.

(7.) The Pentecostal baptism was something earnestly *sought* on the part of those who received it. Three forces were at work: (1) *Christ's promise.* He had never deceived them. He said: "Not many days hence." His word could be trusted; besides, His Spirit was opening their eyes, guiding their hearts into the truth and creating *great hunger* in their souls. Through Him they saw and felt the *necessity* for such a work. (2) *Christ's command.* "Tarry ye in the city of Jerusalem." (3) *The equipment.* They reasoned thus: "We are to go into all the world, to stand before kings and rulers; to suffer for his sake. Within us are elements of weakness; the solidarity of the Spirit has not been realized; cowardice, a lingering love of the world, the fear of death, and especially of martyrdom. Moreover, 'power' is promised. Whatever that may mean, we need it." They, therefore, went calmly, deliberately into the Upper Room to *seek* this equipment, not simply for the Day of Pentecost, but for all after life. Did they obtain it? Read the record. They *found* what they *sought* "by prayer and *supplication.*"

What was it? A *transient* effusion of the Spirit—a passing breeze? Such as comes now to many believers, as they listen to a great sermon, or mighty prayer, or on revival occasions? Nay, nay; but the *abiding* Christ came. Peter, days afterward, stood up "*filled* with the Spirit;" and "filled with the Spirit," "fulness of the Spirit," "filled," etc., became familiar expressions in all after time.

(8.) Now, for the words themselves which describe the occasion: "And when the Day of Pentecost was fully come, they were all with one accord in one place, and *suddenly* there came a sound from heaven as of a rushing mighty wind, and it filled all the house where they were sitting. And there appeared unto them cloven tongues like as of fire, and it sat upon each of them; and they were all *filled* with the Holy Spirit and began to speak with other tongues as the Spirit gave them utterance." (Acts 2:1-12.) Phenomena, such as "visible flames," "cloven tongues," "and speaking with other tongues," the Head of the Church intended should be transient; but the cleansing and filling, by the Spirit, were the abiding features of the day. We know this to be true from passages scattered through the Epistles of Paul and of the Gospel by John. The *changed lives* of the "Holy Twelve" settle the question as to what was done. Read carefully and see what their subjective states before Pentecost were, and it will not be difficult to understand what was taken out and what was put in. Whatever it was, they did not grow into it; they "*received*" it. We grant that the Pentecost was a moment toward which they moved for three or more years; that it had been held steadily before them as their right and privilege; but the life imparted was far and away in advance of any life mortal man had ever reached. How could such a life be obtained by any law of growth known in physics, in mind, or in morals? Processes which lead to the new birth may go on in the penitent for years; but he can grow into neither justification nor regeneration. He reaches these as a penitent by a supreme act of faith; they are blessings handed down to him as free unmerited gifts. Faith, in the heart, becomes the hand which reaches out and takes what Christ has to give.

How, then, could such a life as the Pentecostal be obtained by study, development, or even culture? These might become helps, but the Pentecostal life is on a *divine plane.* Jesus Christ must be the giver and teacher. It can only be grasped by faith; its conditions are "prayer and supplication."

These Pentecostal Christians were *"changed"* that day "into the same image, from glory to glory, as by the Lord the Spirit." (II Cor. 3:18.)

Their lives were glorious before Pentecost; far in advance of what they were the day that Christ called them to be his disciples. True, they but dimly comprehended Him; were slow of heart to believe! Peter, Nathaniel, and others, in a rudimentary sense, understood something of Him; but the value of their faith lay not in its maturity, or accuracy, but in this, that, however imperfect, it brought them into fellowship with Him. As learners, disciples, they were immeasurably above what they were as fishermen of Galilee.

Their association with Him at Cana, Capernaum, and
in the coast of Cesarea-Philippi, had begun in them a
change which ended, doubtless, in making them the
sons of God.   Indeed, amid the shadows of the crucifixion and of the burial, they were higher, grander,
nobler than when they came down from transfiguration
scenes.   The "Forty Days" made them still more glorious.   From the glory of ante-Pentecostal days, they
were changed into the perfect image of Christ "as by
the Lord the Spirit."   "The Image of the Heavenly"
was stamped upon their spirits, and souls, and bodies;
or, in other words, perfected.   Christ lived henceforth
in them; reproduced himself by the Spirit.   A quaint
old commentator said: "The one *dying* Christ on Good
Friday *re-appeared* on the Day of Pentecost in the form
of three thousand one hundred and twenty LIVING
Christians."   *He lived in them!*   For that purpose He
both died and revived.   He was their life; as He is the
life of all "wholly sanctified" men and women.

Having stated the Wesleyan doctrine, will the
reader put it along side Pentecostal phenomena, and
see how it harmonizes with the facts: (1) pardon; (2)
regeneration; (3) witness of the Spirit; (4) sanctification begun; (5) growth in the direction of entire
sanctification (Pentecost); (6) the realization of the
blessing in its fulness "*suddenly*" and by faith; (7) the
blessing *sought*, and who can say it was not obtained?

A few reflections on Pentecost must close my chapter:

1. Why should this day have come to the Holy
Twelve?   Go back in the life of Jesus and the answer
is furnished.   He was born of the Spirit and *developed*

under the Spirit; but when thirty years old, on the banks of the Jordan, He was baptized with the Spirit —came in possession, strangely as it may sound, of the *fulness* of the Spirit. Need we attempt to prove this? The proof is in God's word written.

2. He was to be the Head of the body, the Church. As the Head, He had his Pentecost, "as the second Adam, the Man from heaven." "The Holy Ghost descended upon Him in the form of a dove"—"the symbol of perfect organic life."—*Godet.*.

3. *His body*, the Church, like himself, militant, must have a Pentecost—come as he did in possession of "all fulness." He, therefore, after his own Pentecost, began to promise one to the Church, his body. By this He would complete, crown the work begun in them. The descending flames of Pentecost bear a striking resemblance to the "Dove of Fire" which came upon Him at the Jordan. He through the Holy Ghost gave himself to his Church.

4. Each individual came, that day, in possession of Christ. He gave himself for each, and therefore each could say: "The life which *I* now live in the flesh *I* live by the faith of the Son of God who loved *me* and gave himself for *me*." Each Christian, born of the Spirit, developing under the Spirit, must, nevertheless, have his Pentecost. Fulness of life is ENTIRE SANCTIFICATION.

5. The Lord repeat the Pentecost in all Churches— in all souls—"by many an ancient river, by many a palmy plain." Return, O days of heaven, and let us know that Jesus has been glorified.

CHAPTER VI.

Christian Perfection.

BY REV. RUMSEY SMITHSON, D. D.,
Of the Baltimore Conference.

I wish in this article to present what I understand to be the Wesleyan and Methodist view touching the doctrine of Christian perfection or entire sanctification as found in the teachings of the church.

1. Methodism teaches that all men are born in sin, or with a sinful or depraved nature, inherited from our first parents, by reason of their fall. We sing:

> "Lord, we are vile, conceived in sin,
> And born unholy and unclean;
> Sprung from the man whose guilty fall
> Corrupts his race and taints us all."

In our Seventh article of Religion this inherited depravity is called "original sin," and is described as "the corruption of the nature of every man, that naturally is engendered of the offspring of Adam, whereby man is very far gone from original righteousness, and of his own nature inclined to evil, and that continually."

2. Justification and regeneration are concomitant and co-extensive. In the former the penitent believer is pardoned of all his past actual sins, and in the latter he is cleansed from the pollution of the same. When

these two things are accomplished our justification and regeneration are complete. Both justification and regeneration are instantaneous works.

3. After justification and regeneration there still remains in the believer this inherited corruption of our nature, called by Methodist writers, inbred sin, inborn sin, and is referred to in the Bible as the "flesh," the "old man," and the "carnal mind." All churches agree touching the existence of this evil, or depravity of our nature after regeneration, as also to the necessity of its removal as a qualification for heaven. All agree also that when this original sin, or depravity, is entirely removed, the work of sanctification is complete. The Calvinists believe that this work is accomplished in death. The Roman Catholics maintain that it is done after death, in purgatory. The Methodist doctrine is, that it is a work wrought in this life, and that is the privilege of every child of God to be wholly sanctified instantaneously by faith. This doctrine of instantaneous sanctification by faith is distinctly Methodistic. Expunge this doctrine from the records of our church and there is nothing left to differentiate us from other Christian denominations touching this subject. It is apparent, therefore, that the few Methodist preachers who have assumed to write against the doctrine of instantaneous sanctification by faith, have inveighed against the doctrine of their own church.

4. From the moment of regeneration it is the duty and privilege of all believers to grow in grace, but, growing in grace is not entire sanctification. It is simply necessary as a preparation for its attainment.

and as a condition of its retention after it is attained. The moment a Christian ceases to grow in grace he is in a state of spiritual decline, and consequently is in no condition to receive the blessing of entire sanctification. He must go on to perfection if he would reach the goal. Growing in grace does not eradicate inbred sin or depravity from the heart, but simply enables us the more easily to overcome the evil propensities of our nature. No growth, no works, no purgatorial flames can remove this moral taint. Nothing but the blood of Christ can cleanse from moral pollution, and the very instant the child of God exercises sanctifying faith, this work is accomplished in him. A man may grow up to entire sanctification, but he can not grow into it. It is as impossible for one to grow into entire sanctification as it is to grow into regeneration. Both regeneration and entire sanctification are works of the Holy Spirit, wrought in the heart the very moment the suppliant exercises unwavering faith in the promise of God. No man can exercise sanctifying faith while in a state of spiritual declension, and so a regenerate person must be on the advance in order to receive this blessing. But his advancing is not entire sanctification any more than repentance is regeneration.

5. Christian perfection is not a perfection of knowledge, neither of judgment, nor of understanding. It is not a state of exemption from infirmities or mistakes, nor is it a state from which one may not fall. It is not absolute perfection, for God only is absolutely perfect. Neither is it angelic perfection, nor that of Adam prior to the fall. What, then, is this perfection taught

by the Methodist Church? It is simply the perfection of love. So Mr. Wesley defines it. Mr. Fletcher says: "Christian perfection is a spiritual constellation made up of these gracious stars, perfect repentance, perfect faith, perfect humility, perfect meekness, perfect self-denial, perfect resignation, perfect hope, perfect charity, for our visible enemies, as well as for our earthly relations; and above all, perfect love for our invisible God, through the explicit knowledge of our Mediator, Jesus Christ. And as this last star is always accompanied by all the others, as Jupiter is by his satellites, we frequently use, as St. John, the phrase, 'perfect love,' instead of the word perfection; understanding by it the pure love of God shed abroad in the hearts of established believers by the Holy Ghost." (Works, Vol. 2, pp. 492, 493.) Here Mr. Fletcher, in the language of St. John, defines "Christian perfection" as "perfect love," which he says is shed abroad in the heart by the Holy Ghost, thus making it the instantaneous work of the Spirit, and not the result of the slow process of growth. He further says that, when this work is wrought in the heart, that it is "accompanied by the perfection of the other graces," "as Jupiter is by his satellites."

11

CHAPTER VII.

Christian Perfection.

BY REV. E. M. BOUNDS.

Mr. Wesley affirmed that Christian perfection is the grand *depositum* of Methodism; that the Methodists were raised up for this special purpose, and that they had this distinctive mission to spread this scriptural holiness over these lands.

The clearest expression and enforcement of this doctrine was put into the Methodist Discipline at the beginning, the doctrine being incorporate in the very life of the Church. The statement of this doctrine as believed, taught, practiced by primitive Methodists is found in the Discipline of 1798, from which we quote. The section is headed: "Of Christian Perfection." The statement is as follows: "Let us strongly and explicitly exhort all believers to go on to perfection. That we all may speak the same thing, we ask once for all, Shall we defend this perfection, or give it up? We all agree to defend it, meaning thereby, as we did from the beginning, salvation from all sin, properly so-called, by the love of God and man filling our heart. Some say this can not be attained till we have been refined by the fire of purgatory. Others: 'Nay, it will be attained as soon as the soul and body part.' But others say it may be attained before we die——a moment after is too late. Is it so or not? We are all agreed we may be saved from all sin before death—*i. e.*, from all sinful tempers and desires. The substance, then, is settled. But as to the circumstances—is the change gradual or instantaneous? Is it both the one and the other. But should we in preaching insist both on one and the other? Certainly we should insist on the gradual change, and that earnestly and continually. And are there not reasons why we should insist on the instantaneous change? If there be such a blessed change before death, should we not encourage all believers to expect it? And the rather because constant experience shows the more earnestly they expect this, the more swiftly and steadily does the gradual work of God go on in their souls; the more careful are they to grow in grace; the more zealous of good works, and the more punctual in their attendance on all the ordinances of God. Whereas, just the contrary effects are observed whenever this expectation ceases. They are saved by hope, by this hope of a total change, with a gradual increasing salvation. Destroy this hope, and that salvation stands still, or rather decreases daily. Therefore, whoever would advance the gradual change in believers should strongly insist on the instantaneous.''

This covers the whole doctrine in a practical way, and is of the utmost importance to every Methodist who is in earnest about securing the highest eminence of Christian experience, the fullest blessedness and usefulness on earth and in heaven.

This statement defines Christian perfection as taught by Methodists to mean salvation from all sin, without and within; salvation from all sinful tempers and desires as well as from all outward sin; so that these tempers and desires are molded into the most stringent demands of God's law. Love, perfect love, fills, inflames, purifies the soul, and reigns supreme; long-suffering, harmony, sweetness, temperance, gentleness, goodness are its obedient and ever-attendant handmaids.

This statement shows the distinction between Methodism and other systems on this point. The Roman Catholics hold to a perfection, but they say it can only be secured by the fires of purgatory, which will purge away our dross, and fit us for heaven. Others say that this perfection will be obtained by death. Methodism says it can and must be obtained before we die —that neither purgatory nor death have any purging flames or power. Methodism holds that this perfection is not designed simply to fit the Christian for heaven, but it is the preparation for the fittest and most useful service we can render God, either on earth or in heaven. That while it is the necessary condition of entering heaven, and for performing its high and holy service, yet without it the service of earth is lame, and but half a service. But the most vital point to us as Methodists is the last one stressed, which declares that this perfection is both a gradual and an instantaneous process. It is both a growth and a transition. It is an advance and a climax. It is development and perfection. It is a running and a getting there—a groaning after and an obtaining. It is generally neither the whole of the one nor the other. God's power is illimitable; the work may be cut short in righteousness, in a moment; in the twinkling of an eye; but while the climax may be reached in a mighty effort and exaltation of faith, we are always to be in the school of perfec ion—always learning its difficult lessons; always in His highway, marking an advance by eager, if by toilsome, weary steps.

We must insist on the gradual change; in this we are all agreed, but the fathers of Methodism pressed the other point, that we insist on the instantaneous work, that the two are interdependent, and must co-exist. That to ignore the one or to discount it, is to ignore the other and discount it. These Methodist fathers who were very wise in the things of God, stress with great force the fact that the gradual work depends for its being and growth on the constant urgence and expectation of the instantaneous work. They say that constant experience shows that the more earnestly they expect the instantaneous work, the more swiftly and steadily does the gradual work of God go on in the soul. And they also say that those who are anxiously looking for the instantaneous work, are the more careful to grow in grace, the more zealous of good works and in their attendance on the ordinances of God. They further state that the contrary is true, that where the instantaneous work is neither urged nor expected, that the gradual work stands still, or rather, decreases daily. Therefore, whoever would advance the gradual change in believers, must strongly insist on the instantaneous.

These are weighty deliverances from men who were

master-builders for God, and laid these foundations of Methodism with adamant. For one, we do not hesitate to declare our belief in the truth and wisdom of these statements. Our observation, extending over many years, and embracing many localities, and every variety of spiritual manifestations; an observation actuated by the most tender solicitude for the spiritual prosperity of the people under our charge, substantiates these views. Our experience is corroborative of our observation, and also of these vital deliverances of the Methodist fathers. We have fully realized that this gradual work of perfecting holiness only advances with vigor as we are looking for and groaning after the instantaneous and complete work. We do believe that the absence of that deep groaning after this perfection in its mightiness and completeness is the never-failing sign of a feeble or decayed experience among our Methodist people.

SECTION III.

SANCTIFICATION AS RELATED TO OTHER BIBLE TRUTHS.

CHAPTER I.

The Nature of Sin and Holiness.

REV. R. H. MAHON, D. D.

Sin is at the bottom of this whole order of things. If there were no sin, there would be no sorrow and no death and no need of a Savior and no plan of redemption and no judgment and no hell. To comprehend, therefore, the fullness of the salvation that is through Jesus Christ we must have a just estimate of the nature and consequences of sin. For lack of this nearly all the great mistakes in doctrine and religion are made.

What, then, is sin? Answer this properly, and a flood of light is poured on many questions which would otherwise remain in perpetual doubt. Let us seek an answer to this question, then, "not in the words which man's wisdom teacheth, but which the Holy Ghost teacheth."

In the Bible the words "sin," "unrighteousness," "iniquity," and "ungodliness" are used almost synonymously, but the monosyllable, "sin," is the one emphatic word which denotes all that is meant by any and all these words put together.

"Sin," says the Apostle John, "is the transgression of the law." No more condensed statement of it can be made. The transgression of the law—that is sin. But in order to understand this more fully we must know something of the nature and demands of the law. "Wherefore the law is spiritual," says Paul. It is ordained for the regulation and government of the will and the desires and the affections of the heart, and not merely the outward conduct. And the law is just and holy and good. If there be impure desire or evil affection or purpose, contrary to the demands of the law, then there is sin. "Lust, when it hath conceived, bringeth forth sin." The Savior taught that murder consists in hatred, and adultery in lust. An evil desire, accompanied by a purpose or intention to gratify it, is sin, because it is the transgression of the law; and such seems to be the fallen state of the race that men by nature invariably consent to the gratification of their lusts.

Sin is usually treated under two heads—viz., actual transgressions or sins of volition, and original sin. By actual transgression is meant what the words indicate—sins committed by the will and consent of the transgressor. Original sin can not be better defined than in the language of the Seventh Article of our Church. It is "the corruption of the nature of every man, that naturally is engendered of the offspring of Adam, whereby man is very far gone from original righteousness, and of his own nature inclined to evil, and that continually." Thus we see that sin, according to the teaching of the Church, does not consist alone in actual or voluntary transgression, but is a thing of our nature as well as of our practice. It consists primarily in the *corruption of the nature* of every man. We may call it depravity, misfortune, moral evil, or whatever else we please, but the Article speaks of it as "sin." I suppose there are few orthodox theologians who deny the innate depravity of the human heart, although there be many who deny that this corruption of nature entailed by the trangression of the first man is, in any proper sense of the word, sin. Let us inquire into this. Is it sin, or shall we call it something else? The Article, which is the exponent of the doctrine of the Church, calls it sin. It speaks of "original sin," not of original depravity or inherited misfortune, but sin, and then goes on to define wherein this sin consists, which is not in willful estrangement from the law, but the "*corruption of the nature* of every man." "But," says one, "let us not call it sin; call it depravity or anything, only let sin be understood to mean voluntary transgression." I do not see why we should thus narrow down the definition. The Church has been calling this inherited corruption sin through all the ages, and it seems to accord precisely with the definition given by the apostle: "The transgression of the law." There are no qualifying words. Wherever there is a want of conformity to the law sin abounds, for, says the Book: "All unrighteousness is sin." It is the corruption of the nature, hence it is called unrighteousness, the state or condition of being unrighteous or not right. If this be true, then let us call it sin. This corruption of nature is certainly not too good to be called by that name.

The most masterly discourse that was ever written on the doctrine of sin is the Epistle of Paul to the Romans. He speaks of sin after this fashion: ''For we have before proved both Jews and Gentiles, that they are *all under sin.*'' And again: ''Wherefore, as by one man sin entered into the world, and death by sin; and so death passed upon all men, *for that all* have sinned.'' Then, quoting the fourteenth Psalm, he affirms: ''There is none righteous, no, not one.'' If there are none righteous, they are all unrighteous, and if so, then they are sinners, whether guilty of actual transgression or not. But the apostle is even more specific. He not only declares that all have sinned, and calls it by that name, but he mentions in detail a long list of the grossest of the sins of which the world is guilty. ''Being *filled* with *all unright-eousness*, fornication, wickedness, covetousness, maliciousness; full of envy, murder, debate, deceit, malignity; whisperers, backbiters, haters of God, despiteful, proud, boasters, inventors of evil things, disobedient to parents, without understanding, covenant-breakers, without natural affection, implacable, unmerciful.'' Will any man say that these, which are the universal qualities of the human heart, are not sins? And yet they have distinguished and dominated the whole race of mankind from the introduction of sin into the world. Observe that the apostle does not say all are depraved or that they have inherited an evil disposition. He emphatically says, ''that there is none righteous,'' and ''that all have sinned.'' It is *sin*, not misfortune, that he is seeking by his great argument to establish and convict the world of, and if words are to be taken for what they are worth, he does it.

So far from sin being restricted to voluntary transgressions of the law, we are told in this same epistle that sin was in the world before the law: "For until the law sin was in the world." The announcement or publication of the law might give occasion to sin, but it did not create it. Sin was in the world all the time. The law was given by Moses more than two thousand years from the foundation of the world, but sin was in the world working its awful results of misery and death from the day that Adam sinned. The apostle speaks of those who had sinned without law: "For as many as have sinned without law shall also perish without law; and as many as have sinned in the law shall be judged by the law." The very nature of the race was corrupted, so that it is inclined to evil, and that continually "Out of the *heart* proceed evil thoughts, murders, adulteries," etc. They originate there, and this corrupt state of the heart is of the nature of sin,

I have said that sin exists without the law—that is, where there is no knowledge of the law. The law does not create sin. It is simply a standard of right. Where there is no knowledge of the law one may feel himself to be quite good enough perhaps; but when his life is compared with the law, then the turpitude of his sins appears. "For I was alive without the law once: but when the commandment came, sin revived, and I died." "For without the law sin was dead." There may be no remembrance of guilt on the part of the sinner, although he is living in sin continually. But this absence of a sense of sin is no proof that sin does not exist. Apply the law, and sin will appear. "When the commandment came, sin revived, and I died." Before the law is consulted, there is little or no knowledge of sin, because there is no dread of it, sin being dead, so to speak; but when the law, by which is a knowledge of sin, appears in contrast with the life and character, then sin revives, and the self-righteous Pharisee dies. Still the law did not create the sin; it was there. The law simply enlightened the sinner as to its presence and guilt, and carried conviction to the heart.

We sometimes hesitate to call this innate depravity sin, because the word "sin" somehow implies the idea of guilt and responsibility. But this association of ideas is the result of our own metaphysical reasonings on the subject. The Bible does not palliate our moral delinquencies with soft names. It denominates "all unrighteousness" as sin. But then we are given to understand that God is not unreasonable. "Sin is not imputed when there is no law." It is there; men commit it, live in it; but those who have not the law are not condemned by the law. Human accountability is clearly defined without making any apology for sin, with or without the law: "For as many as have sinned without law shall also perish without law; and as many as have sinned in the law shall be judged by the law. . . . For when the Gentiles, which have not the law [of Moses], do by nature the things contained in the law, these, having not the law [of Moses], are a law unto themselves; which show the work of the law written in their hearts, their conscience also bearing witness, and their thoughts the meanwhile accusing or else excusing one another.'' It appears that in all the wide world, even where the law of Moses and the gospel have not gone, men have a knowledge of right and wrong. We know by nature, to some degree at least, the things contained in the law. If depravity is deep, so is the intuition of right, and therefore this inclination to evil that we feel continually is accompanied by a painful sense of guilt. Says Horace Bushnell: '' Reason as we may about human depravity, apologize for men or justify them as we may, they certainly do not justify themselves. Even in the deepest mental darkness concerning God, stifled—we may almost say as regards their proper humanity—under the sottish and debasing effects of idolatry, still we see the conscience struggling with guilty fears, unable to find rest. An indescribable dread of evil still overhangs the human spirit. The being is haunted by shadows of wrath, and tries all painful methods of self-pacification. Vigils, pilgrimages, sacrifices, tortures, nothing is too painful or wearisome that promises to ease the guilt of the mind. Without any speculations about justification, mankind refuse to justify themselves. A kind of despair fills the heart of the race. They have no courage. Whether they know God or not, they know themselves, and they sentence themselves to death.''

In the seventh chapter of Romans Paul speaks of sin as an ''entity,'' an indwelling something that is independent of the will and a proper sense of right. "What I hate, that I do. . . . Now then it is no more I that do it, but sin that dwelleth in me." This is that law in the members which wars continually against the law of the mind. It dominates the nature, independently of the will. A man may choose the right, but he is powerless to execute his choice. With his mind he may see the excellence and delights of a life of piety, but to walk in that way he is utterly unable of himself; for when he would do good evil is present with him. The carnal mind is not subject to the law of God, neither indeed can be. It is inbred and sinful. Men seek to apologize for it and excuse it because it is inherited. They say: "We were born this way, and are not responsible." Nevertheless, in every man's bosom there is a sense of accountability and guilt, an awful dread of the consequences of the present condition. We feel sure that, while we are in no degree responsible for the moral condition that we find ourselves in, unless we can somehow obtain deliverance from this corruption that reigns within, the end will be dreadful; "for to be carnally minded is death." The truth is, then, the whole world is in sin, both Jews and Gentiles, because corrupt and with no fear of God before their eyes. And not only so, but the world is condemned in their own eyes in the sight of God. This thing that we call depravity, which is little other than "inbred sin," and which we generally condone or excuse, carries with it a sense of guilt and condemnation, and will inevitably end in death unless deliverance is obtained.

Sin, then, in its very nature and essence, is "the corruption of the nature of every man." The next question in order, and a most important one, is, "What is the remedy for this great evil?" Is it possible by any means to be delivered from so deep and so radical a disease, and if so, how?

If original sin be the corruption of the nature, then of course deliverance from sin must necessarily lie in a change of nature. Nothing short of this can avail. The remedy, to be effectual, must reach the roots of the disease. No outward applications can effect a cure. "The leprosy lies deep within." Hence we find the change from a state of sin and death to a state of righteousness continually presented in the Scriptures as a "birth," "born of God," "born of the Spirit." "Except a man be born again, he can not see the kingdom of God." "For neither circumcision availeth any thing, nor uncircumcision, but a *new creature.*" As this corruption of nature is innate, so nothing short of a new birth can deliver from it. "That which is born of the flesh is flesh; and that which is born of the Spirit is spirit." Like begets like. A carnal, sinful nature can produce nothing better, while the Holy Spirit alone, who is the Source of all life and purity, can renew a right spirit within. This work we call "regeneration," because it is the "new creature" begotten by the Spirit of God. "And you hath he quickened, who were dead in trespasses and sins."

An important question to be determined, and one which has agitated the Church not a little, is whether this work of the Spirit called regeneration, or the new birth, destroys invariably and at once all the remains of the corrupt nature. In other words, is all sin destroyed in the moment that the new life is quickened within by the Divine Spirit? or do some of the elements of the carnal nature remain ordinarily in those who are born of God? Observe that the inquiry is not whether at the moment of justification all *guilt* is taken away. This is conceded. "There is therefore now no condemnation to them which are in Christ Jesus." Neither have they any longer the guilt of sin in their conscience. But are those who are born of God invariably delivered, and wholly so, at the moment of regeneration from what the Scriptures call the carnal mind? Concerning this there are at least three opinions, all claiming the sanction of the Holy Scriptures.

1. There is the Calvinistic theory, which holds that this infection of nature doth remain in them that are regenerated even until death, and that entire deliverance from it can not be obtained in this life—no, not even through the blood of Christ.

2. Then there is the Zinzendorfian theory, so-called from Count Zinzendorf, who seems to have been about the first person of any note to advocate the doctrine which holds that in the moment of regeneration the work of the Spirit is complete and the change so thorough that there is absolute deliverance from all sin, both actual, so to speak, and original. This view is entertained no doubt by many at this day and time in all the Churches. Not a few Methodists have fallen in with it. Instead of calling it Zinzendorfianism, they call it the *non*-residue theory.

3. Then there is what is known as the Wesleyan theory, which is a distinctive doctrine of Methodism in all the world. It is that in believers—that is, those who are converted, born of God—there remains (I will not say in all such, for there may be exceptions) what may be called the seeds of evil, the infection of nature, or some of the elements of what the Scriptures denominate the carnal mind, and which we have defined to be sin. Of course it is not meant by this Wesleyan doctrine that believers have any further sense of guilt for sin, because in the moment of justification a gracious pardon is granted for all past offenses. But the roots of the sinful nature remain even in believers like pernicious seeds in the fertile soil. They stock the ground, and, under favorable conditions, may spring up again to mar the purity and disturb the peace of the soul. Deliverance from the remains of this corrupt nature, sometimes called "inbred sin," is what Wesley termed sanctification or Christian perfection, and which he taught to be attainable in this life by faith, and to be attested by the Holy Spirit. This was one of the distinctive features of the Methodist movement, and subjected Wesley and his associates in the work to the sharp criticism of being self-righteous and bigots and fanatics. If any man doubts that this was the teaching of Wesley, let him read Wesley's sermon on "Sin in Believers" and his "Plain Account of Christian Perfection."

I know that it is said, after a hundred years have gone by, that Mr. Wesley greatly modified his views on this subject, if he did not change them altogether.

12

There is not the least shadow of evidence that Mr. Wesley did any such thing. No authentic word or syllable of his can be found upon record contrary to what is taught in the works mentioned above. The only inference—and it barely admits of being an inference—that Wesley's mind underwent any change on this subject was the omission of certain words from the Ninth Article of the Church of England when he came to prepare a system of doctrine and belief for the Methodists in America. The editor of the *Quarterly Review* of the M. E. Church, South (January, 1889), gave such a satisfactory explanation of that action that I can not do better than quote his laconic statement of the reason which influenced Mr. Wesley in his abridgment of the Article. He says: "The language of the Article is Calvinistic. It affirms not only that sin does remain in the soul after the new birth, but that it must continue there during life, until death comes to the relief of the soul and perfects the holiness which the grace of God could not accomplish in the earthly life-time of the believer. This doctrine Mr. Wesley did not teach. He believed that the grace of God could, and did in many cases, so root out and destroy the 'roots of bitterness' that the soul was *entirely* sanctified, holy in thought, desire and act. He saw very clearly that the language of this Article could be used to antagonize his doctrine of Christian Perfection, and he wisely omitted it."

It was to purge the Article of those words which were liable to be construed against the doctrine of Christian perfection, and not to recant his life-long teaching, "that this infection of nature doth remain, yea, in them that are regenerated." He wanted to do away with those words in the Article which seemed to teach that it must *necessarily continue to remain;* for he advocated the doctrine that, while there is an infection of evil nature remaining, even in the regenerate, yet there must be deliverance from it. It is part of the Christian life to seek and obtain *full* salvation through Jesus Christ—in other words to go on to perfection until we are complete in him. This view of the case was beyond all question the sole motive that controlled Mr. Wesley in his abridgment of the Article.

That the Wesleyan theory is in accord with the Scriptures I shall now attempt to show by reference to a few plain texts bearing directly on the subject.

I Corinthian 3:1: "And I, brethren, could not speak unto you as unto spiritual, but as unto carnal, even as unto babes in Christ." This scripture has, strangely enough, been interpreted to mean precisely the opposite to what the apostle intended. Is not a babe a perfect man, having all the members and parts of a full-grown man, only in an infantile state? All that is needed is *growth*, development, by which the babe shall come to the full stature of a man. So we are told that every babe in Christ is a perfect Christian, weak in faith and knowledge as yet, but needing only the graces of the Spirit developed in ordinary growth to arrive at the stature of the fullness of Christ. Now such was not the meaning of the apostle at all. He addressed the Corinthians as babes in Christ to denote not alone their weakness and debility, but their low degree of spiritual-mindedness. They were indeed born of the Spirit, and so were babes in Christ; but there remained in them much of the carnal mind, which manifested itself in "envying, and strife, and divisions," the very things which belong to the flesh. Being the subjects of such ungodly tempers and uncharitable divisions about their ministers, they were carnal, and the apostle addressed them as such, hardly venturing to speak of them "as spiritual" at all. Two things are settled: First, these Corinthians were born of God, for they were "babes in Christ." Second, they were not yet freed from all sin, for they were "carnal." And we know that the "carnal mind is enmity against God." So that their infantile state, instead of being a proof of their perfection in weakness, is intended to denote just the opposite. It means a *want* of perfection, a *lack* of spiritual-mindedness and the prevalence of carnal tempers.

A somewhat parallel text occurs in I Peter 2:1: "Wherefore laying aside all malice, and all guile, and hypocrisies, and envies, and all evil speakings, as newborn babes, desire the sincere milk of the word, that ye may grow thereby." All of which is addressed to believers in Christ who are for the reasons given above styled "newborn babes." They are born again. But let it be observed that growth, the development of the grace already obtained, is not the only thing recommended to these infants in Christ, but the laying aside or getting rid of all malice, *guile*, hypocrisies, envyings, evil speakings, and such like. These are not accidents or infirmities or weaknesses; they are bad things. Neither can there be any healthful growth while these,evil principles infest the heart; hence the very first work urged is complete deliverance from these things. which is not by growth. *They must be laid aside*—which, as all Christian experience attests, is not without a struggle. Common observation teaches that this is the state of most young converts. No sooner do the ecstacies of the first love subside than the motions and feelings of the former self are discovered in some measure; and while there is a sense of peace and joy for what has been done, there is also a conciousness that a further struggle is needed in order that these newly discovered affections and lusts may also be crucified with Christ. Some sincere souls, I dare say, have even been led to doubt their conversion by the discovery of such affections and tempers within, and it may be some for the same reason, not aware of the operation of the Spirit, have lost their hold on God altogether. Feeling the motions of sin within, they have hastily concluded that they were under a delusion. Let all such take comfort from this text; not indeed to be content in sin, but to seek and to find deliverance from sin by laying aside whatever thing is hurtful.

It is impossible to read aright Colossians 3:5 without being impressed with the same doctrine. Speaking to such as were "dead to the world," and whose "life was hid with Christ in God," Paul says: "Mortify therefore your members which are upon the earth; fornication, uncleanness, inordinate affection, evil

concupiscence, and covetousness, which is idolatry ''
Such things had occupied their whole life in times
past; but, having been delivered from the guilt and
bondage of these degrading lusts, it remained for them,
by a course of constant self-denial, to seek and obtain
entire deliverance from the indwelling of these base
elements. Mortify, put to death your members which
are upon the earth. The work is progressive. As
the apostle says, "And have put on the new man,
which is *being* renewed in knowledge," etc. Our
heavenly Father intends that we shall be co-workers
together with him in this process of destroying the
flesh. Only as we see and feel the motions of sin in
the flesh shall it be crucified. We ourselves must
mortify, condemn, insult, put to death by the aid of
the Spirit our members which are in the flesh. Thus
power of will, strength of resolution, and force of
character, as well as the love of God, are developed
mightily within us.

Another text much in point is Hebrew 12:1: "Let
us lay aside every weight, *and the sin which doth so
easily beset us.*" Will anyone say that this is not
addressed to believers? And yet these are exhorted
to seek deliverance from sin, some specific sin, as if it
were a common or universal thing among believers to
have some troublesome remnant of the corrupt nature
until it is destroyed by an extraordinary act of faith
and consecration to God. It is not willful and habitual sin that we are urged to renounce, but the *"beset-
ting sin."* In most, if not all, who are born of the
Spirit there remains what is very properly called "inbred

sin." This is ordinarily some peculiar sin that has dominated the life more than all the rest. While the guilt of former trangressions is canceled, the "original sin," as it is called, may remain in some degree, and, rising at times, may become a besetment. Some are pleased to call this a susceptibility to temptation. But the Bible does not dignify it by any softer appellative than "sin." It is not the *liability* to sin that we are to lay aside, which we can never do, but the *sin* itself. "Let us lay aside every weight, and *the sin.*"

There is another text that I can not forbear to quote—Hebrews 12:14, 15: "Follow peace with all men, and holiness, without which no man shall see the Lord; . . . lest *any root of bitterness springing up* trouble you." That roots of bitterness do often remain even in those who are born of God is beyond question, The apostle speaks as if it were a general rule. Personal altercations more than anything else are likely to give occasion to such roots of bitterness. We ourselves know that we can hardly feel charitably toward those who differ from us in opinion. How much more shall bitter feelings likely rise toward any who may be unfriendly toward us! Hence peaceful relations are to be preserved toward all men, lest roots of bitterness *spring up;* they are there. But this is not all: *holiness* must be pursued also. This implies that all such roots of bitterness must be eradicated. Their very presence is a menace to the purity and peace of the soul, and their continuance in the heart greatly endangers its final salvation. Is it not said: "Without which [holiness] no man shall see the Lord"?

There is one other text which is eminently in point,
II Corinthians 7:1: "Having therefore these promises.
dearly beloved, let us cleanse ourselves from all filthiness of the flesh and spirit, *perfecting holiness* in the
fear of God." Comment is hardly necessary. If the
work was complete and the cleansing thorough, where
were the necessity for this exhortation? Holiness is
the ultimate aim of all who are born of God. And
this word "holiness," which primarily means "sound,"
"safe," "*whole*," is pre-eminently the one word to express the want and need of poor, fallen, corrupt human
nature. Nothing short of heart purity can avail.
There is no theory of sanctification or holiness that is
in such perfect accord with the Scriptures and sound
reason and experience as the Wesleyan theory. Start-
ing with the truth that sin is the corruption of the
nature of every man, it culminates in the doctrine that
if we confess our sins Jesus Christ is faithful and just
to forgive us our sins and to *cleanse us from all unrighteousness.* Some have taken fright at the words "second blessing," and have turned from the doctrine of
holiness altogether, hardly making use of the word.
Whether there be a second blessing or a third blessing
or a continuation of blessings matters little. The
question is to be delivered from "inbred sin," and thus
"perfect holiness in the fear of God." Those who
"expect to be made perfect in love in this life," and
who are "groaning after it," may expect to endure
criticism. But to such I can not do better than repeat
the language of John Wesley himself: "Avoid all
magnificent, pompous words; indeed, you need give

it no general name; neither perfection, sanctification the second blessing nor the having attained. Rather speak of the particulars which God has wrought fo you. You may say: 'At such a time I felt a change which I am not able to express; and since that time have not felt pride or self-will or anger or unbelief, o anything but a fullness of love to God and to all mankind.' "

CHAPTER II.

Christian Perfection—What, When, and How Is It?

REV. H. O. MOORE.

Text: "To the law and to the testimony; if they speak not according to this word, it is because there is no light in them."—Isaiah 8:20.

I do not write for *controversy*. I am not at the task of defending a theory. I labor not to collate the *opinions* of men. I want "the *truth* in love." I want to set forth "that which we have *seen and heard*." I want to speak, "not in the *words* which *man's wisdom* teacheth, but which the *Holy Ghost teacheth;* comparing spiritual things with spiritual."

I come to this "labor of love" feeling my unfitness for it, and pleading the Spirit's guidance in every sentence. I desire to write alone to His glory whom I

In preparing a paper on *Christian Perfection*, a theme that has employed the best minds from the days of Wesley till now, it is needless to say that I do not claim originality. I am content to follow in the footsteps of the safest expositors and holiest people earth has known in my work.

Permit me to say that the title, Chirstian Perfection, is a phrase made of two words used by the Scriptures, and, "unless we would send the Holy Ghost to school, and teach Him to speak," we must accept it and do our best to know what it means when translated into Christian *experience*.

Allow me to further state that according to Mr. Wesley, "*Perfection . . .* is only another term for *holiness*. They are two names for the same thing." *Holiness* and *Sanctification*, in our English Bible, are from one word in the Greek (*hagiasmos,* and must mean the same thing. So it comes to pass that most writers and speakers use these three words interchangeably. I shall, therefore, do so in this article, satisfied that I follow the Spirit in so doing.

I. *I can not conceive of the pure, perfect, holy God being content with less than the holiness of his intelligent creatures.* I can not think of Him stopping in Redemption's work short of "the perfecting of the saints." He tells us in his word of his holiness and says to us: "Be ye holy; for I am holy." (I Peter 1:16.) He reveals to us the fact that angels are our companions (Psalm 91:11-12), and affirmed that they are "holy." (Matt. 25:31.) He assures us that all his "prophets" were "holy men." (Luke 1:70; II Peter 1:21.) He declares that in olden times there were "holy women." (I Peter 3:5.) He proclaims that there are "spirits of just men made perfect." (Heb. 12:23.) He brings out in Revelation the following facts:

(1.) Holiness is a possibility on earth. (Gen. 6:9; Job 2:3; Luke 5:40; Heb. 2:11, 12; Jude 1.)

(2.) The covenant made with Abraham contemplated our holiness. (Luke 1:72-75.)

(3.) The Scriptures were written to show us how to be made perfect. (II Tim. 3:16, 17.)

(4.) Christ gave Himself to a bloody death that He might sanctify and make us pure. (Ephesians 5:25-27; Titus 2:13-14.)

(5.) Preachers and preaching are intended to lead us to perfection. (Ephesians 4:11-13; Col. 1:28.)

(6.) The greatest prayers in the Bible were for the perfecting of God's people. (John 17:16-20; Ephesians 3:14-19.)   The above texts abundantly sustain the statement that the Bible is a treatise on Christian Perfection.   We, therefore, come to inquire of this Book:

II. What is Christian Perfection? It frequently occurs that a question can best be answered affirmatively by first answering it negatively.   Let us, therefore, briefly see what this perfection is not.

(1.) It is not Divine perfection.   God is absolutely holy, therefore His holiness does not admit of growth or loss.   We are to "grow up into Him" to all eternity.

(2.) It is not Angelic perfection.   Angels are not in fallen bodies, nor are they in a sinful world.   As they were never sinners, and as we can never reach a place where it can be said that we never were sinners, it is evident that ours is not angelic perfection.

(3.) Nor is it Adamic perfection.   He had not known sin or its power.   His body was no clog to his mind.   He reasoned accurately at all times.   And as these things can not be affirmed of us on earth, we dare not hope for Adamic perfection.   Mr. Wesley says, in answer to the question, "In what sense are Christians not perfect?"   "They are not perfect in knowledge.   They are not freed from ignorance, no, nor from mistakes.   We are no more to expect any living man to be infallible, than to be omniscient. They are not free from infirmities, such as weakness or slowness of understanding, irregular quickness or heaviness of imagination. From such infirmities as these none are perfectly freed until their spirits return to God. There is no perfection of degrees, none which does not admit of a continual increase."— (Plain Account, page 22.)

It is a washing that makes us clean. "Christ also loved the Church, and gave himself for it, that he might sanctify and cleanse it with the washing of water by the Word." (Eph. 5:25-26.)

It is freedom from sin. "Being then made free from sin, ye became the servants of righteousness."— (Romans 6:18.)

It is a crucifixion that destroys the body of sin. "Knowing this, that our old man is crucified with him, that the body of sin might be destroyed." (Romans 6:6.)

It is a circumcision of the heart. "And the Lord thy God will circumcise thine heart, and the heart of thy seed, to love the Lord thy God with all thine heart, and with all thy soul." (Deut. 30:6.)

It is a Divine purging that is needed. "Every branch in me that beareth not fruit He taketh away, and every branch that beareth fruit, he purgeth it, that it may bring forth more fruit." (John 15:2.)

It is a baptism with the Holy Ghost. "Ye shall be baptized with the Holy Ghost. . . . Ye shall receive power, after that the Holy Ghost is come upon you." (Acts 1:5-8.)

It is a divine filling. "That Christ may dwell in your hearts by faith; that ye, being rooted and grounded in love, may be able to comprehend with all saints what is the breadth, and length, and depth, and heighth, and to know the love of Christ which passeth knowledge, that ye might be filled with all the fulness of God." (Eph. 3:17-19.)

It is our love made perfect, so that tormenting fear is cast out of the soul. "Herein is our love made perfect, that we may have boldness in the day of judgment. . . There is no fear in love, but perfect love casteth out fear, because fear hath torment. He that feareth is not made perfect in love." (I John 4:17-18.)

The above propositions and texts bring out these facts:

(1.) The sanctifying act is one of cleansing, separating, and destroying.

(2.) The sanctified experience is one of expansion, enlargement, and increasing fulness. Thus Rev. F. G. Hibbard, D. D., says: "It is hence, Mr. Wesley, and also Mr. Fletcher, distinguish sanctification into two stages, the lowest degree is to be emptied of all sin; the highest to be filled with God. To be emptied of all sin, to be cleansed from all unrighteousness, is a work to be done by the Spirit of God immediately acting on the soul, through the truth. It is done at once, according to the faith of the believer, through the meritorious blood and righteousness of the Redeemer. But to bring forth the Christian graces to the highest measure of maturity or perfection compatible with this earthly state, or with the moral capabilities of the believer, is a work of time, to be carried forward and performed, till the day of Jesus Christ.''—Quoted in *Purity and Maturity*, p. 154.

Having in this brief way had an answer to the question, What is Christian Perfection? we proceed to ask:

III. When is Christian Perfection to take place in the soul?

Most Protestants believe that as soon as we die we go to heaven or to hell. But as we must follow ''holiness, without which no man shall see the Lord'' (Heb. 12:14), all admit that, in some way, we become perfect before we go out of the body. Yet I am sure that the majority of Christians have no clear-cut views of God's promises or the capacities of the soul at this point, and so, they do not think it possible to reach perfection until near death. I am convinced that most Christians do give all up to God and lean on him alone in death's valley, and are then made perfect. But I do not think this is the best or the safest course to pursue, and I, therefore, call upon God to show you now ''a more excellent way.''

It is unnecessary to argue at length that Perfection is not the same in fact or in time as regeneration. On this point Mr. Wesley says: ''It has been observed before, that the opposite doctrine, that there is no sin in believers, is quite new in the Church of Christ; that it was never heard of for seventeen hundred years; never till it was discovered by Count Zinzendorf. I do no remember to have seen the least intimation of it, either in any ancient or modern writer; unless, perhaps, in some of the wild, ranting Antinomians."—*Sermon on* "*Sin in Believers.*"

It is a remarkable fact that the few who do maintain that sanctification is but a name for the separating, purifying work of regeneration, do regularly testify to their regeneration, but they can not be induced to say they are sanctified, or made holy or perfect. The only reasonable explanation of such conduct on their part is that they are conscious of regeneration as an experience, but do not consciously experience sanctifying grace.

Neither the founders of Methodism nor the Bible represent the two terms as standing for one experience. Mr. Wesley declares: "It is not so early as justification; for justified persons are to 'go on to perfection.'" (Heb. 6:1.) In our Discipline, the pastor after being satisfied "of the genuineness of their faith," etc., is to bring candidates "before the congregation" and after recognizing them "as members of the Church of Christ," he exhorts the "brethren" in these words: "Do all in your power to increase their faith, confirm their hope, and perfect them in love." And in the same Discipline we are told concerning the "admitting preachers into full connection:" "After solemn fasting and prayer, every person proposed shall then be asked, before the Conference, the following questions . . . namely: Have you faith in Christ? Are you going on to perfection? Do you expect to be made perfect in love in this life? Are you groaning after it?"

To these quotations from the founders agree the Scriptures. Paul, in writing to the Corinthians, says,

they were "brethren," "saved," "saints," "in Christ,"
etc. Yet he tells of imperfect Christians living by
them, leading to "contentions," "envying, and strife,
and divisions," and an unseemly conduct at the Lord's
table. He, therefore, exclaims: "This also we wish,
even your perfection." (II Cor. 13:9.)

St. Paul writes to the Thessalonians thus: "And ye
became followers of us, and of the Lord, having received the word in much affliction, with joy of the
Holy Ghost; so that ye were ensamples to all that
believe in Macedonia and Achaia. For from you
sounded out the Word of the Lord not only in Macedonia and Achaia, but also in every place your faith to
God-ward is spread abroad; so that we need not to
speak anything." (I Thes. 1:6-8.) Still after showing
conclusively that these Christians have a high standard
of religious experience, he goes on to affirm that they
lack perfect faith (I Thes. 3:10); that they are not yet
unblameable in holiness before God (I Thes. 3:13); and
that God will entirely sanctify them in the future
(I Thes. 5:23, 24.)

Yet in the face of the fact that the Bible makes
sanctification subsequent to regeneration, we are assured
that Job was a perfect man (Job 2:3). We learn that
God made David's way perfect (II Sam. 22:33). We
find that certain Philippians were perfect (Phil. 3:15).
We are told that some Hebrew Christians were sanctified (Heb. 10:10). And we are informed that Jude
wrote to them that are sanctified (Jude 1). As these
were all living persons, we are compelled to admit that
Christian perfection is possible in this life.

13

A careful study of the Bible brings out these truths: (1) No unconverted sinner is ever required to seek sanctification. (2) No unsanctified Christian is authorized to wait until death for that blessing.

Mr. Wesley says: "As to the time, I believe this instant generally is the instant of death, the moment before the soul leaves the body. But I believe it may be ten, twenty, or forty years before death. Do we agree or differ here?

"I believe it is usually many years after justification, but that it may be within five years, or five months after it."

Christian perfection is for the Church, and for it while on earth. It is the Church that is to be sanctified (Eph. 5:25-27). It is the man of God who may be perfect. (II Tim. 3:17.) The ministers of truth are given for the perfecting of the saints (Eph. 4:11-13). Our love is to be made perfect in this world (I John 4:17). And, finally, God intends "that we, being delivered out of the hand of our enemies, might serve him without fear, in holiness and righteousness before him, all the days of our life." (Luke 1:74, 75.)

We come to inquire:

IV How is Christian perfection to become ours?

In the science of salvation this truth is patent—it is all of grace (Eph. 2:8, 9). It is Jesus who redeems (I Peter 1:18, 19). It is God who quickens (Eph. 2:1). We are born of God (I John 5:1). The Spirit of God reproves of sin, and guides into all truth (John 16:7-13). "It is God that justifieth." (Rom. 8:33.) And so, also, we "are sanctified by God the Father." (Jude 1.)

Sanctification being a divine work in the soul, we can only receive it in meeting the conditon of its reception, as that condition may be revealed to us in his word.

Mr. Wesley says: "I have continually testified (for these twenty and five years) in private and public, that we are sanctified as well as justified by faith. And, indeed, the one of those great truths does exceedingly illustrate the other. Exactly as we are justified by faith, so are we sanctified by faith."

Christ said to Paul that he sent him to the Gentiles "To open their eyes, and to turn them from darkness to light, and from the power of Satan unto God, that they may receive forgiveness of sins, and inheritance among them which are sanctified by faith that is in me." (Acts 26:18.)

These extracts from the founder of Gentile Christianity, and of Methodism, forever explode the idea of growing, working into perfection. No one ever grows into regeneration. No one ever works into any grace. We always enter by faith. By work and growth we stay in that state or experience into which we entered by faith. As soon expect a garden to grow the weeds and grass out of it as to expect a Christian to grow "original sin," "the carnal mind," "the body of sin," "the old man which is corrupt" out of him. The work in either case is a destroying, cleansing work performed by another party.

The Christian studies his Bible and sees that God has promised to make him free from sin, and to fill him with all the fulness of God. He hungers and thirsts for this freedom and filling so intensely that he is led to present his body a living sacrifice unto God (Rom. 12:1), and to cleanse himself trom all filthiness of flesh and spirit (II Cor. 7:11), so that, in conduct, he purifieth himself, even as He is pure (I John 3:3). All the desires are for God's likeness; all the activities are given up to God's glory; and all the prayer of the consecrated soul, "thy will be done in earth, as it is in heaven." This is entire consecration. After this work of complete surrender to the will of God faith is to be made perfect (James 2:22). In the study of the word I am led to believe that Christ "is able also to save them to the uttermost that come unto God by him." (Heb. 7:25.) I am also brought to understand that "this is the will of God, even your sanctification." (I Thes. 4:3.) I see clearly that "Jesus also, that he might sanctify the people with his own blood, suffered without the gate." (Heb. 13:12.) I understand "that the offering up of the Gentiles might be acceptable, being sanctified by the Holy Ghost." (Rom. 15:16.) I come to know that "these are written, that ye might believe," and that "faith cometh by . . . the Word of God." Thus God perfects that which is lacking in my faith, "and the blood of Jesus Christ his Son cleanseth us from all sin." (I John 1:7.)

The steps leading up to the sanctifying act were of necessity to a greater or less extent progressive, but the cleansing work was performed in that very day that I exercised perfect faith in my Omnipotent Sanctifier. "Wherefore the Holy Ghost is also is a witness to us." (Heb. 10:15.) Hallelujah!

So far as I know, the testimony of all who are clear in the experience and witness of purity, is that it was sought as a distinct blessing, was obtained by letting go every dependence but Christ, and trusting alone in his cleansing blood; and was received in a moment.

The words of Wesley on this point are: "In London alone I found six hundred and fifty-two members of our society, who were exceeding clear in their experience, and of whose testimony I could see no reason to doubt. . . . And every one of these (after the most careful inquiry, I have not found one exception either in Great Britain or Ireland) has declared that his deliverance from sin was instantaneous; that the change was wrought in a moment. Had half of these, or one-third, or one in twenty, declared it was gradually wrought in them, I should have believed this in regard to them, and thought that some were gradually sanctified, and some instantaneously. But as I have not found, in so long a space of time (more than thirty years a single person speaking thus; as all, who believe they are sanctified, declare with one voice, that the change was wrought in a moment; I cannot but believe that sanctification is commonly, if not always, an instantaneous work."—*Sermons, Vol. II, p. 223.*

Let no soul say: "It can not be thus." The God who regenerated us in the minute we trusted him for pardon, and who shall awake and change all earth's millions in a moment (I Cor. 15:52) can sanctify us in one day as well as in a thousand years (II Peter 3:8), "according to the working whereby he is able even to subdue all things unto himself." (Phil. 3:21.)

Neither dare affirm: "It can not last, but will soon die out of the soul." "He is able to keep that which I have committed unto him against that day." (II Tim. 1:2.) He "is able to keep you from falling, and to present you faultless before the presence of his glory with exceeding joy." (Jude 24.) He "is able to do exceeding abundantly above all that we ask or think, according to the power that worketh in us." (Eph. 3:20.)

Think of a cork saying to old ocean, "You can't float me." And think of a man in the face of God's love and the above texts declaring, "Christian Perfection is a moral impossibility." Let us trustingly look up into a merciful Father's face and say, "Thou wilt keep him in perfect peace, whose mind is stayed on thee: because he trusteth in thee." (Isa. 26:3.)

This is the what, when, how, of Christian Perfection. It is simply "the fulness of the blessing of the gospel of Christ." (Rom. 15:29.) It is Wesleyan Methodism. Wesley says: "It is the doctrine of St. Paul, the doctrine of St. James, of St. Peter, and of St. John; and no otherwise Mr. Wesley's, than as it is the doctrine of every one who preaches the pure and the whole gospel. I tell you, as plain as I can speak, where and when I found this. I found it in the oracles of God, in the Old and New Testament; when I read them with no other view or desire, but to save my own soul."—*Plain Account.*

Here we stand. This doctrine of post-regenerate sanctification is in the Bible. It is in Methodism to stay. In the early days the Methodist people accepted certain "standards of doctrine," and, by the "first Restrictive Rule," made it utterly impossible for the Church ever to select or establish other "standards of doctrine" contrary to the ones already established. That man would stultify himself who would dare affirm that sanctification, as an experience subsequent to regeneration, is not clearly taught in Wesley, in Watson, in the Hymn Book, and in the Discipline. No ecclesiastical power can ever get it out. It must continue in "our standards" till earth passes away. We stand right on the standards, the first Restrictive Rule, the Bible and a blessed experience, and confidently expect to bring all Christians to accept the doctrine of Christian Perfection, obtain the "like precious faith," and "walk with Him in white" to all eternity Amen

CHAPTER III

The New Birth.

REV. JOHN S. KEEN.

"Ye must be born again." This is not one way, but the only way. What is it to be born again? This is a spiritual birth, and is wrought by the Holy Spirit. It is not so much a radical change of the spirit that is in men, as it is the introduction of the "new man," or of divine life into the dead soul. By sin, man as a subject has dethroned God as a King, and as He is the life of the soul, without His indwelling it is dead. "And you hath he quickened who were dead in trespasses and sins." (Eph. 2:1.) You observe that, "hath he quickened," as it occurs in the Bible, is in italics. That means that it is not in the original text. But it is no harm to supply it here, as it is brought in by the Spirit in the 5th verse. The word *quicken* means to "make alive." Regeneration means to re-life the dead soul. Born of the Spirit, or divine life begotten in the dead soul by the Spirit: "Christ formed within." It is love shed abroad in the heart. God is love—God shed abroad in the heart.

Are you born again? Does God dwell in you?

"Be ye holy, for I am holy." "Without holiness no man can see the Lord." The term holiness in this passage is from the Greek word usually translated sanctification. Holiness is as necessary to the preparation for our coming Lord as the new birth. What is holiness or sanctification? It is the cleansing of the believer from indwelling sin. Entire sanctification is the theme of the inspired writers in their letters to the churches. They had preached Christ and the new birth to the multitudes and organized the young converts into churches, and now they are writing to these babes (yet carnal) on holiness.

By overlooking this fact, we have failed properly to interpret the New Testament writers. Indeed, the entire Bible is a revelation of God to the church directly; and only to the sinner indirectly. God's inspired epistles are written to Christians, and the Christians are God's epistles to the world.

There is no immediate appeal in the Old or New Testament to the heathen, or to the sinner, to be holy. The voice of God to the sinner is, ''Repent;'' to the Christian, ''Be ye holy.'' Jesus gives the key-note to the Father's New Testament saving plan when he says, ''I pray not for the world,'' and then prays, ''Sanctify them through thy truth.'' When he prays for sinners he prays, ''Father, forgive them.'' When he prays for believers, he prays, ''Sanctify them;'' that is, cleanse, or purify them, ''that they may be perfect in one.''

When did this take place? ''When the day of Pentecost was fully come.'' Peter, some time after this, in referring to Pentecost, says to his brethren in defense of his ministry to Cornelius, ''The Holy Ghost fell on them, as on us at the beginning. Then remembered I the word of the Lord, how that he said, John indeed baptized with water, but ye shall be baptized with the

Holy Ghost. . . . God gave them the like gift as unto us, who believed on the Lord Jesus Christ." Later on, in referring to this occasion again, Peter says, "God . . . bear them witness, giving them the Holy Ghost even as unto us; and put no difference between us and them, purifying their hearts by faith." The believing disciples who were "not of the world," in answer to Christ's prayer, were "suddenly" sanctified; and years afterward, under inspiration, Peter testified to this as purification. "Christ also loved the Church, and gave himself for it; that he might sanctify and cleanse it with the washing of water by the word, that he might present it to himself a glorious Church, not having spot or wrinkle, or any such thing; but that it should be holy and without blemish." (Eph. 5:25, 26, 27.)

This is what we are to be, or, not having the pure wedding garment on when he comes, we will be "speechless"—lost without excuse. Have you repented? Have you been born again? Have you been wholly purified? Are you without spot or wrinkle, or any such thing?

Having considered the states and steps to this complete deliverance from all actual sins, and entire purification from all moral corruption, we now come to consider what we are to do in order to be accepted of Jesus when he comes. In the regenerated state there is life, and life will bear fruit. But the presence of indwelling sin in the heart prevents faultless fruit. The divine life is sown, but it is sown among thorns and in stony ground, and in general uncleanness, and a struggle for life begins, which is only ended by death to the spiritual life, or by the Gardener's second work, which is one of cleansing. The figures of fruit growing, and of agriculture, are freely used in both Testaments to teach and explain the two blessings. The hindrances that exist in the first are removed in the second. When removed, the clean branch bears more fruit, and the cleansed ground brings forth some thirty, some sixty, and some an hundred fold. The fight is transferred from the heart to the external world—from a civil to a foreign war. But it is a war. The three principal foes are: The world, the flesh, and the devil.

The world includes everything that is material which can be used by Satan to tempt the soul. Sinful and carnal men are included in the world.

While in sin the entire man has been impaired, and evil habits have been formed. While the root of these habits, which is in the spirit, is destroyed, the effects of the habits still linger in the region of the body. All acquired appetites, passions, and habits can and must be destroyed. All natural appetites and passions are to be regulated. The devil is an unrelenting foe, and while we may have continual victory over him, he is an ever present antagonist.

This warfare is both defensive and aggressive. It involves resistance to the devil, and the courageous discharge of duties in the face of these foes. In this unceasing battle, ''be thou faithful unto death, and I will give thee a crown of life.'' Not simply until, but unto death. Ponder these things, as you and the writer must soon meet them in the presence of the Judge, whose coming will put an end to the war. Jesus must reign till he has put all enemies under his feet. Are you on his side?

CHAPTER IV.

Holiness—Negative and Positive.

REV. L. M. RUSSELL,
Of the Louisville Conference.

1. Entire sanctification does not transform a man into an angel, but it does endow him with such moral dignity as that in God's estimation he is only a little lower than (a little while inferior to) the angels.

2. It does not free a person from being tempted; temptations to the sanctified, if not multiplied in number, are more subtle and intense; but it does wonderfully quicken the spiritual perceptions, and takes everything out of the heart disposing to sin, thus making it more easy to resist and overcome the evil one.

3. It does not affect the possibilities of forfeiting our relationship to God, but it does diminish the liabilities to backsliding and apostasy, making such forfeitures less probable.

4. It does not fix one at a point in experience beyond which there is no development, but it does remove the hindrances to growth in grace, and makes development more sure, rapid and systematic.

5. It does not rid people of infirmities nor insure them against errors of judgment and mistakes in conduct, but it does keep them from making a cloak of infirmities by which to cover their faults and excuse sin, and also makes them less liable to errors in judg-

ment and mistakes in conduct. Such mistakes as may be made by one who is perfectly sincere, prayerful and prudent are consistent with the highest possible state of grace in this life. Infallibility of judgment or con-duct is not taught in the Holy Scriptures as belong-ing to any state of grace in this life.

6. It does not destroy natural affection nor lessen human love, but it does regulate said affection and intensify said love, and keeps one from being enslaved by mere passion or infatuation.

7. It does not take a man out of his natural body, nor disqualify him for the duties of this life, but it does give him perfect dominion over himself, and pre-pares him as nothing else can for the duties of every rightful relationship in this life.

8. It does not deprive a man of his necessary phys ical appetites and propensities, making it indispensa-ble for him to subsist on ethereal matter (for he still requires food, drink, sleep, etc., as other men), but it does regulate all natural, and destroys all abnormal, appetites.

9. It does not deprive one of the powers of speech, nor of the right to express himself, but it does keep one from levity, vulgarity, gossip and backbiting. It makes some folks less loquacious and makes all who have it talk for God.

10. It does not divest folks of the use of their ears, but it does make them sensitive to the voice of God, and keeps them from lending their ears to be used as funnels through which tattlers pour the scum of society into the mind.

11. It does not deprive people of the use of their eyes, but it does keep them from winking for the devil, from gazing with desire after the fashions, amusements and ways of the world; and saves men and women from looking with evil eyes upon each other.

12. It does not destroy one's love for intellectual food, but it does estrange one from fiction and wed him to fact. It keeps one from hankering after unholy literature, novels, etc., and makes him passionately fond of the Word of God, and pure, elevating literature.

13. It does not precipitate death upon an individual, but it does extract the sting and take away the fear of death, and blessedly qualifies a person for living a holy life here, and for an abundant entrance into heaven, when the time of his dissolution may come.

14. It does not put one where he may not conscientiously pray "the Lord's prayer," but it does enable him to pray it with all the sincerity of an innocent and pure soul. One wholly sanctified may commit involuntary transgressions (commonly called errors or mistakes), of which inexorable justice must take account, and for which specific provision was made under the law, and knowing that the atonement of our Lord Jesus embraces the same efficacious need under the dispensation of grace, and knowing that his conduct is not infallible, he cheerfully and humbly prays, "Forgive us our tresspasses," etc.

And being taught of the Holy Spirit that an answer to the prayer directly applies to himself (I Thes. 4:3), and through him affects his fellows, he intelligently prays, "Thy will be done on earth as it is in heaven."

His entire submission to God implies not only a **willing-ness** to receive, but also to do and to suffer His holy will. Dear reader, can you pray "the Lord's prayer"?

15. It does not bring a man into a state where he does not longer need the personal benefits of the meri-torious blood of Christ, but it does place him where there is a continuous affusion of the precious blood upon his love-inflamed and fire-baptized being. Halle-lujah!

CHAPTER V.

What Do You Believe About Sanctificatio.1?

REV. THOMAS M. COBB,
Of Southwestern Missouri Conference.

"That the regeneration which accompanies justifi cation is a large approach to this state of perfect holi ness, and that all dying to sin and all growth in grace advances us nearer to this point of *entire* sanctity, is so obvious that on these points there can be no reason able dispute. But they are not at all inconsistent with a more instantaneous work, when the depth or our natural depravity being more painfully felt we plead in faith the accomplishment of the promises of God."— *Richard Watson.*

I have been asked to state just what my views on sanctification are. I know no better or more Method-istic way than to answer in the words of Richard Wat-son. The work of grace in the human heart, leading np to holiness without which no man can see the Lord, is a progressive work. Progressive in the sense that certain states go before certain other states. The Methodistic, and as we all believe, Bible doctrine, is conviction, penitence, faith, justification, regeneration, sanctification. This order can not be inverted or in any wise changed. That sanctification is subsequent to regeneration is just as apparent as that regeneration is subsequent to justification. As regeneration begins in justification so sanctification begins in regeneration.

The one does not end in the other, however. Holiness implies the presence and perfection of all other graces, perfect in the sense that all necessary preparation is now had for the crowning work—the entire sanctification of soul, body and spirit. Romans 12:1 is the Scriptural statement of how it is done on our part. A man may be a year or ten years reaching this entire consecration of faith that he may know the good and perfect will of the Lord. Then, as Mr. Watson teaches, there may be, there ought to be, a more instantaneous work. The fact is, our sanctification, like our justification, must be sought after and obtained by faith. The blessing itself comes instantaneously, as at Pentecost, though the evidence of it may not always be so satisfactory. But if the sacrifice is made, if it be living, *holy*, and of faith, the fire will come down, and the heart will be melted into sweetness and love. There is no better test of its genuineness than the fruit it bears. The mind that was in Christ will also be in the sanctified one. Humility (study that word) will dominate all words and ways. Intelligent, sanctified people are always careful to magnify the Christ and to keep self out of view. What Jesus has done for my soul is the theme, not what I was then and what I am now. It is enough to say that "I am chief of sinners, but He has saved me and made me feel the least of all the saints." The less one esteems himself, the more he realizes his own weakness and unworthiness, the nearer he is to God. I know that many accuse Methodists of boasting, claiming to be more holy than others. This comes of the fact that

14

they teach and preach a more perfect salvation. We believe in salvation from *all* sin; that a man may so give himself to God and so believe in the blood of Christ as to not only be pardoned and cleansed, but be kept by the power of God unto perfect and eternal salvation.

The revival of this doctrine in the Church is one the most hopeful signs of the times. To be sure there has been, and will be, much controversy as to theories and measures. All are not agreed about these things. If we can only agree to disagree about minor and non-essential things and press the battle for the Lord and the purity of the Church, a great and glorious victory awaits us in the future. Our God is merciful. He can and will hear prayers, and if his holy ones will only agree touching this one thing, a mighty baptism on all the Church, and cry mightily to God for it, *it will come*.

I am on the superannuated list, a hopeless invalid, can no more enter the battle as an effective soldier, but from my place of suffering, watching and writing, I lift up my heart to God for the spirit of power upon our preachers and people. I am in full sympathy with every movement that looks to deliverance from worldly lust and sinful pleasure. Let us be true to our form of government, stand by those in authority over us, do everything through the regular channels of the Church, defend our system of doctrines, and persist in spreading scriptural holiness over the land. God is with all who are for holiness, and the number of sanctified ones is being multiplied. Victory is coming. Glory to God in the highest! The blood—the blood of the Lamb—is my only plea. It cleanseth me from all sin.

CHAPTER VI.

Entire Sanctification.

BISHOP ELIJAH HEDDING.

The difference between a justified soul **who is not** fully sanctified, and one fully sanctified, I **understand** to be this: the first (*if he does not backslide*) is kept from *voluntarily committing* know sin, which is what is commonly meant in the New Testament by *committing sin*. But he yet finds in himself the remains **of** *inbred corruption*, or *original sin*, such as *pride, anger, envy, a feeling of hatred* to an enemy, a rejoicing **at a** calamity which has fallen upon an enemy, etc. The second, or the person fully sanctified, *is cleansed from all these inward involuntary sins.*

The degree of *original sin* which *remains in some believers* though not a transgression of a known law, is nevertheless sin, and must be removed before one goes to heaven, and the removal of this evil is what we mean by full sanctification.

Though the Christian does not feel guilty for this depravity, as he would if he had voluntarily broken the law of God, yet he is often grieved and afflicted, and reproved at a sight of this sinfulness of his nature.

Regeneration also, being the same as the **new**

birth, is the beginning of sanctification, though not the completion of it, or not *entire sanctification.* Regeneration is the beginning of purification; entire sanctification is the finishing of that work.

_____

It is as important that you (the ministers of the New Jersey Conference) should experience this holy work, as it is that the sinners to whom you preach should be converted.

_____

The faith which is the condition of this entire sanctification is exercised only by a penitent heart, a heart willing to part with all sin forever, and determined to do the will of God in all things.

SECTION IV.

SANCTIFICATION AND THE OPPOSITION.

CHAPTER I.

A Plea For Righteous Judgment.

REV. H. B. COCKRILL.

Much has been said against the doctrine of the second blessing unto sanctification and against its promoters. There is no use for either side to become unduly excited. We all agree that it is truth, not error, that we want; peace, not strife; love, not hatred; gentleness, not harshness; liberality, not prejudice.

That God in the last few years has sent us a great revival of religion we can but see, and in this we can but rejoice. All over the Church hundreds and thousands have been converted and sanctified. The Church has come upon a higher plane spiritually. Yet none of us feel that enough has been done. We doubtless greatly desire that the work go forward unhindered. Where we have had hundreds of souls converted and perfected in love we desire to see thousands and hundreds of thousands.

God forbid that any of us should say one word, or do one thing that would in the remotest degree hinder this work. That God is with us, and mightily wit.. us, who can doubt but the unbeliever?

All we ask is to be judged fairly in this matter. What have we done to merit censure? It has been charged upon us that it is our purpose to "rule or ruin;" that we have designed to alienate the people from the Church; that we are un-Wesleyan, and un-Scriptural, riding a human hobby; that it is our stock in trade to abuse the Church of Christ; that it is our purpose to organize a new Church. From the general trend of opposition it would appear that we are unworthy of a place in the Methodist Church or ministry. We have not space to reply at length to all these serious charges, but we trust to show by our lives of devotion to God and the Church that they are all totally unfounded. But we wish to submit to your candid judgment the following. God being our judge, we wish to mislead no man, our object being to get the sinner converted, the believer sanctified and the kingdom of God built up.

IS THE SECOND BLESSING SCRIPTURAL?

We believe that it is. In this we stand with our founder, who says: "In 1729 my brother Charles and I, reading the Bible, saw we could not be saved without holiness, followed after it, and incited others so to do. In 1737 we saw that this holiness comes by faith. In 1738 we saw likewise that men are justified before they are sanctified."

Here John Wesley, reading the Bible, saw justification as a first blessing, sanctification as a second or subsequent blessing.

Again he says: "I tell you as plain as I can speak, where . . . I found this [doctrine.] I found it in the oracles of God, in the Old and New Testament."— Plain Account.

This shows that John Wesley thought he saw sanctification as a second blessing in the Bible. Let none be too hasty in saying it is not there.

Richard Watson, whose Systematic Theology is in our Course of Study, says: "We have already spoken of justification, adoption, regeneration, and the witness of the Holy Spirit, and we proceed to another as distinctly marked and as graciously promised in the Holy Scriptures: This is ENTIRE SANCTIFICATION or the perfected HOLINESS of believers; and as this doctrine, in some of its respects, has been the subject of controversy, the Scriptural evidence must be appealed to and examined. Happily for us a subject of so great importance is not left in obscurity." (Theological Institutes, p. 611.)

Here you see our greatest theological writer believes that "distinctly marked and as graciously promised in Holy Scriptures" is this second blessing unto sanctification, that is, that it is another blessing distinct from justification, adoption, regeneration and the witness of the Spirit. Let us not be too ready to say this great man was wrong in saying it was Scriptural. We believe in independent investigation, but not in rash conclusions.

Dr. T. N. Ralston, whom we all remember with tenderness, after dealing specifically in his Elements of Divinity with regeneration, says: "What we her* propose is a brief view of the doctrine in question [Christian Perfection] as exhibited in Scriptures. It is expressed in the New Te tament by three different words—holiness, sanctification and perfection." Again. "When we are justified, we *may*, from that hour, go on to perfection; and whenever we comply with the conditions prescribed in the gospel—that is, whenever *we exercise the requisite degree of faith*, be it one day or ten years after our conversion — *that moment* God will *cleanse us from all unrighteousness.*" (Elements of Divinity, p. 468.)

Dr. Ralston thought it Scriptural, and a second blessing to be received *that moment we believe, one day or ten years after our conversion.* Should not all consider well before they pronounce this doctrine un-scriptural?

Dr. Miley, of the M. E. Church, and Dr. Tigert, of the M. E. Church, South, modern theologians whose scholarship all acknowledge, conclude that the second blessing is Scriptural.

Dr. Miley says: "Indeed the attainableness of sanctification according to this definitely-wrought doctrine [second blessing], as above stated, is a truth which lies in the soteriology of the Scriptures, as a whole."

Dr Tigert, in a late *Methodist Review*, declares: "We have never been wedded to the much-ridiculed phrase 'second blessing,' but we have always contended that better than any other phrase, it sums up the essentials of the Wesleyan and Scriptural doctrine."

These men of acknowledged ability declare the doctrine to be Scriptural. We would be unwarranted in denying their statements without a thorough investigation.

Is it not clear that there are two distinct blessings taught in the Bible? The first, pardon of sin, the second, cleansing from all unrighteousness; the first, justification; the second, sanctification; the first, regeneration; the second, entire sanctification; the one, the acceptance of Christ as a Savior, the other, an acceptance of Christ as a sanctifier? That converted persons may have this second blessing, or entire cleansing, we refer you to the prayer of Jesus for his disciples. John 17:15-23; I Thes. 5:23; Acts 2:38-39; 26:18; Gen. 17:1; Titus 3:3-6; I John 1:7-9; Titus 2:14.

There are a great many other passages showing that converted persons are commanded to *perfect holiness in the fear of God*. Now it seems to us that if, as you claim this experience of sanctification is by growth, it would yet be a *second blessing*, being the first distinctly marked blessing after conversion. Much more then may it appropriately be called a second blessing since it is the gift of God and obtained by faith; may be experienced now, and is the removal of indwelling sin.

You understand that any justified person receives many blessings while living in the converted life, as they sometimes say, "a thousand of them," but by entire sanctification we mean that blessing which cleanses us from *all unrighteousness*, which removes indwelling sin from the heart, which makes us "free indeed."

This is what Mr. Wesley meant by the second bless-

ing.   Is it right for any Methodist to keep our meaning
hid, and ridicule the phrase "second blessing" in order
to prejudice people against the great doctrine of Methodism, and the promoters of it?   Let us judge righteously.

IS THE SECOND BLESSING WESLEYAN?

John Wesley and the early writers of the Church
were very clear in pronouncing Christian Perfection to
be a second blessing.   They commonly spoke of it as
such.

Mr. Wesley in his Journal speaks of the experience
of sanctification thus: "Within five weeks five in our
band received the second blessing."   Again: "This
morning one found peace and one the second blessing."
Writing to a lady he says: "You have evidently received the second blessing properly so-called."   Again
he says: "Insist everywhere on full salvation received
now by faith.   Press the instantaneous blessing."

A volume might be filled with extracts from the
writings of Mr. Wesley along this line.

Tyerman in his Life of Wesley says that Christian
Perfection was generally known and spoken of as the
second blessing in early Methodism.   Mark the statement of Mr. Wesley that sanctification is "the second
blessing *properly so-called*."

Richard Watson, as we have seen, declares it to be
distinctly marked from regeneration and adoption.

Hence we see that Mr. Wesley is responsible for the
phrase second blessing.   He thought it was properly
called a second blessing.   Why should any Methodist
object to us on this account?

The Methodist doctrine as stated many times by Mr. Wesley, was substantially this: Christian Perfection is the gift of God bestowed upon a truly regenerated person in answer to the prayer of faith, and is received instantaneously. A gradual work of growth in grace precedes it and follows it. The work accomplished by this blessing he clearly teaches is the destruction of the old man, the removal of indwelling or inbred sin. To substantiate this we point you to Wesley's Sermons on "Sin in Believers," "Repentance of Believers," and "Patience." Also to his "Plain Account of Christian Perfection," and his Journal. Mr. Wesley combatted with great vigor the doctrine that we are wholly sanctified at conversion.

We give a few brief extracts from his Journal: "Several of our friends declared that God saved them from *inbred sin* with such exactness, both of sentiment and language, as clearly showed us they were taught of God."—Journal, 1785. This was written after he gave the American Church her articles of faith. "Many children, chiefly girls, were indisputably justified; some of them likewise sanctified, and were patterns of holiness."—Journal, 1788. "Many have been convinced of sin; many have been justified; some perfected in love."—Journal, 1789.

"I have continually testified," says Mr. Wesley, "for these five and twenty years, in private and in public, that we are sanctified as well as justified by faith."

"Press the instantaneous blessing," said John Wesley to his brother Charles.

But we do not believe now that any will question

that Mr. Wesley, Watson, Clarke, and Fletcher taught the second blessing unto sanctification—that it is subsequent to regeneration, by faith, instantaneous, and removes inbred sin.

Now what real offense can we have committed as Methodists, in preaching this second blessing, since it it is clearly the Methodistic doctrine or view of sanctification?

DO WE WANT A NEW CHURCH?

We say most emphatically we do not. That is said to be our purpose. We utterly disclaim any such purpose. What could we want with a new Church? The Methodist Church, distinctively a holiness Church, is good enough for us. Hear John Wesley: "It (holiness) is the grand *depositum* which God has given to the people called Methodists, and chiefly to propagate this, it appears, God has raised them up." Here is where we want to live and work, and here is where we want to die.

We believe the doctrinal teachings of our Churc_ from conviction to perfect love. We could have no design in organizing a new Church. You might suspect those who differ in doctrine from the Church, but not those who are in perfect harmony therewith. A few have left us who professed holiness, but they have received no encouragement from the great body of those who have sought and obtained perfect love.

And it might be well to inquire into the real causes which led these to withdraw from us. We can not believe it was the second blessing unto sanctification, the distinguishing doctrine of Methodism. We are to look elsewhere for the causes. The main cause is no doubt to be found in the bitter opposition of those in our Church who fight the Wesleyan doctrine of the second blessing unto sanctification. Many professing holiness in other denominations have, under the pressure of opposition, come to us, hoping to find a refuge from strife, but sad to say they have not always found it. Ought we not to make our Church an asylum for those who are persecuted for Jesus' sake? Or shall we join hands with the worldly, the indifferent, the formal, the vicious, and become "despisers of those that are good?"

Have not the promoters of the second blessing unto sanctification the right in the Methodist Church to testify and preach the doctrine with vigor without being subjected to the suspicion that they want a new Church? It does seem to us they have.

ARE WE RIDING A HOBBY?

We are not. None but the most reckless and inconsiderate could get his consent to call this *grand depositum of Methodism* a hobby. If it is, our founder, and those who helped him establish our Church, are guilty of riding a hobby. Some of the best men that ever lived, including bishops and other worthies of our Church, stand convicted of hobby riding. And by whom? Better men, or wiser? Who will say so?

Are we charged with hobby riding because we are zealous in promoting this doctrine? Listen to the instructions of our founder on this point: "Therefore, let all our preachers make it a point to preach Perfec-

tion to believers constantly, strongly and explicitly."
To Mr. Garrettson he wrote in 1785: "The more
explicitly and strongly you press all believers to aspire
after full salvation, full sanctification, as attainable *now*
by simple faith, the more the whole work of God will
prosper."

Ought we to be called hobby riders because we take
this excellent advice of Mr. Wesley? Suppose all
Methodist preachers, North and South, should begin
to press full sanctification on all believers, now, by
simple faith. All will agree that we would soon be in
the midst of the greatest revival that ever blessed our
land. Our danger is not that we make a hobby of this
great and full salvation, but that we fail to preach it
as faithfully as we should.

Is it meant by this charge that we preach Perfection
exclusively? We do not preach it to the exclusion of
conviction, repentance, justification by faith, adoption
and regeneration. Indeed, we make these the necessary foundation for Perfection. It can be built upon
no other.

Do we alienate the people from the Church?

This charge has been made but without foundation
in fact. Among the most zealous supporters of the
institutions of the Church, the most efficient revival-
ists, the most zealous Sunday-school workers, the most
scrupulous and faithful in observing family prayer and
working for the conversion of sinners, are found those
professing the second blessing unto sanctification. We
reprove worldliness, we rebuke sin. We urge people
to get converted and go on to perfection, and receive

thousands into the Church. Indeed, thousands who were only nominal members before become efficient supporters of the Church through the work of the promoters of holiness.

If any are alienated from the Church, it comes from their being opposed. It does not lie in any fault of the doctrine taught, or of those who teach it. Instead of an alienating spirit in holiness there is really a mighty drawing power. And if there were no opposition in our Church all the good people in the world would be drawn toward us.

DO WE WISH TO FORM A FACTION OR PARTY IN THE CHURCH?

We do not. Of course we feel that we must glorify God by telling our experiences on all proper occasions. The fact that we testify makes it appear (not designed on our part) that we are clannish.

Then another thing. Opposition will make people of the same mind appear clannish. Nothing grieves the promoters of the second blessing more than that they should be taught not to love their brethren, or to wish to be separated from them in any sense. This they greatly deplore.

DO THE ASSOCIATIONS ANTAGONIZE THE CONFERENCES?

We ask you to calmly consider this question. Wherein? Why, not at all. The Association antagonizes the Conference at no point. Each has its respective work not contemplated by the other. The Conference attends to the business of the Church, the Association is organized (in the simplest way) to promote holiness. There is as much difference and yet as little conflict between the Quarterly Conference and the public service connected with it. There is absolutely nothing done at the Association that conflicts with the Conference in the remotest degree. The Association is simply a reviving of the band meetings Mr. Wesley organized for the promotion of holiness. There is no strife between them, and it is not right for the opposers to make this unfounded charge.

Is God with those who are teaching the second blessing unto sanctification?

You can not deny this. Many are mightily converted in their Associations, their camp-meetings, their revivals. Many church members are brought upon a higher plane of joy and peace and rest in the Holy Ghost. This is the great work of God. We feel that men ought to be very slow in their opposition to that which God honors. If you can not indorse it, be at least like Gamaliel who advised the Jews not to persecute the early Christians, "for," said he, "if it be not of God it will come to naught. If it be of God you should be careful lest you be found fighting God."

Are the promoters of this doctrine beardless youths? This has been charged. But they are not. Men of deep piety, of learning, of ability are among the zealous advocates of this doctrine. Also men of age and sound judgment. It is folly to try to discount this doctrine because only the young and unlearned are its advocates. If that were true, it would make it all the more marvelous that they have had such great success.

Now we submit it to your calm judgment, Have we not the right to peaceably preach our views, to live unmolested in the Methodist Church? Why should Isaac be driven from his own house? If anybody must go in order to secure peace let it be Ishmael. If we can be proved un-Wesleyan or unscriptural, we are willing to vacate in favor of the truth. But if neither can be shown, we ask of all fair-minded men if we ought not to be let alone?

We can not believe our church organs are promoting the cause of sanctification or of the true interests of the Church by fighting the second blessing either as a phrase or as a doctrine, for both are Wesleyan and it is believed can be clearly and satisfactorily proved by the word of God.

Brethren, we can not get rid of this Methodist doctrine. It will not down. If every Association were disbanded, every camp-meeting deserted, every promoter of the second blessing excluded from the Church, we would still have it in our standards of doctrine. And others would rise up in your midst to seek it and preach it. To get rid of it there would of necessity be an unending process of exclusion. or change of our standard literature on this subject of sanctification; a task which can not be accomplished.

Besides, no man is offering us anything better than the Wesleyan theory. Indeed, most of us feel that this is, after all, the best theory of sanctification ever

15

formulated. Then let us fall back to this, preach it with all our might, and we will soon see the world in a revival flame, and the knowledge of the Lord covering the earth as waters cover the sea.

Let Mr. Wesley first answer this. He says: "But we do not know of a single instance, in any place, of a person receiving in one and the same moment, remission of sins, the abiding witness of the Spirit, and a new and clean heart."—Plain Account.

Dr. Clarke says: "I have been twenty-three years a traveling preacher, and have been acquainted with some thousands of Christians during that time who were in different states of grace; and I never, to my knowledge, met with a single instance where God both *justified and sanctified* at the same time."

Rev. Wm. Bramwell writes to a friend: "An idea is going forth that when we are 'justified we are entirely sanctified,' and 'to feel evil nature after justification is to lose pardon,' etc. You may depend upon it *this is the devil's great gun*. We shall have much trouble with this, and I am afraid we can not suppress it."—Memoirs.

How did Mr. Wesley regard the view that we are entirely sanctified at conversion?

He repudiated it as a dangerous heresy. It was to correct this error that he wrote his sermon on "Sin in Believers." He says: "I retired to Lewisham and wrote the sermon on 'Sin in Believers' in order to

remove a mistake, which some were laboring to propagate—that there is no sin in any that are justified.''

He further says: ''I can not therefore, by any
means, receive this assertion, that there is no sin in a
believer from the moment he is justified:

''1. Because it is contrary to the whole tenor of
Scripture.

''2. Because it is contrary to the experience of the
children of God.

''3. Because it is absolutely new, never heard of in
the world till yesterday.

''4. Because it is naturally attended with the most
fatal consequences; not only grieving those whom
God hath not grieved, but perhaps dragging them into
everlasting perdition.''

IS IT THE REMOVAL OF INBRED SIN?

Let Mr. Wesley answer this first.   He says: ''Sanctification begins the moment a man is justified.   Yet
sin remains in him, yea, the seed of all sin till he is
sanctified throughout.''

Mr. John Fletcher says: '' This fault, corruption,
or infection doth remain in them who are regenerated.''

Bishop Hedding says: '' Regeneration is the beginning of purification; entire sanctification is the finishing of that work.''

Bishop Foster says: '' The merely regenerate are
not sanctified; they are not entirely free from sin, they
are not perfect in love.''

Mr. Wesley further says: '' By all the grace which

is given at justification we can not extirpate them. Though we watch and pray ever so much we can not wholly cleanse either our hearts or hands. Most sure we can not till it please our Lord to speak to our hearts again — to speak the SECOND time, be clean; and then ONLY the leprosy is cleansed. Then only the ROOT, the CARNAL MIND is destroyed; INBRED SIN subsists no more.''

IS IT INSTANTANEOUS?

Mr. Wesley declares: '' But if there be no such SECOND CHANGE; if there be no instantaneous change AFTER justification; if there be none but a GRADUAL work of God (that there is a gradual work none denies), then we must be content, as well as we can, to remain full of sin till death.''—Sermons.

Again he says: ''To talk of this work (entire sanctification) as being gradual, would be nonsense, as much as if we talked of gradual justification.

''As to manner, I believe this perfection is *always* wrought in the soul by a SIMPLE ACT OF FAITH: consequently IN AN INSTANT.''

Again he says: '' Certainly, sanctification (in the proper sense) is an INSTANTANEOUS DELIVERANCE FROM ALL SIN.''

Lest some should not understand what is meant by a gradual work, to which Mr. Wesley refers, it may be well to explain that he means here, growth in grace. He teaches that if there is nothing but growth in grace, no instantaneous work, that then the Christian must go to his grave with sin in him.

SHOULD IT BE TESTIFIED TO?

Rev. William Bramwell says: "I think such a blessing (entire sanctification) can not be retained without professing it at every opportunity; for thus we glorify God, and with the mouth make confession unto salvation."

John Fletcher lost this grace several times. He says: "I received this blessing four or five times before, but lost it by not observing the order of God who has told us 'with the heart man believeth unto righteousness and with the mouth CONFESSION is made unto salvation.' But the enemy offered his bait under various colors to keep me from a PUBLIC DECLARATION of what my Lord had wrought.

"When I first received this grace Satan bid me wait awhile, till I saw more of the fruits. I resolved to do so. But I soon began to doubt of the witness which before I had felt in my heart, and was in a little time sensible I had lost both.

"A second time after receiving this salvation (I confess it with shame) I was kept from being a witness for my Lord by the suggestion, 'thou art a public character; the eyes of all are upon thee; and if, as before, by any means thou lose the blessing, it will be a dishonor to heart holiness,' etc. *I held my peace and again forfeited the gift of God.*

"At another time I was prevailed upon to hide it by reasoning, How few even of the children of God will receive this testimony. . . . Now, my brother," he continues, "you see my folly."

It does good to profess sanctification in the presence of those who are unprejudiced. Dr Adam Clarke says: "It has been no small mercy to me, that in the course of my religious life I have met with many persons who *have professed* that the blood of Jesus Christ had saved them from all sin, and whose profession was maintained by an immaculate life."—Theology.

Mr. Wesley encouraged the profession of sanctification. He says: "One reason why those who are saved from sin should freely declare it to *believers* is because nothing is a stronger incitement to them to seek after the same blessing."

Again he says: "At the love feast Mr. C. related the manner how God perfected him in love,—*a testimony which is always attended with a peculiar blessing.*" This is always true, unless the profession is made in the presence of a lot of old Pharisees.

Bishop Asbury says: "I think we ought modestly to tell what we feel to the fullest. For two years past, amidst innumerable trials, I have enjoyed almost *inexpressible sensations.* Our Pentecost is come in some places for *sanctification.* I have good reasons to believe that upon the eastern shore *four thousand* have been converted since the first of May last, and *one thousand sanctified.*"—Journal.

Rev. Henry Boehm gives an account of the work of God in the days of Asbury in the following statement taken from his diary: "There were one hundred and forty-six converted and seventy-six sanctified during the day. . . . During the meeting there were reported thirteen hundred and twenty-one conversions, and nine hundred and sixteen sanctifications."

So we see that the early American Methodists had just such meetings as we are now having, only greater ones. When will our Church quit fighting their own precious doctrine and go to seeking it with all their might? Again this writer says: "At sunset they reported three hundred and thirty-nine conversions and one hundred and twenty sanctifications. . . . There were eleven hundred conversions and nine hundred and sixteen sanctifications." Truly Bishop Asbury could say, *"our Pentecost is come in some places for sanctification."*

CHAPTER II.

"History Repeats Itself."

REV. H. R. WITHERS, D. D.

Since the day the Pharisees expelled from Israel the precious hope, the result has been an effort of ecclesiastical authority to check the movements of Providence. Jesus saw what was coming and made an organization to meet the emergencies, but He had hardly more than shaped it, when the same spirit of jealous dominance showed itself among the apostles. "Master, we saw one casting out devils in thy name and we forbade him, because he followeth not with us." "Forbid him not," the Lord replied, and then laid down a rule of church government applicable to all ages and conditions of religious government.

The ill judgment of the Pharisees, and later of the Pope in his treatment of Luther, down to the expulsion of Wesley's societies from the Church of England and the refusal of the New Connection Methodists to recognize the evangelism of Booth, who now, in thirty years, heads a church stronger than that which pushed him off, are but repetitions of the bigotry which he suffered in his own person and rebuked in his disciples. "No man can do a miracle in my name and lightly speak evil of me." "He that is not against us is for us." Here is a liberal and broad constitutional provision for church administration.

(244)

Suppose the Jews had correctly read the signs of
their times. All those great prophecies of national
splendor and universal influence would have been ful-
filled. Judea would have become the first and greatest power on earth. All nations would do reverence
to the grand old power. With Israel thoroughly
Christianized, with the glory of the present century
fully anticipated, what a base of union the gospel
would have had. Every synagogue in Asia and
Africa would have been a Christian church and there
would have been no Jews — "Lewd fellows of the
baser sort" — to stir up the Gentiles in antipathy to
the gospel. I fear the Jew will never appreciate the
terrible significance of the Lord's words, "The kingdom of God shall be taken from you and given to a
people bringing forth the fruits thereof." It is now a
moral derelict, floating without aim, dark and deserted
of God and man, a wretched curse and monumental
of the danger of crossing the purpose of God.

The blind eyes of Israel, I fear, will never be able
to see what was implied in the Lord's words when he
said, "The kingdom of God is taken from you and
the vineyard shall be given to others who shall bring
forth the fruits in their season." And with equal
blindness the Pope rejected divine overtures tendered
Rome in the proposed reformation of Luther. I have
a strong conviction that the seven thunders uttered
and sealed contain the glory of the Church as it would
have been if Rome had accepted this tender of mercy.

The angel with foot on sea and land — Church and
State — appears with a trumpet — next to the last —

swearing "time shall be no more." Not the fina dissolution, of course, for another trumpet, with its long history, was yet to sound. It referred to the character of the times, the slavery and degradation of the true church, "The City of God," and of letters and civil governments. But what history presents to us, I think, bears little comparison to that which might be read could we but open the pages of those sealed thunders. Unbind your imagination and ask, What might the Church of Rome not have done had she given herself wholly to God's will when he called her by Luther? She held much of the world's great treasures. They were tributary to her hand. Kings were obedient to her will. Many nations bow at her feet. All she needs is to be washed in the blood of the Lamb, and take the world by the hand leading it to Christ. God had practically destroyed idolatry, leaving the world in the hands of the Church. But O, it is the saddest thought of history! The Church was not ready. Once more history is repeated. "The kingdom of God shall be taken from you." "Ye can not discern the signs of the times." They "Cast out the heir and seized upon the inheritance." Now God will seal up the thunders and raise a church of Protestants.

And behold another spiritual "derelict" floating on the ocean's current. A great imperial hull, dark and bloody, dashed by billows, deserted by the Holy Spirit. The church of Germany and England now come into view. It was the best God could do. The faith of the Reformers was not perfect. Like Peter before he was sanctified, they leaned too much on the sword. Luther is the lone exception. His motto is: "Fight Rome with the Bible. It is the only thing she dreads."

But there was a political element in the work he could not control; it appealed to arms, and resulted in the organization of a church on the imperfect creed of justification by faith. The church was filled up with great blocks of ignorance and religious superstition, torn from the bosom of Rome by the German sword. The same occurred in England by the English sword, from motives in Henry VIII. of the most dishonorable grade. But God's work can not be wholly obstructed, although it may and often is hampered and hindered. The gospel has not been successful in France because the sword was used.

Many truly great men were in this vast mass of British ignorance called the Church of England. It has steadily declined in the sanctity of its ministry till the light on the altar was extinguished. When Mr. Wesley was born her ministry did not know the doctrine for which their fathers had died at the stake: Justification by faith alone. They did not know the church held such doctrine. Were they ignorant? Far from it. They were masters, classical, great writers, and scholarly as they are to-day in our church. Thorough in everything but their own church's doctrines. We have to-day in Methodism men in holy orders who are ignorant in nothing but the standard doctrines of their own church. Does the statement seem irreverent, uncharitable, and shock you? You do not deny it was true of the Pharisees when Jesus came; true of the Church of Rome when Luther came; true of the Church of England when Wesley came. The ministry were not all corrupt in that day. Many of them were truly devout, and some of them were justified, enjoying a working degree of spirituality; but in England they were so rare that Mr. Wesley had long been an ordained priest before he found one who could give him just views of the doctrines of justification by faith; and he — Peter Bohler — of a different church — the Moravian. The church had never been raised high enough; the reformation had not been completed. Faith alone, even unto entire sanctification, was then, as now, and ever has been, and must forever be, God's one and only method for perfect salvation.

Luther started well, but politics fastened itself on his scheme and he could not control it. Then it was the thunders were sealed up. Among the last words of Christ was the solemn warning given to Peter for the Church: "They that take the sword shall perish with the sword." Christ does not need the sword. He will use a far greater power. What hindered him from commanding "more than twelve legions of angels" to defend his cause if he would use a carnal weapon? The German governments made the mistake of joining the sword to the doctrine of justification by faith, thus weakening the arm of the Lord. They did perish by the sword. Defeated by Charles V., the whole Protestant movement would undoubtedly have been lost but for providential political complications, which promoted the independence of Germany.

One of the saddest scenes of the wars of the Reformation is that of a poor Zwingle, dying of wounds on the
battlefield, begging water from the enemy who had
stricken him to the earth. For hours the charging
cavalry had ridden over his prostrate form, still conscious, but helpless. They knew not that, next to
Luther, the chief promoter of the world's greatest
Reformation lay bleeding on a carnal sword, beneath
their horses' feet, dying, in the camp of the enemy.

But few of those great leaders had risen as high in
spiritual knowledge as God designed. The Reformation was conducted on the plan of a compromise with
works and was extended so far as to include war as a
part of its works on some occasions. The Reformation must be reformed. It can never be considered as
finished till works of all kind are eliminated from the
divine system as having any merit in the production
of either justification or Christian perfection. The
Reformation halted on the doctrine of justification.
One always backslides who stops at this point. The
only way to make justification safe is to keep it pressing forward to the end, perfection. Failing of this.
it is sure to lapse into open sin or devotional Pharisee-
ism — most generally the latter. Such were the ministry of the Protestant churches, long after persecution
ceased. And the masses, alas! they were more the
fruit of the sword than of the Spirit. Here was work
for the second Reformation, the work in which the
Reformation was to be reformed; the time and the
field for Wesley.

The providential purpose in this great movement

was to eliminate, not only the sword as a means of grace, but works of all kinds as a condition either of justification or entire sanctification. This latter grace was not really to be discovered, for the church had always acknowledged it, even in its darkest and most idolatrous age; but it was to be defined, delivered from mysticism, æstheticism, and restored to its New Testament place as the finishing of the grace given in regeneration, and, like it, by faith alone.

These doctrines are the corner-stone of the great Wesleyan Reformation. As the work progressed, more and more clearly did this great apostle of truth perceive the truth. It is well to observe here how easy it is for honest and devout men and women to be deceived; and learning is no protection whatever.

It is amazing how deeply and earnestly religious one may be without being religious at all in the right sense. If John Wesley, the brilliant scholar, A. M., D. D., M. D., Moderater of Classes in Oxford, Fellow of Lincoln, and "Father of the Holy Club," is not wise, learned and religious, who is? And he is so zealous. Was anyone ever more so? He says of himself, when speaking of the unconverted preachers of his day, "Are they in philosophy? So was I. In ancient or modern tongues? So was I, also. Are they versed in the science of divinity? I, too, have studied it many years. Can they talk fluently on spiritual things? The very same I could do. Are they plenteous in alms? Behold I give all my goods to feed the poor. Do they give of their labor as well as of their substance? I have labored more abundantly than they all. Are they willing to suffer for their brethren? I have thrown up my friends, reputation, ease and country. I have put my life in my hands wandering into strange lands.''

Does all this give a claim to the holy, heavenly, divine character of a Christian? By no means. He also says: ''But what have I learned myself in the meantime? Why (what I least of all supected), that I, who went to America to convert others, was not myself converted.'' If a man so learned, so honest, so holy in outward life, so charitable and so kind, bearing persecution, scoffed at by companions, ridiculed as the ''Father of the Holy Club,'' should be deceived, it certainly behooves those who do not *know* they are holy, as he afterwards came to know, to begin a careful inspection of their religious standing. In this supreme business—that of knowing whether we stand right with God, guessing or hoping is of business matters most inappropriate and dangerous. I believe a disposition to criticise, and especially to obstruct measures calculated and designed to promote holiness, to be an infallible evidence that the person thus exercised, is not sufficiently holy to bear the test of divine judgment, however good one's motives may be.

One must be truly spiritual to be holier than Mr. Wesley's description of himself before his conversion. Reading it, I can but think of that noble Centurion, who was devout, gave alms, fasted, prayed, and saw a vision by an angel before he had received the Holy Ghost; and Paul, who kept the law with a good conscience; and a "young man" who had kept the law from his youth, but was not "perfect."

One who is wholly sanctified will never oppose holiness either in fact or in theory. One who is not wholly sanctified, knows it, and ought not in any way to oppose that which he does not know, when what he opposes glorifies God.

To resume: In our day history is again repeated. After the days of Methodist poverty and persecutions had gone by, the Church once more began to retrograde. Her liberal conditions of membership soon filled her with a mass of worldly-mindedness, but Wesley had erected her standards so high, and guarded the pulpit so well, that it is almost impossible for her to fall to the lower depths as a whole Church. She has much further to fall than had the churches of the first reformation. Her ministry must first fall from entire sanctification, but they may yet maintain regeneration, which is itself a great evangelizing force when kept on an ascending grade, but even if it fall so low as to give little comfort, and inspire but little zeal, it is nevertheless kept so prominently before the eye, by the forms of the Church, that one can hardly lose sight of it, thanks to the wise building of the Church by Wesley.

The doctrine of regeneration must be preached whether the preacher enjoys it or not. Many preachers who are esteemed holy by the people, as was Mr. Wesley, are, nevertheless, really backslidden in heart (so I've often heard them confess) which, no doubt, in many cases means they are actually not justified, even in Wesley's day.

I neard a presiding elder once say he was sorry the word "assurance" was in our Standards.) But their outward life is good, and they preach justification by faith alone. Some are not converted, but it is the truth that does the work, not the preacher; not the spirit that is in the preacher, but the Spirit that is in the gospel he preaches.

The gospel is the power of God. It will always be useful, even if preached by contention, but its best fruit is seen when the spirit of the holy truth is in the preacher as well as in the word he preaches.

Colonel DeGampart (formerly of Alabama), professed sanctification while I was explaining the doc· trine, long before I experienced it myself. I believed it, and preached it, and God blessed it, even when I did not enjoy it. So with the doctrine of regeneration I am fully persuaded that numbers of preachers in ai, churches are resting in an outward piety while they preach a higher doctrine. God be praised that they preach it!

It is that which keeps the Church alive. But it is sad to think of one preaching, but doing not. It is now, as it was in the days of the incarnation. "They sit in Moses' seat; whatsoever they bid you, that observe and do. But do not after their work, for they say, and do not.' They teach the truth. Oh, that they were sanctified wholly! Then would you see the same difference as that between Peter when he first went out under the limited commission, before the Holy Ghost was given, and Peter on the day of Pentecost; or, as that between Carradine as a regenerated pastor at

16

New Orleans and Carradine as a sanctified evangelist.

The great majority of Methodist preachers are truly regenerated, but with gaps, alas! too many and too long, of lapses, backslidings and loss of preaching power. As a whole, the ministry and the Church are far below the status of the Church one hundred years ago.

Rev. W. W. Hopper, of Mississippi, was awakened, I know not how. By providence he read in a "secular paper" (why did he not see it in the Church papers?) of holiness work a lady was doing nearly one thousand miles away in Stanford, Kentucky. Knowing of no one nearer to instruct him, he took train for Stanford and was there taught how to trust Christ. Does that sound like the days of Carvosso, Hester Ann Rogers, or of Asbury?

Our Church sustains to-day a relation to the Standard doctrine of entire sanctification, like that the Church of England sustained to the doctrine of justification by faith when John Wesley was born. This is obvious to the most superficial reader, and here history again repeats itself. Like Lutheranism, the English Church was founded on the doctrine of justification by faith alone. This was an article of her religion, and her standards were filled with it. Many of the fathers and founders of the Church, fresh from the flaming horrors of Smithfield, enjoyed the holy communion of a justifying faith. But alas! in Wesley's day only a trace of it could be found here and there in all the world. While many, no doubt of those earlier fathers were sanctified Christians, they erred in judgment, and one of the chief errors was in failing to organize the Church on the higher doctrines of entire sanctification, distinctly stated and defined, as Mr. Wesley did after them. They no doubt enjoyed that state themselves; at least some of them. Luther certainly did, but his eyes were evidently never fully opened to sanctification in the light of a distinct and higher work of grace to be specially sought, professed and maintained by faith alone, works being at most only a condition of faith, or evidence of it. He magnified justification but wavered on the higher work. Why was this?

1. Luther had re-discovered the lost grace of justification by faith alone. It worked wonders in his own heart and proved itself a great working force, capable of revolution in man and nations. It plunged him headlong into a bloody strife with the Pope, at that time the greatest power on earth, which, with the reformatory effects of the doctrine he preached, gave Luther more to think of and to do, than usually falls to one poor mortal. That he should be unequal to all the work is not wonderful.

2. Revivals of genuine religion are generally accompanied with more or less exaggerations in one form or another. "Possessions," "sorceries," "witchcraft," and "deceivers" preceded and followed the genuine outing of the Holy Ghost. Now that Luther had shaken the powers of earth, and with the smooth pebble of truth had smitten the great Giant of Error, he had also aroused the slumbering spirit of fanaticism. Very soon he had co-workers in the great Reformation

as dangerous on that side as Rome is on this side. They have "prophets" and "inspirations" above the Bible, and are so holy and divine they can not sin. Some good men from the Moravian Church demand of him a higher standard of holy living for his followers—a wise and timely suggestion—but Luther's reply tells the story of the spiritual failure of his Church: "With us things are not sufficiently ripe for introducing such holy exercises in doctrine and practice as we hear is the case with you." Such sentiment could never have escaped from John Wesley's lips after once the live coal had touched them.

What is the matter with Luther? Just this: He was afraid to risk the highest doctrines lest they might produce fanaticism, till the people were generally prepared and brought to a point of religious intelligence that would appreciate and approve the high doctrines and practices referred to—a method of grace unknown to history. The reverse is always true. Thus it was, that his Church was organized on the lower order or grade, and not on the higher. He did not raise the Church even to the standard of his own highest experience. He did not understand the doctrine of entire sanctification, though I do not doubt that, at several periods of his life, he enjoyed it; but for want of specific knowledge of it, he was irregular in its victories. His Church took ground even below his teaching.

The Church of England was formed on the same model, and took the same type—both dead.

The historians say of it: "This imperfection of the Reformation on the continent was not lessened by the manner of its introduction into England. . . . The truth of God will make its way under many and heavy disadvantages. Two years later an English version of the Bible was printed, and the doctrines of the Reformation were about this time faithfully preached by Cranmer, Ridley, and Latimer, and other pious ministers.''—McTyeire's History of Methodism.

But in the short lapse of about one hundred years, England is as dark a scene—religiously—as a Christian land under Protestant control may be. The history of the Reformation was practically unknown; its doctrines wholly so. Enmity to Rome seems to have been the only thing preserved. Even the priests of the Church of England did not know their own Church held to the doctrine of justification by faith alone. The Bible seemed not to be a material part of a priest's study. ''Natural religion,'' says Mr. Watson, ''was their principal study on which the candidate was to be examined.''

Years after his ordination, Mr. Wesley himself said: ''Who would believe our Church was founded on this important article of justification by faith alone? I am astonished I should ever think this a new doctrine, especially while our Articles and Homilies stand unrepealed.'' His father, an able divine, and mother, little less distinguished, did not understand the doctrine; few did in that day.

It is well known that Methodism was organized on the higher doctrine of entire sanctification, stated plainly and reiterated in conference minutes, and in all the standards of the Church. The power of the churches of England and Germany—the little they had—was soon lost in the mass of their unjustified multitudes. Building a church on justification alone is like building a city upon a slope where land-slides are imminent —liable any day to slide to the bottom. The English Church soon touched the bottom, her masses degraded, her ministers, for the most part, wicked, and the best of them ignorant of her doctrines, with lives, when not vicious, no better than that of a Pharisee.

True, no such dark picture can be drawn of any Protestant community today as that of Kingwoods and the mobs of Bath in Wesley's day, because civilization is higher, education is more general, and there are many faithful witnesses of the truth and many fearless ministers. But it is just as true that a large class of our ministers have wholly forgotten—if they ever knew—the history of our origin, and are just as illy informed of our standard doctrine of entire sanctification by faith alone, as Mr. Wesley was of the standard doctrine of his church when he was going about to establish his own righteousnes. Many of the leaders now who admit that entire sanctification by faith is a doctrine of the church, are like Luther, afraid of its effect lest it produce fanaticism, and caution those who preach it to be careful and to always omit the theory; because, it is in the obtainment and practice of it, all its power lies. There is neither good nor bad in it when the theory is omitted. So the bishops used to caution Mr. Wesley, and were constantly pointing to the extravagances that followed his ministry.

Once more, history had brought forward a class of

men "who turn the world upside down." Men rushed forth in surprise asking— "What new doctrine is this?" A doctrine as old as the prophets, but Mr. Wesley was not afraid of it. If extravagances appeared, as did occur with the society under the ministry of Maxfield, he was prompt to investigate them, and, if real, rebuked them; and if persisted in, the leaders were severely disciplined even to expulsion. He would not tolerate worldliness, nor formality on the one side, nor fanaticism either, in the form of spurious spirituality, nor mysticism, on the other; but at all times he would patiently investigate before he condemned. If the thing tended to the futherance of Christ's cause, even though it did not quite suit his views of propriety, he gave it encouragement. "Lay preaching," "field preaching," "watch-night meetings" were all gross departures from custom, and grated harshly on his sense of propriety until he saw that God had set his seal on them, then he wisely exclaimed, "What was I, that I should withstand God!"

In about 1819, a number of godly persons in New York, and also in Philadelphia, organized societies in the interest of our missionary work. They performed so successfully that the church soon after adopted the society as an arm of its service. That was quite in line with Mr. Wesley's uniform policy, and the rule laid down by the Lord. Nearly every institution of the church has come to us that way. If Mr. Wesley were living today, and was informed that certain brethren, having observed a great destitution of vita;

holiness in many parts of the church, had organized a
society for the purpose of holding revival services;
that the society had but one rule, that of meeting to
preach holiness; that it had no officers, except a president, who is, in truth, only a committee whose duty is
to provide a place and fix a date for the meeting; that
only the gospel in its purity was preached, and great
revivals occurred and many professed the all-cleansing
grace, God greatly blessing the meetings, backsliders
being reclaimed, and the church at large was being
vitalized by them, who can doubt what would be
Mr. Wesley's answer to all this? "What am I, that I
should withstand God!" He would fail to see danger
where no danger is. Holy eyes see holiness in a holy
light. The scene is lovely. Oh, that the Spirit which
gave Wesley his wise administrative ability might now
rest on the rulers of Methodism!

Had our Lord's rule, "Forbid him not," been
observed, holy men would never have been driven out
of Wesleyan Methodism for their godly zeal in holding camp-meetings, from which has sprung their great
body called the New Connection Methodist, now almost
equal to the cruel mother in numbers, setting up altars
beside hers everywhere.

Only a little more than a century before, the English
Church was chasing their fathers from hill to valley
with rancorous thongs for preaching in the open air;
now they are pursuing with caustic lash their brethren
for casting out devils without following the general
custom.

In less than fifty years a zealous young preacher of

the New Connection Church finds himself called on for special services in numerous places of need. It is "irregular;" cannot be allowed; he is thrust out. In thirty years that young man is at the head of the Salvation Army wielding perhaps a larger influence in the world than the church that hurled him forth upon the slums of earth.

No church government is of Divine Sanction, nor to speak of authority, that is not sufficiently flexible to admit the administrative feature commanded and enjoined on his disciples by the Lord. And this feature has a simple test, "He that doeth a miracle in my name." If it is Christ's work it may be claimed by Christ's church. "*My name*" properly signed to any work will give it currency in heaven, and it should not be protested on earth.

CHAPTER III.

Holiness and Its Opponents.

BY REV. L. L. PICKETT.

Every great truth has had to fight its way into recognition through all the ages. That wicked trio, the world, the flesh and the devil, have ever been arrayed against the progress of truth in all its phases. Satan and his cohorts are essentially and eternally opposed to God and everything that He favors. Abel was murdered by his own brother because his sacrifice was more acceptable to God than that of the murderer. Lot was despised in Sodom, and the Isrealites were persecuted in Egypt. Caleb and Joshua were unpopular with the ten faithless spies, and Moses was frequently discounted by the people whom he loved and delivered. David was as a thorn in the side of Saul and a subject of the maledictions of the ungodly The three faithful Hebrew children were thrown into the furnace and Daniel into the den of lions in Babylon, while Jeremiah and other prophets were maltreated in Israel. Jesus was hated by the world and rejected by His own people; His name was cast out as evil and His followers were driven forth into poverty and want. His mistreatment, as that of many of His best followers, came from the hands of the ecclesiastics of His time.

It is a fact that the chief opposition to gospel truth

has commonly shown itself in the ranks of the church, and in its leaders at that. The Romans would not crucify Christ until they were instigated by the Jews. If the reader were to study the history of all great spiritual upheavals, he would find that their greatest opposition came from those who should have been their staunchest friends. Study the Acts of the Apostles and you will find that it was the Scribes and Pharisees who strove hardest to counteract and overthrow the gospel as preached by the apostles. When they entered Gentile communities, they were frequently well-received until the Jewish leaders instigated rejection and persecution. Follow this thought and you will find that every spiritual movement was opposed by the churchites of the times. Savonarola, Wycliff, Huss, in fact the martyrs of all the ages, encountered their bitterest opposition within the ecclesiastical lines, by which they were surrounded.

Martin Luther, tired of the follies of Romanism and its nonsense, sought the Christ by faith and found Him precious. At once he began preaching the word of God in simplicity, and declaring that we are justified by faith alone, as is so amply taught in the Word. Instead of welcoming him; instead of preachers and people bowing around the altar and seeking by faith the conscious knowledge of sins forgiven, they branded him as a heretic, denounced him as an enemy of the church and sought by wicked means to overthrow his work and even to burn him at the stake. But truth triumphed, the cursed shackles which Rome has been forging around the souls and bodies of men for ages

were severed with the two-edged sword of righteousness. The Bible was brought from its hiding place
and spread out before the hungry souls of men, the
Spirit of God gilded its pages with the halo of eternal
light, the life of heaven accompanied its inspired
truths. The Reformation was the result.

A little more than two centuries from the birth of
Luther, God sent John Wesley to arouse lethargic
England to that further great truth that the Spirit bears
witness to our acceptance with God. With the witness of Spirit, he also inaugurated what has since
developed into the great holiness revival of the present
century. But Wesley was scarcely more kindly
received than Luther. He was called a disturber of
the church, an enemy of the established order, a promoter of riot and anarchy, an ecclesiastical tramp. He
was shut out of the churches, even having to preach
the gospel at one time on his father's tombstone
because the Epworth church was locked against him.
Driven to the open fields, he preached to the dirt
begrimed miners and the ignorant hoodlums of England
and Wales in the open air. At one time, having no
house open to him, he was forced to sleep in the open
air upon a plank, and live on berries gathered by the
roadside. The common people heard him gladly, as
they would his Lord and Master, but the be-titled,
ease-loving, salary-drawing ecclesiastical lords of his
time looked down on him as the promoter of schism
and the enemy of those whom they were pleased to
term his superiors in the church. But little did Wesley and his coadjutors stand on ceremony, or care

the maltreatment of their self-constituted censors. They held to the truth of God, and knew it. They read their Bibles and loved them. They were filled with the Spirit and rejoiced therein. They were consciously converted and baptized with the Holy Ghost. Through grace, they mightily prevailed. In the knowledge of their risen Lord they had abiding victory.

It is too late in the day to deny that Wesley advocated what is commonly known as the second blessing view of sanctification. A few years since some attempted this; but light has been turned on. It has been found that he actually used the word and declared the experience of sanctification to be a "second blessing, properly so-called." He said that if a local preacher or leader in the Methodist Societies should be found antagonizing this gracious experience, he should be unfrocked and allowed no longer to retain his leadership. If Mr. Wesley were living to-day, there are men in high official positions, calling themselves Methodists, who would either turn up out of the Church or be expelled by him.

There is the same kind of opposition now to the "Holiness Movement" and the blessed doctrine of the nearness of the coming of Jesus, that there once was to justification by faith, and the witness of the Spirit. The opposers of these vital themes have never been noted as soul-winners. They have simply been ecclesiastical top-heavies. Their one duty has been to magnify their office and themselves in it. They have thought more, as a rule, of the honors and emoluments

of their position than they have of the deep spiritual
life of Zion and the souls of perishing men. I have
yet to see the first man who had won five hundred souls
to God in the twelve months preceding, arraying himself against the experience of entire sanctification.
Man is naturally, in his carnal state, devoted to his own
self-aggrandizement, his ease and ambition, but the
doctrine of holiness requires the emptying of self, the
crucifixion of the "Old Man." Men who are unwilling
to be little and obscure, to be looked upon as the filth
and offscouring of the world, to forego carnal pleasures, and consecrate all things to the redemption of the
lost world, can not be sanctified wholly, and they will
naturally antagonize that doctrine which is opposed
to their selfish desires. It is therefore an historical
fact and a philosophical necessity that men resting in
carnal security and seeking earthly glory, and who are
using the ministry as a position of ease and emolument,
will oppose the doctrine which means death to all sin,
and an entire devotedness to God.

The Apostolic Church was lost in the mazes of
worldliness when civil honor and wealth were heaped
upon it. In all ages, as wealth and numbers have
increased, fine churches have been built, ecclesiastical
honors have accumulated, and worldly men have
crowded the folds of the Church, she has degenerated
into that condition described by Paul when he speaks
of some "having the form of godliness, but denying
the power thereof."

This is an age of wealth. Riches, learning and
influence are heaped upon the Church. The conse-

quence is, entire sanctification is theorized out of many pulpits, and its humble professors are condemned as heretics and frequently driven from the membership of the Church of their choice.

Let us cultivate the spirit of meekness and seek all the fulness of God. In kindness, but in faithfulness and with great energy, let us press the whole truth of God upon the hearts and consciences of men.

CHAPTER IV.

How To Treat Enthusiasts.

REV. DANIEL STEELE, D. D.

Says Lord Macaulay: "It is impossible to deny that the polity of the Church of Rome is the very master-piece of human wisdom. She thoroughly understands, what no other church has ever understood, how to deal with enthusiasts. She knows that when religious feelings have obtained the complete empire of the mind they impart a strange energy, that they raise men above the dominion of pain and pleasure, that obloquy becomes glory, that death itself is contemplated only as the beginning of a higher and happier life." He asserts that this is one of the secrets of her great strength to withstand all the assaults of the past forty generations. To illustrate, he supposes a tinker or coal heaver hears a sermon and becomes alarmed about his sins, and after days of earnest prayer, under the illumination of the Holy Spirit applying such truth as the Roman Church has lodged in his mind, "he emerges from the Valley of the Shadow of Death" into the sunshine of a joyful Christian experience. He feels impelled to exhort his neighbors, and being a man possessing native gifts, especially the talent of persuasion, he wishes to devote his whole life to teaching the religion of his church. What does she do? "She bids him nurse his beard, covers him with a gown and hood of coarse, dark stuff, ties a rope round his waist, and sends him forth to teach in her name." He costs her nothing, nor does he take a dollar away from the revenues of the salaried clergy. Though he does not preach like Massillon, he moves myriads of the uneducated whom the classical periods of the pulpit orator can not arouse; and all his efforts strengthen his church. Thus Rome bridges the gulf between the classes and the masses, uniting in herself all the influence of "the hierarchy above and all the energy of the voluntary system below." Millions who would have been alienated by the selfishness, sloth and sensuality of the priests and bishops have been held loyal to the church by the zeal of begging friars. Her sagacity is seen in "assigning spiritual functions, dignities and magistracies" to women. At Rome, instead of a new sect taking its name from Lady Huntingdon, we would have had the order of St. Selina; and a Latin Mrs. Fry, instead of being an untitled Quaker, would have been the foundress and first Superior of the Blessed Sisterhood of the Jails.

Our great English essayist and historian proceeds to show that the Church of England has ruinously lost by her bungling treatment of enthusiasts. When the converted coal-heaver applies for a license to preach, he is coldly repulsed because he can not exhibit a college diploma, construe a Greek sentence, or write a Latin thesis. He is told that if he remains in the church he must be a hearer only, and that if he will be a preacher he must begin by becoming a schismatic. He prefers schism to stagnation, mounts a

17

horseblock and exhorts sinners to flee from the wrath to come, organizes a society, obtains from it a license, builds a chapel, and in a month has drawn away from the church a hundred families who, with their descendants in all future generations, are lost to her forever. If one of her own episcopally ordained priests is baptized with the Spirit and ordained by a mightier Hand to preach to colliers, sailors, and the paganized outcasts, telling them they must be born again, although they may have been baptized with water, every church door in England is closed against him, and he must be silent or lift up his voice in the streets and fields. He courageously makes his choice of the slums of London rather than its "society:" and draws away from the Established Church millions of people, including its most spiritual members. If John Wesley had been reared a Roman Catholic, with his intense love of his church, he would have received, not a red-hot persecution, but rather the red hat of a cardinal as a reward for a new society of which he was the founder, a body celebrated for its zeal in spreading the faith.

Now arises the question: In the footsteps of which church is Methodism following in her treatment of enthusiasts? In her earlier history she seemed to be endowed with the wisdom of Rome, but in later years she seems to evince the fatality of short-sighted Anglicanism. What are our proofs? We answer: First, the growing disfavor towards earnest and demonstrative persons in large sections of the Methodist Episcopal Church. Our preaching has become so proper and nice that a hallelujah in the pews is deemed an impertinence, and the "amen corner" in our prayer-meetings has gradually diminished till it has finally vanished.

Secondly, an increasing number of enthusiastic women testify that the Holy Spirit has anointed them to preach the gospel. I do not boast of the wisdom of my church when I see a procession of gifted women with university diplomas in their hands, with lingering and reluctant steps leaving Methodism for Congregationalism or some other church in which they may find a sphere for the exercise of gifts which God has given and Methodist co-educational institutions have at great cost developed. This loss to our church will greatly increase, seeing that the women are rapidly becoming the educated class, all our high schools, academies and many of our colleges graduating more women than men. General Booth has demonstrated their superior efficiency in the great problem of saving the unchurched and submerged masses in our rapidly growing cities. Yet Methodism unwisely, if not stupidly, refuses to put the gospel trumpet to the lips of her maidens, when she knows that three of them can be supported by the salary paid a married man. We have about 1,500,000 women in the Methodist Episcopal Church, and we could in a single day double our corps of preachers in all our city missions.

Again, testimonies to the efficacy of the blood of Christ to cleanse from all sin, are regarded with suspicion by many of our preachers and laity; and those who persist in such a testimony are stigmatized as

fanatics and cranks, and they are made to feel that
they are not wanted any longer. They usually join
the Salvation Army, the so-called Pentecostal Church,
the Christian Alliance, the Free Methodist Church, or,
in New England, the Evangelical Association. Thus
the church planted by Jesse Lee, George Pickering,
Timothy Merritt, Wilbur Fisk, and other advocates
and professors of Christian perfection, is being depleted
by the loss of some of its most spiritual members, because she is not wide enough in her charity, warm
enough in her sympathy, and astute enough in her
sagacity to retain them in her communion.

Are we not repeating the blunder of the Anglican
Church? I contend that our Methodism ought to be
wide enough and warm enough to have retained these
her own children in her own bosom.

SECTION V.

DIVERS DELIVERANCES ON SANCTI-FICATION.

CHAPTER I.

The Different Theories.

BY MR. JAMES E. SCHOOLFIELD.

Definition—Dr. Adam Clarke says: "The word 'Sanctify' has two meanings: 1. It signifies to conse-crate, to separate from earth and common use, and to devote or dedicate to God and His service. 2. It sig-nifies to make holy or pure."

Mr. Webster defines sanctification as follows: "The act of God's grace by which the affections of men are purified, or alienated from sin and the world, and ex-alted to a supreme love to God; also the state of being thus purified or sanctified."

He defines sanctify: "To make holy or free from sin: to cleanse from moral corruption and pollution: to make fit for the service of God and the society and employments of heaven."

When does the soul reach the state of entire sancti-fication?

We quote from "The Book and Its Theme," by

Rev. L. L. Pickett: "This question is, after all, the real battle-ground of Christendom on the subject of holiness. It is granted by all believers in the Bible, as it is definitely declared therein, that 'without holiness no man shall see the Lord.' The idea of man entering the sacred city of God, and standing in the august presence of our Maker, who is holiness itself, with any of the pollutions or defilements of sin upon him, is not to be entertained for a moment by any believer in our holy religion. 'Blessed are the pure in heart for they shall see God,' is accepted as truth by all churches; and so is that declaration of the apostle, 'Without holiness no man shall see the Lord.'

"Entire holiness as a necessary qualification for admission to heaven, is not, therefore, an open question, or a matter of debate among Christian people. The only questions are: When and how can entire sanctification or perfect holiness be reached? There are five answers given. The five theories may be briefly stated as follows:

"1. The Catholic theory of sanctification in purgatory, after death.

"2. The Calvinistic theory of sanctification in death.

"3. The theory of sanctification by growth, held by some Presbyterians and others.

"4. The Zinzendorf theory of entire sanctincation at conversion.

"5. The Methodist theory of partial sanctification at conversion; entire sanctification a second blessing.

"These theories, we think, cover the entire ground."

The Methodist Church was organized for the avowed

purpose of spreading Scriptural holiness throughout the world, and was, therefore, a holiness movement. What was the Scriptural holiness referred to? An appeal to the standards, it seems to me, would be the proper way to obtain an answer to the question. We quote from Dr. Adam Clarke:

"In no part of the Scriptures are we directed to seek holiness *gradatim*—we are to come to God as well for an instantaneous and complete purification from all sin as for an instantaneous pardon. Neither the *seriatim* pardon nor the *gradatim* purification exist in the Bible. It is when the soul is purified from all sin that it can properly grow in grace and in the knowledge of our Lord Jesus Christ; as the field may be expected to produce a good crop, and all the seed vegetate when the thorns, thistles, briars and noxious weeds of every kind are grubbed out of it."

Again: "If the Methodists give up preaching entire sanctification (*has that day come?*) they will soon lose their glory. This fitness to appear before God, and thorough preparation for eternal glory, is what I plead for, pray for, and heartily recommend to all true believers under the name of Christian perfection. Let all those who retain the apostolic doctrine that the blood of Christ cleanseth from all sin in this life, pray every believer to go on to perfection and expect to be saved, while here below, unto fullness of the blessing of the gospel of Christ."

Mr. Wesley says: "It (sanctification) is the grand *depositum* which God has given to the people called Methodists, and chiefly to propagate this it appears

God has raised them up." We quote again from Mr.
Wesley: "But what is that faith whereby we are sanctified, saved from sin and perfected in love? It is a
Divine evidence and conviction, first, that God hath
promised it in the Holy Scripture. Till we are thoroughly satisfied of this, there is no moving one step
farther. And one would imagine there needed not one
word more to satisfy a reasonable man of this than the
ancient promise: 'Then will I circumcise thy heart and
the heart of thy seed, to love the Lord thy God with
all thy heart and with all thy soul and with all thy
mind.' How clearly this impresses the being perfected
in love! How strongly it implies the being saved from
sin! For as long as love takes up the whole heart,
what room is there for sin therein? It is a Divine evidence and conviction, secondly, that what God hath
promised he is able to perform. Admitting, therefore,
that 'with men it is impossible' 'to bring a clean thing
out of an unclean,' to purify the heart from all sin and
to fill it with all holiness, yet this creates no difficulty
in the case, seeing 'with God all things are possible.'
And surely no one ever imagined it was possible to any
power less than that of the Almighty." Again: "But
does God work this great work in the soul gradually
or instantaneously? Perhaps it may be gradually
wrought in some. I mean in this sense they do not
advert to the particular moment wherein sin ceases to
be. But it is infinitely desirable, were it the will of
God, that it should be done instantaneously, that the
Lord should destroy sin 'by the breath of His mouth,'
in a moment, in the twinkling of an eye. And so he

generally does, a plain fact of which there is evidence enough to satisfy any unprejudiced person. Thou, therefore, look for it every moment; look for it in the way above described, look for it, then, every day, every hour, every moment. Why not this hour, this moment? Certainly you may look for it *now*, if you believe it is by faith. And by this token you may surely know whether you ask it by faith or by works. If by works, you want something to be done *first before* you are sanctified; you think I must *be or do* thus or thus. Then you are seeking by works unto this day. If you are seeking by faith you may expect it *as you are;* and if as you are, then expect it *now*. It is of importance to observe that there is an inseparable connection between these three points—expect it by *faith*, expect it *as you are*, expect it *now*. To deny one of them is to deny them all; to allow one is to allow them all. Do you believe we are sanctified by faith? Be true then to your principle and look for the blessing just as you are, neither better nor worse—as a poor sinner that has still nothing to pay, nothing to plead but Christ *died*. And if you look for it as you are, then expect it *now*. Stay for nothing.''

The doctrine was reiterated by the General Conference of the united churches in 1832. We quote from Dr. Lovick Pierce, in a sermon to the General Conference of the M. E. Church, South: ''Just so far as our Church has ceased to believe in entire sanctification and to seek after it as the only phase of religion revealed in the New Testament that saves us from all sin, just so far are we a corrupted and God-forsaken Church.

and it is useless to try to sustain ourselves on what we have been.''

Were these words prophetic?

We quote from Dr. William Arthur, author of the ''Tongue of Fire'': ''Methodism was not in its original life more marked by seeking justification by faith than by seeking sanctification by faith.''

Now we quote from an article written by W. F. Tillett, D. D., and published in the *Sunday School Magazine* of February, 1896:

''*The real question at issue* among Methodists concerning sanctification, seems to be this: *Does the Bible teach, and Christian experience confirm the doctrine, that there is, subsequent to regeneration, a second radical and instantaneous work of divine grace within and upon the moral nature of the regenerate believer which must take place before death in order to his complete salvation from all sin?* The solution of this, the only real point at issue, will carry along with it the solution of all other important points. That the primitive and generally recognized 'Wesleyan Methodist doctrine of sanctification' answers this question affirmatively, admits of easy and abundant proof, by an appeal to Wesley, Fletcher, Watson and others. An influential and continually increasing majority of modern Methodists, however, answer this question negatively, feeling that they thereby deny nothing that is essential to that high and lofty ideal of Bible holiness which it is the part of all true and genuine Methodists to believe, experience, practice and preach. They feel that the doctrine of *instantaneous* sanctification lacks that Scripture proof which alone can justify its being regarded as a part, least of all an essential part of the true Bible doctrine of holiness.

"It is plain that the primitive Methodist Church was a holiness movement to '*spread Scriptural holiness*' throughout the world. This holiness included repentance, justification by faith, regeneration, the witness of the Spirit and *instantaneous sanctification by faith as a second work of grace and the witness of the Spirit thereto.*"

The modern holiness movement, so-called, is a movement in the Methodist Church to *retain intact all her doctrines.* As to whether there is any occasion for this movement, let the reader determine for himself by reading the quotation above given from Dr. Tillett, also some of the articles that have recently appeared in our Church organs. Dr. Tillett's article, from which the above quotation is taken, is a very strong paper, written in excellent spirit and is like everything from his pen, conservative, and I most heartily concur in many things he says; and while I have great respect for him and his opinion, yet I am very slow to believe that Wesley, Fletcher, Watson, Clarke, and others, could have been so deluded as to preach and insist‧ upon a doctrine that is heretical and not in the Scriptures.

What is it that the "influential and continually increasing majority" ask us to do? To give up a doctrine that gave Methodism her glory and revolutionized the world? Would it not be expedient for intelligent Methodists to ¦ponder well before surrendering any of the great principles which brought us into being as a Church, and has given us a glorious history?

It is easy to say a doctrine is unscriptural, but surely John Wesley and Adam Clarke were as able interpreters of Scripture as any of our modern theologians. When a doctrine has stood for one hundred and fifty years and all the opposition which has been brought against it has been as stubble to the fire, I confess that I am loath to believe it false. In this connection I quote from a private letter now before me from one of the leading men of the Western North Carolina Conference, a man of deep piety and long experience as a minister of the gospel:

"I have for some time felt that the theory of our latter day Methodist Church has grown out of her experience or rather *lack of experience on that line.* I believe we have departed from the *faith* of Wesley because we have lost this *experience.*"

A leading member of the Baltimore Conference said to me recently in Washington City, "after a careful study of this question," he was convinced that "the bitterness engendered by the agitation of the slavery question, and the war following, caused the church, North and South, to lose the experience to a very large extent, hence the opposition to the doctrine."

Both of these men were members of the late General Conference, and neither of them had professed the second blessing or are identified with the holiness movement.

The true Wesleyan doctrine, as I understand it, is this: Regeneration is sanctification begun—sanctifica•

tion is regeneration completed. Then comes growth, fertile growth and development in all the Christian graces throughout time and eternity. Sanctification is one thing, *maturity* is quite another. Neither Mr. Wesley nor any of the modern advocates of any prominence whatever of the primitive Wesleyan doctrine, so far as I know, or have reason to believe, teach "an arrested development," nor do they teach angelic, physical, or Adamic perfection, nor do they hold that one in the blessing can not sin or will not be tempted. On the other hand they urge constant watchfulness lest the experience be lost. What they *do* claim is that ...e "old man of sin" is destroyed, and that the temptation is no longer from within, but from without. They claim "a heart from sin set free," a "life hid with Christ," that sanctification is the "secret of the Lord" revealed in the inner life, and the difference between the justified and the sanctified experience is clearly set forth in the two ways of rendering the old hymn: The justified experience:

> "Prone to *wander*, Lord, I feel it;
> Prone to *leave* the God I love."

The sanctified experience:

> 'Prone to *love* thee, Lord, I feel it;
> Prone to *love* thee and adore."

Shall the doctrine be preached, the experience sought and professed? Modern Methodism says *No!* Let us appeal to the fathers and hear what they say. We quote from a letter of Mr. Wesley to John King in 1787: "It requires a great deal of watchfulness to retain the perfect love of God: and *one great means of retaining it is frankly to declare what God has given you and earnestly exhort all the believers you meet with to follow after full salvation."*

We quote again from Mr. Wesley: "Therefore let all our preachers make it a point to preach perfection to believers constantly, strongly and explicitly. I doubt not we are not explicit enough in speaking on full sanctification, either in public or private."

We quote from a letter of Mr. Wesley to L. Caughland in 1768: "Blessed be God, though we set a 'hundred enthusiasts aside, we are still encompassed with a cloud of witnesses' who have testified, and do testify, in life and death, that perfection I have taught these forty years. This perfection can not be a delusion, unless the Bible be a delusion too. I mean loving God with all our heart and our neighbor as ourselves. I pin down all its opposers to this definition of it. No evasion. No shifting the question. Where is the delusion of this? Either you received this love, or you did not. If you did, dare you call it a delusion? You will not call it so for all the world. If you received anything else, it does not at all affect the question."

And a letter from Mr. Wesley to Miss Chapman in 1773: "You can never speak too strongly or explicitly upon the head of Christian perfection. If you speak only faintly and indirectly, none will be offended and none profited; but if you speak out, although some will probably be angry, yet others will soon find the power of God unto salvation."

Dr. Adam Clarke says: "If men would but spend

as much time in fervently calling upon God to cleanse by the blood that which he has not cleansed, as they spend in decrying this doctrine, what a glorious state of the Church should we soon witness. Instead of compounding with iniquity, and tormenting their minds to find out with how little grace they may be saved, they would renounce the devil and all his works, and be determined never to rest till they had found that He had bruised him under their feet, and that the blood of Christ had cleansed them from all unrighteousness.''

Bishop Asbury wrote to Henry Smith: ''Preach sanctification directly and indirectly, in every sermon.'' He wrote to another: ''O purity! O Christian perfec· tion! O sanctification! It is heaven below to feel all sin removed. Preach it whether they will hear or for · bear. Preach it.''

I am not identified with the ''holiness movement,'' and am not classed as a ''holiness evangelist,'' but am in sympathy with all who are earnestly contending for the faith of our fathers. Especially am I inclined to this way when I find that the arguments used to dis- prove the doctrine are almost identical with the argu- ments used by some of the theologians of the Calvin- istic school to disprove the doctrine of assurance and apostasy or falling from grace, as taught by the Meth- odist Church. I find also that the same arguments used to discredit the experience of sanctification are often used by ritualists and worldly people to discredit the doctrine and experience of conscious conversion and witness of the Spirit. To instance, a Presbyterian minister a few months ago said to me he doubted not but that we were sincere in preaching assurance, but he did not believe that one could know that he stood in a saved relation to God.

I preached in a town a few years ago where a bishop of the Episcopal Church had said in a sermon a few days before that "the doctrine of conscious conversion and the witness of the Spirit, as taught by John Wesley and his followers, was a perversion of the Bible and a delusion of the devil."

Because I have not been consciously converted is no proof that others have not been, or that the Bible does not teach conscious conversion.

Because I seek the blessing of sanctification and do not receive it, does not prove that others have not received it, or that the doctrine is unscriptural. The fact that some profess sanctification, who do not show a sanctified spirit, is no more an argument against sanctification than that some who profess conversion, and do not exhibit the Christian spirit, is an argument against conversion. My investigations on this subject have covered more than ten years. In that time I have met with some who are cranks on the subject, but by far the larger part of those with whom I came in contact, who professed to be in the blessing, exemplified it in their life and walk; and I have often been struck with one peculiarity, *they seem to have something that the vast majority of professing Christians do not seem to have.* My investigations have also convinced me that the experience called "Entire Sanctification," "Christian Perfection," "Perfect Love," and "Second

Blessing '' by Wesley, Watson, Clarke, Asbury, Lovick Pierce, Bishop Key, Dr. Carradine, and others, is identical with the experience taught by Moody, Pearson, Torrey, Dr. Gordon, and others, and called ''Enduement for Service,'' or ''Baptism with the Holy Ghost.'' While they differ in *theory and name, all agree that it is a definite work of grace wrought in the heart of the believer subsequent to regeneration,* and that absolute consecration and a specific act of faith are the prerequisites to this ''Cleansing,'' ''Infilling,'' or ''Baptism.'' I would say to all interested in this question, if you want the blessing meet the conditions —*Consecration and Faith.* Never mind about theories, but do as a friend once said to me, ''Send your heart on to heaven by lightning express.'' Get the baptism and call it what you please. Get it, whether necessary to salvation or not. The *experience* I know to be real, for it tallies with my own, and it can not be a delusion, for it transformed my own life and made me an evangel of the cross.

If you ask me what it was I received, what it is I have, I answer, ''JESUS, BLESSED JESUS, whose blood now cleanseth from *all* sin and gives me victory.''

We can only be ''complete in Him.'' He alone is our ''wisdom, righteousness, sanctification and redemption.'' Claim Him, brother, as your Savior from *all* sin, and claim Him *now*.

'' 'Tis the promise of God FULL salvation to give.''

This ''O-wretched-man-that-I-am'' experience is not the language of a soul ''from sin set free,'' but is legal bondage.

18

"He breaks the power of canceled sin,
  He sets the prisoner free;
His blood can make the foulest clean,
  His blood avails for me."

"Put ye on the Lord Jesus Christ, and make not provision for the flesh." "Whatsoever ye do, do all to the glory of God."

Get the Savior and you are saved; get the Baptizer and you will have the baptism; get the Sanctifier and you are sanctified. "For God hath not called us unto uncleanness, but unto holiness." "And the very God of peace sanctify you wholly; and I pray God your whole spirit and soul and body be preserved blameless unto the coming of our Lord Jesus Christ. Faithful is he that calleth you who also will do it." This I believe to be the true remedy for the dead formality and worldliness in our churches. Let the old-time doctrine be preached, experienced, urged constantly, anywhere, everywhere, and soon our pulpits would flame with the old-time fire. Our altars would be crowded with penitents, and the glory of the latter-day Methodism would rival that of the early churches.

The class-meeting would take the place of the card table, ball-room and theatre, and our prayer-meetings would resound with the hallelujahs of praise. Then would the Church walk "in the Spirit," obeying the commandments of God; "looking for that blessed hope and the glorious appearing of the great God and our Savior Jesus Christ, who gave himself for us that He might redeem us from all iniquity and purify unto Himself a peculiar people zealous of good works."

CHAPTER II.

Heart-Purity, and Our Reasons for Urging It.

BISHOP J. S. KEY.

Would to God ye could bear with me a little in my folly: and indeed bear with me. For I am jealous over you with godly jealousy: for I have espoused you to one husband, that I may present you as a chaste virgin to Christ.—II Corinthians, 11:1, 2.

Our theme to-day is *heart-purity, and our reasons for urging it:* beautifully brought to view under the figure of an espoused bride, of whom the supreme demand is that she be a "chaste virgin."

Nothing can be more needful than this state. The holy Bridegroom demands it; the "many mansions" fitted up for their dwelling place give welcome only to the "pure in heart;" the yearning heart of the engaged bride pants for purity that she may thus be adorned for her Lord; the commissioned minister, "jealous with godly jealousy," and earnest even to the appearance of folly and fanaticism, strives that he "may present a chaste virgin to Christ."

Most surprisingly this urgent presentation of heart-purity promotes objection and stirs up criticism. It has been ever thus. St. Paul encountered it; and his reference to it in the text is made with a touch of rarest delicacy. His tone is apologetic. He knows his zeal is counted by many as folly, and he well appreciates the

(275)

condescending charity with which his "folly" is excused.
He is called a " crank " and extreme, and yet somehow
they bear with him.   Our text is his appeal to his impatient and fault-finding brethren.   Notice: "Would
to God ye could bear with me a little in my folly: and
Indeed bear with me."   The margin reads: "*Indeed ye
do bear with me.*"   Much opposed as they were to his
crazy zeal for purity, they nevertheless excused and
bore with him because he was consistent, and they
thought him a good man, though misguided.   This
was fortunate.   He could well bear their criticism if
amid it all he held their confidence.

Indeed, upon reflection, this opposition to heart
purity does not appear wholly unaccountable.   Purity
antagonizes impurity; holiness, unholiness.   Light reveals darkness.   And he who by precept and example
stands for the highest experience of holy living, may
expect to be misjudged and ridiculed and caricatured
and condemned.

In May, 1762, Mr. Wesley makes this entry in his
Journal: "We begin now to meet with opposition from
every quarter.   Some say this is rank enthusiasm.
others, that it is a cheat or mere pride; others, that it
is a new thing, and that they can find no such a thing in
the Bible.   The Lord increases his work in proportion
to the opposition it meets with."

In the nature of the case, intensity and urgency
must characterize those who are themselves saved to
the uttermost, and have invested all for the salvation
of others.   Again and again the question is repeated,
'Why such zeal in propagating holiness?   Why so

many and such novel methods? Why not be content with the regular and established services?"

Our first answer is, we are under commission, charged with a special care. "A dispensation of the Gospel is committed to us," and we are straitened till it be accomplished. "We are ambassadors for Christ," and as such must be inspired and controlled by our instructions. "He gave some, apostles; and some, prophets; and some, evangelists; and some, pastors and teachers; for the perfecting of the saints, for the work of the ministry, for the edifying of the body of Christ: Till we all come in the unity of the faith and of the knowledge of the Son of God, unto a perfect man, unto the measure of the stature of the fullness of Christ." No marvel if a saved and consecrated servant of Christ should in his zeal, sometimes overstep the devil's limit of propriety and receive censure.

There is a touch of exquisite beauty in the figure employed by the apostle in the text: "I have espoused you to one husband, that I may present you as a chaste virgin to Christ." No inexperienced mind can adequately appreciate this responsibility and anxiety. Sent of God to choose and prepare a bride for his Son, what carefulness, what delicacy, how numerous the possibilities of mistake and failure, what trembling heart-yearnings and jealousies for his Master!

The eldest servant of Abraham's house, sworn and sent by his master to find and bring a bride for Isaac. is the typical representative of every Christian minister. "Put thy hand under my thigh," said the patriarch, "and I will make thee swear by the Lord, the

God of heaven, and the God of the earth, that thou shalt not take a wife unto my son of the daughters of the Canaanites among whom I dwell. But thou shalt go unto my country, and to my kindred and take a wife unto my son Isaac.''

The Canaanites were impure. Virtue was well nigh unknown among them, and chastity was not. A bride worthy of Abraham's son must come from the land of his fathers, and a long journey and patient search be made. That commissioned messenger had in his keeping the honor and happiness of his master. More delicate his office than if he intended marriage for himself. In his own case he might take some risk. In his master's none. ''A chaste virgin'' must be found, and on him was laid the duty. He was literally saturated with his mission. Thoughtfully, prayerfully. instantly, urgently, unceasingly he gave himself to it. At the well whither the women gather to draw water at the time of the evening, he waits and prays and finds Rebekah. He follows her to her home, and refuses to eat or sleep until he can open his errand and press it to a consummation. His mission accomplished, the dawn of the morning finds him returning with the chosen bride.

It is this sing.e and exclusive work which our Lord has confided to us, his blood-washed messengers, that fills us with enthusiasm. He has put great honor on us in this appointment. We must give ourselves absorbingly to its execution. To formal, cold and calculating eyes our methods may sometimes appear irregular and extreme, but the hope of bringing a chaste virgin as the espoused bride of Christ, is the inspiration of all. Surely in this case the end accomplished will justify the means.

Another and very controlling reason for our intensity in "spreading scriptural holiness over these lands," is found in the *definite and exclusive mission of Wesleyan Methodism*.

"What was the rise of Methodism?" asked John Wesley, in his Conference of 1765. This is his answer: "In 1729, my brother Charles and I, reading the Bible, saw we could not be saved without holiness: followed after it and incited others so to do. In 1737 we saw that this holiness comes by faith. In 1738 we saw likewise that men are justified before they are sanctified, but still holiness was our object: inward and outward holiness. God then thrust us out to raise up a holy people." To this statement, found in your Discipline of 1882, are signed the names of Bishops Paine, Pierce, Kavanaugh, McTyeire, Keener, Wilson, Parker, Granbery, Hargro

In 1790—just two years before he died—he wrote: "This doctrine is the grand *depositum* which God has lodged with the people called Methodists; and for the sake of propagating this chiefly he appears to have raised us up."

I affirm to-day, with all possible emphasis, that salvation from all sin, received now by faith, is the distinguishing doctrine which differentiates Methodism from all other churches. Leave this out and your Church is indefensible. No Church can be sustained or tolerated that does not hold a place unoccupied by any other, and teach doctrines untaught by others, and employ agencies and methods unused by others. Partisanship and passion may for a time maintain rival organizations holding and teaching the same points, but inevitable reaction will sweep away the surplus. Study your Church then in the life of this postulate.

Every great Church that has survived a hundred years, and is fit to live another century, has a grand principle out of which its life comes. Fidelity to that alone is the guaranty of perpetuity. For example:

Roman Catholicism claims its place, and demands a following by its bold and defiant assumption of being the only authorized Church of Christ on the earth. Through all the centuries she has remained the same, exclusive, intolerant, uncompromising. "The Pope is the vicegerent of Christ, and the priesthood are the successors of the apostles." The very audacity of the statement has terrorized the multitudes, and in this way Rome has held an acknowledged sway.

The Church of England and her descendant, the Protestant Episcopal Church in America, build on this same foundation of arrogance and assumption, hoping to divide with Rome solely by charging corruption and apostasy upon the hoary pretender. It is alone a revolt from the vices and oppression of the ages as seen in Rome that opens a door to the Episcopal Churches and makes them possible.

The Presbyterian Church stands for Calvinism in creed, and qualified congregationalism in polity. Her attitude is definite and her voice unvarying. She is fixed, stern, and somewhat severe in her teaching, but her devotion to the Sabbath, and pure private morals, and her trained ministry defending the authority of the word of God, have established her claim to Church-hood and won recognition.

Our Baptist brethren are differentiated by a single point of faith, viz: exclusive immersion and its derivatives. Their Calvinism and congregational government would liken them to several other numerous and influential churches, but their peculiar view of water baptism distinguishes and sets them apart. On this question they are neither silent nor equivocal. Immersion in water is their glory, and they allow no compromise. They deserve the place they occupy in the sisterhood of churches, because of their straightforward consistency and fidelity.

What now of Wesleyan Methodism? Arminian in theology, episcopal in government, and non-ritual in polity, she so far presents no claim to a separate and independent place. The vision of a great Church moving on through the ages and bearing his name never lodged in John Wesley's mind. When once his soul felt the pulse of a new spiritual life his eyes opened on a scene that stirred his deepest sensibilities, and drew him out of himself in sublime self-consecration for the neglected millions around him.

He saw in his native England the frame work of a grand and mighty Church, but death had fixed its grasp upon it, and all the marks of decay were visible. He saw magnificent cathedrals with vast endowments and splendid appointments, and titled noblemen in gorgeous dress thronged the aisles and filled the pews, while a dead priesthood ministered at the altar. Card-playing, horse-racing, amusements of all sorts, and self-indulgence generally characterized the people, both clergy and laity, while the teeming multitudes wandered over the fields with no folds and no shepherds.

Out of the womb of this necessity, with the birth-agonies of a great heart moved by the Holy Ghost, Methodism came into being, a mission to the masses, the Church of the poor. Her distinctive theology involves only matters of experience, justification by faith alone, regeneration by the Holy Ghost without the intervention of water, or priest or bishop—sanctification, and witness of the Spirit.

Abel Stevens, the great historian of the Church, says: "Methodism has reversed the usual policies of religious sects, who seek to sustain their spiritual life by their orthodoxy. She has sustained her orthodoxy by devoting her chief care to her spiritual life, and for more than half a century has had no serious outbreak of heresy, notwithstanding the masses of untrained minds gathered within her pale, and the general lack of preparatory education among her clergy."

Now, then, I repeat with an added stress that Methodism, this child of Providence, embodies and holds forth a new, definite and distinguishing statement of scriptural holiness.

Romanism and its progeny hold and teach that entire deliverance from the stain and guilt and power of sin comes only after death in purgatorial purifying.

Calvinism of every name refuses to allow heart-purity and holiness, except *in articulo mortis*.

Wesleyan Methodism alone, in all the sisterhood of churches, claims it now. In 1766 John Wesley wrote to his brother Charles: "Insist everywhere on full salvation received now by faith. Press the instantaneous blessing." A heart-yearning after this high experience drew together in Christian sympathy and finally organized that band of godly men, by some called "Methodists," and by others, in mockery, the "Holy Club." These our fathers banded together, as they said themselves, "seeking the power of godliness." They "hungered and thirsted after righteousness." They sighed and cried to be cleansed from all sin, outward and inward, and to be "filled with all the fullness of God." They organized class-meetings where they might open hearts one to another, and tell their conflicts and triumphs, their joys and sorrows, and thus mutually stimulate and assist. They met in foundries and workshops and in the open air to pray and sing and exhort. In love-feasts they told of their growth in grace, and of their yearnings after holiness of heart and life. They were filled and ruled by one supreme, overmastering desire: to be holy themselves and urge others to the same experience. They preached it, prayed for it, professed it, sang of it, illustrated it in their lives, and died testifying "the blood of Jesus Christ his Son cleanseth us from all sin." When these holy men crystalized into Church organization, it was for experimental holiness as the grand result.

The vows of Church membership look to a final and total consecration. "Dost thou renounce the devil and all his works, the vain pomp and glory of

the world, with all covetous desires of the same, and
the carnal desires of the flesh, so that thou wilt not
follow or be led by them?''

''Will thou obediently keep God's holy will and
commandments, and walk in the same all the days of
thy life?''

Complete surrender was demanded at the very
threshold of the Church. The purpose of your Church
was announced to each applicant at the very beginning
of his career. None were invited to join who did not
set out with a purpose to experience hearty-purity and
practice holy living. And so they formulated the
''General Rules of the United Societies'' as their
conception of Bible religion, and the directory of all
true Methodists, affirming ''all these we are taught of
God to observe, even in his written word, which is
the only rule and the sufficient rule both of our faith
and practice. And all these we know his Spirit writes
on truly awakened hearts. If there be any among us
who observe them not, who habitually break any of
them, let it be known unto them who watch over that
soul as they who must give account. We will admon-
ish him of the error of his ways; we will bear with
him for a season; but if he repent not he hath no
more place among us; we have delivered our own
souls.''

When a ministry was to be called and set apart,
these spiritually minded fathers said: ''How shall we
try those who profess to be moved by the Holy Ghost
to preach?

''Answer.—Let the following questions be asked:

Do they know God as a pardoning God? Have they the love of God abiding in them? Do they desire nothing but God? And are they holy in all manner of conversation?''

When, after a sufficient trial, these licensed preachers came forward to be received into the Annual Conference, Mr. Wesley directed the following questions:

'' Have you faith in Christ? Are you going on to perfection? Do you expect to be made perfect in love in this life? Are you groaning after it? Are you resolved to devote yourself wholly to God and his work?''

The mind and purpose of Methodism are unmis-takably uttered in these questions. Raised up as she was to ''spread scriptural holiness over these lands,'' she would receive and commission no preacher who was doubtful or indifferent on this subject. The representatives of a cause should be strong believers.

One year before he died John Wesley wrote to Dr. Clarke:

''*Dear Adam:* The account you send me of the continuance of the work of God in Jersey gives me great satisfaction. To retain the grace of God is much more than to gain it. And this should be strongly urged on all who have tasted of perfect love. If you can prove that any of our preachers or leaders, either directly or indirectly, speak against it, let him be a preacher or leader no longer. I doubt whether he should continue in the Society. Because he that could speak thus in our congregation can not be an honest man.''

Let me reaffirm. Your Church is for holiness or for nothing. Take that out of your preaching and it

is emasculated. Take it out of your living, and you
have nothing left worth your time and effort. Outside
of heart-purity received and enjoyed now, you hold
to no tenet that is not held and taught by some other
Church, and in many instances can be better urged by
them. "To raise up a holy people" is our peculiar
and exclusive mission. This conviction seems to have
been inwrought into the thought and conscience of our
leaders from the beginning.

In 1768 John Wesley wrote to Charles: "I am at
my wits end with regard to two things—the Church
and Christian perfection. Unless both you and I
stand in the gap in good earnest, the Methodists will
drop them both. Talking will not avail. We must
do, or be borne away. Will you set shoulder to
shoulder? If so, think deeply upon the matter and
tell me what can be done. Come on. Act the man
and do your utmost. Peace be unto you and yours.
Adieu!"

Again he says:

"Let all our preachers make a point of preaching
perfection to believers constantly, strongly, explicitly.
I doubt not we are not explicit enough in speaking on
full sanctification, either in public or private. I am
afraid Christian perfection will be forgotten. A general faintness in this respect has fallen on the whole
kingdom. Sometimes I seem almost weary of striving
against the stream of both preachers and people."

Dr. Adam Clarke says:

"If the Methodists give up preaching entire sanctification, they will soon lose their glory. This fits

them to appear before God; and thorough preparation for eternal life is what I plead for, pray for, and heartily recommend to all true believers under the name of Christian perfection. Let all those who retain the apostolic doctrine, that 'the blood of Jesus Christ cleanseth from all sin,' press every believer to go on to perfection and expect to be saved while here below, unto the fullness of the blessing of the gospel of Christ.''

Bishop Asbury makes this entry in his journal during a season of sickness:

"I have found by secret search that I have not preached sanctification as I should have done. If I am restored, this shall be my theme more pointedly than ever, God being my helper.''

Again he says: "I am divinely impressed with a charge to preach sanctification in every sermon.''

Bishop McKendree wrote to the eloquent Summerfield:

"But superior to all these I trust you will ever keep in view in all your ministrations the great design which we believe God intended to accomplish in the world in making us 'a people that were not a people.' I mean the knowledge, not of a free and a present, but also a full salvation. In other words, a salvation from all sin unto all holiness. Insist much on this; build up the churches herein, and proclaim aloud that 'without holiness no man shall see the Lord.' Under the guidance of the Spirit of holiness, this doctrine will be acknowledged of God: signs will follow them that believe and press after this uttermost salvation, and our people will bear the mark of their high calling, become a holy nation, a peculiar people.''

Let me say, furthermore, that in addition to these individual utterances, the highest and most authoritative councils of the Church have, at various periods, sent forth the most unequivocal and emphatic deliverances.

In 1824 the Bishops of the Church, in their quadrennial address to the General Conference, said: "Never was there a period more momentously interesting to our Church than the present. Do we, as preachers, feel the same child-like spirit which so eminently distinguished our first ministers? Do we come to the people in the fullness of the blessing of the gospel of peace? It is not enough merely to preach the gospel from a full heart, and preach it, too, in demonstration of the Spirit and of power. Above all, do we insist on the present witness of the Spirit and entire sanctification through faith in Christ. Are we striving by faith and obedience to elevate our hearts and lives to the standard of gospel holiness? or are we wishing to have the standard lowered to our unsanctified natures? In short, are we contented to have the doctrine of Christian holiness an article of our creed only, without becoming experimentally and practically acquainted with it? Are we pressing after it as the prize of our high calling in Christ Jesus? If Methodists give up the doctrine of entire sanctification, or suffer it to become a dead letter, we are a fallen people. It is this that lays the axe to the root of the Antinomian tree in all its forms and degrees of growth; it is this that

Inflames and diffuses life, rouses to action, prompts to perseverance and urges the soul forward to every holy exercise, and every useful work. If the Methodists lose sight of this doctrine, they will fall by their own weight. Their success in gaining members will be the cause of their dissolution. Holiness is the main cord that binds us together. Relax this and you loosen the whole system. This will appear more evident if we call to mind the original design of Methodism. It was to raise up and preserve a holy people. This was the principal object which Mr. Wesley, who, under God, was the great founder of our order, had in view. To this end all the doctrines believed and preached by the Methodists tend. Who ever supposed, or who that is acquainted with the case can suppose it was designed, in any of its parts, to secure the applause and popularity of the world, or a numerical increase of worldly or impenitent men. Is there any provision made for the aggrandizement of our ministers or the worldly mindedness of our members? None whatever!''

To this address are fixed the names of Bishops McKendree, Hedding, Soule, George and Roberts.

The General Conference of 1832 issued a pastoral address to the Church, of which this is part: ''When we speak of holiness we mean that state in which God is loved with all the heart and served with all our power. This, as Methodists, we have said, is the privilege of the Christian in this life. And we have further said that this privilege may be secured instantaneously by an act of faith, as justification is.

19

"Why, then, have we so few living witnesses that the blood of Jesus Christ cleanseth from all sin? Among primitive Methodists the experience of this high attainment in religion may justly be said to have been common. Now a profession of it is rarely to be met with among us. Is it not time in this matter to return to first principles? Is it not time that we throw off the inconsistency with which we are charged in regard to this matter? Only let all who have been born of the Spirit and have tasted of the good word of God seek with the same ardor to be made perfect in love as they sought for the pardon of their sins, and soon will our class-meetings and love-feasts be cheered by the relation of experiences of this character, as they now are with those which tell of justification and the new birth. And when this shall come to pass we may expect a corresponding increase of Christian enjoyment and in the force of religious influence we shall exert over others."

The Centennial Conference of American Methodism, which met in Baltimore in 1884, reaffirmed the faith of the Church in all its branches:

"We remind you, brethren, that the mission or Methodism is to promote holiness. This end and aim enters into all our organic life. Holiness is the fullness of life, the crown of the soul, the joy and strength of the Church.

"It is not a sentiment or an emotion, but a principle inwrought in the heart, the culmination of God's work in us followed by a consecrated life. In all the borders of Methodism this doctrine is preached and the experience of sanctification is urged. We beseech you, brethren stand by your standards on this subject. Our founder rightly interpreted the mind of the Spirit, and gave us the truth as it is in Jesus. Let us not turn from them to follow strange lights, but rather let us believe their testimony, follow their example, and seek purity of heart by faith in the cleansing blood, and then in the steady line of consecrated living, go on to perfection ''

Now, then, in this extended review we find the central purpose and inspiration of your Church. Methodism is primitive Christianity revived. It is ''Christ in you, the hope of glory: whom we preach, warning every man, and teaching every man in all wisdom; that we may present every man perfect in Christ Jesus.''

Mr. Wesley and the men of his times grasped this vision and were lifted out of themselves up to fellowship with St. Paul, when he said: ''For whether we be beside ourselves, it is to God; or whether we be sober, it is for your cause; for the love of Christ constraineth us.'' Herein, then, is our defense. We preach heart-purity and Christian perfection, because for this purpose God has raised us up, and on this mission has he sent us forth. Silence would be sin.

An inference of some weight follows now. This Church of ours is no temporary provision; she has a mission for all time and all people. Her rapid growth; her signal triumphs over opposition; her pre-eminent adaptation to human society; and most of all, the marked presence and favor of God in her past brilliant history, make it very clear that she was designed for the whole earth and for all time.

But now mark. If this conclusion be correct, then in tne preservation of her distinguishing peculiarities is to be found the single condition of her perpetuity. In other words, if God called Methodism into being for the single purpose of preaching and practicing holiness, we must do that at the peril of his displeasure and abandonment. We have no latitude of choice. We are shut up to our one mission. We must fulfill the purpose of our being, or pass away. Other churches may live and prosper with different inspirations, because raised up for different ends, but Methodists must be child-like and consecrated and pure, or die.

I have sought the Scriptures diligently for a clear and faithful prototype of Wesleyan Methodism, and I find it accurately drawn out in the character and career of Samson. Study that wonderful life with your own Church in mind.

All the mystery and darkness connected with Samson find their explanation in the Nazaritish vow under which he was born. It was that vow that called him into being; it was that which pointed the course his life should take and urged him forward; it was that which segregated him from all other men, and his work from all other work; it was that which limited and controlled him, and shut him up to God and his work. Adherence to that vow, and compliance, literal and implicit with all its points, was the inexorable condition of success. In his physical constitution, Samson was doubtless small and weak, and his bodily presence contemptible. His enemies never feared him, but ever pursued him, confident they could hold and destroy him. Indeed the Scripture, "out of weakness was made strong," is positive assurance that God chose one of his weakest servants to perform miracles of strength. Why not? If he be the Lord's chosen one, then the instrument is nothing. It was the arm Omnipotent that used him. "This treasure we have in earthen vessels, that the excellency of the power may be of God and not of us."

But weak as Samson was, so long as he with single eye observed and kept the vow of his consecration, he was irresistible — we might say *almighty*. But no sooner did he forget that vow, and turn away to other following—no sooner did his mind become divided, and he begin to live for other ends than those appointed him, than the Lord left him, and with him departed influence and power and glory.

So God has a special work for Wesleyan Methodism. A vow of consecration, as definite and unalterable as Samson's Nazaritish vow, is on her, which differences her from all other churches and people, and devotes her to her peculiar and exclusive work. Our power and glory will be found to follow a faithful execution of this vow.

Methodists started out to be a "peculiar people." In their creed and conduct they were to antagonize all forms of error and vice. In their daily living they were to be exemplary, separate and conspicuously free from worldly love and following. "Holiness to the Lord," was their motto, and salvation to the uttermost their theme. Always and everywhere they were to be pronounced, clearly defined, unequivocal on this subject.

Now, we insist that what the Church started out to be and do, she should continue to the end. Most assuredly, then, in her early spirit and methods we are to find the model and type of what she should ever be. The teaching of the early fathers should be our guide to-day. Their aim should be our aim, and their inspiration should be ours.

How fearful now this conclusion! If the Methodist Church fail to accomplish her given work in her own appointed way, and begin to catch the spirit of the world and formal churches around her, then there is no further use for her Her mission is at an end, and God will raise up some other to take her place and do her work. The history of the past has demonstrated that God can easier raise up a new church than revive a dead one.

Excuse this added thought. If worldliness creep into a church, and a decline of numbers and prestige occur, how natural to overlook the real remedy and resort to popular human expedients? I have known churches under such conditions build a fine house or refit an old one, rent the pews, improve the music, change the pastor, so as to popularize the pulpit. But these are only palliatives that may or may not abate the symptoms. The disease is not reached, and without heroic treatment the patient will die.

Common sense and Scripture both point to one course—*return to first principles*. The ship is off her course. There is danger. She must be brought back or perish on unknown reefs.

"Stand ye in the ways and see, and ask for the old paths, where is the good way, and walk therein, and ye shall find rest for your souls."

A few words now to you, my brethren, who are set for the promotion of the experience of heart-purity.

Satan hates nothing as he does holiness. It exposes his own depravity, and antagonizes his heartless and malignant schemes. He scruples at no means to oppose it. It must be overthrown and defeated at all cost. A favorite device is misrepresentation and perversion. He has succeeded in some instances in seducing the sanctified, and they have fallen away, and "the last state of that man is worse than the first " What a parade he makes of such, and how their fall is used to disparage heart-purity. One of his favorite methods is to send forth his own chosen missionaries to preach holiness. If he can only be allowed to represent purity he will surely, by ridicule and burlesque and extravagance, make it disgusting in the eyes of all. Nothing so shocks the public taste as a high and loud profession of sanctity, coupled with inconsistency and fanaticism and a headlong, fiery spirit. These emissaries of the pit have done us incalculable harm. They have turned good people away from us, and made timid ones afraid to associate with us, and have put the precious doctrine of heart-purity under suspicion if not under ban. We protest to-day against them all. We are not responsible for them. If men and women have

gone through the land, self-appointed and self-seeking,
preaching for gain, bad tempered, and in some instances openly immoral, in heaven's name, we beg, do not
hold Methodism or Christianity responsible for it. Do
not reject purity because it is counterfeited. If in the
run of the ages one heart has been cleansed and kept,
the truth is established, though ten thousand may misrepresent it.

But, brethren, how careful we should be. While a
counterfeit only proves there is a genuine coin, men
are prone to scrutinize and suspect religious profession.
We are ever passing under the eye of the world's criticism. They watch our words and spirit and actions.
Condemn our creed as they may, they expect more of
us than they did before we believed and entered in.
A fault found in us is inexcusable. An inconsistency
is made a reason for rejecting the whole doctrine.

We can not object to the test. We are "witnesses."
Only let us be careful that there be no conflict in our
testimony.

Be loving, brethren. Nothing wins like love. It
is irresistible. Remember our Lord's words: "Love
your enemies, bless them that curse you, do good to
them that hate you, and pray for them which despitefully use you and persecute you. That ye may be the
children of your Father which is in heaven; for he
maketh his sun to rise on the evil and on the good, and
sendeth rain on the just and on the unjust. For if ye
love them which love you, what reward have ye? Do
not even the publicans the same? And if ye salute
your brethren only, what do ye more than others? Do

not even the publicans so? Be ye therefore perfect even as your Father which is in heaven is perfect.''

Again, be patient with those who reject your doc·trine and ridicule your experience. There be many precious brethren in the Lord who do not see heart· purity as an experience, as we do. Sometimes they grow impatient with us because they see no good in our associations and special meetings. How much we need a baptism of patience to love those who do not agree with us, and bear the opposition of those who condemn us. We do only need to recur to our own experience and practice in all the years we wandered in the wilderness of doubt and unbelief and rejection on the subject, to make us forbearing and tender with them. Let us live down the severest criticism, and show by our gentleness and patience and love the reality of our profession. ''Be ye all of one mind, having compassion one of another, love as brethren, be pitiful, be courteous; not rendering evil for evil, or railing for railing; but contrariwise blessing; knowing that ye are thereunto called, that ye should inherit a blessing.''

May I now touch lovingly a delicate matter? Heart· purity implies the death of self. *Ego* retires. The emptied heart is filled with the Holy Ghost, and ruled and guided by him. Oh how important that we speak the right word at the right time and in the right way. ''Walk in wisdom toward them that are without, redeeming the time. Let your speech be always with grace seasoned with salt, that ye may know how ye ought to answer every man.''

In Mr. Wesley's Journal I find the following:

"*Question*. Does not the harshly preaching perfection tend to bring believers into bondage, or slavish fear?

"*Answer*. It does. Therefore we should place it in the most amiable light, so that it may excite only hope, and joy, and desire."

The same is true in the relation of Christian experience. In the rapture of deliverance from sin, and in the transport of joy and love to Christ for what he has done for us, we may sometime speak extravagantly. Untrained ears may be offended at what to them sounds irreverent and familiar. Our strong declarations and confident assurance sometimes grate harshly upon timid believers, and seem boastful and self-assuring.

Brethren, by all means let us magnify the Lord who saves us by his grace. "Let nothing be done through strife or vain-glory; but in lowliness of mind let each esteem other better than themselves. Let this mind be in you which was also in Christ Jesus; who, being in the form of God, thought it not robbery to be equal with God: but made himself of no reputation, and took upon him the form of a servant, and was made in the likeness of men: and being found in fashion as a man, he humbled himself, and became obedient unto death, even the death of the cross." "If any man offend not in word, the same is a perfect man."

To one and all let me make this final appeal for unity and love. If any heart has been sanctified after it was justified, surely nothing haughty or arrogant can dwell therein. It would be unpardonable for that cleansed one to feel "I am holier than thou." No stronger proof of delusion could be offered. Saved himself, he can only yearn with brotherly desire to assist in saving others. Delivered from sin, he is now the servant of all. St. Paul claimed that he was "the least of the apostles and not meet to be called an apostle." And again: "Unto me, who am less than the least of all saints, is this grace given." As we rise in Christian experience, we sink out of self, and are brought closer to every lover of the Lord.

And, then, if I speak to-day to any brother who claims that he was cleansed when he was converted, I know he will be patient and generous toward those of us who were not. There be some who hold and teach that God never does an imperfect work, and that when they were pardoned and regenerated they were also sanctified. To all such, dear brethren, we appeal to-day for charity. Heart-purity we must have. Without it, we are fearfully convicted none of us shall see the Lord. We know, also, by a mortifying experience that we were not purified when we were pardoned. These many years have been years of advance and retreat, success and failure, victory and defeat. The old man of the heart, which Mr. Wesley termed "inbred sin," lingered in us after our conversion. What wrestlings we have had! Now, brethren, we must be holy, and there is no hope for us, except as Mr. Wesley and our Bishops say, "men are justified before they are sanctified." Converted, but consciously not sanctified, how can we reach your blessed attainment if not by another and subsequent work of cleansing? For this we reach up, and pray and believe. Encourage us, brethren. Having reached it yourselves, we know you can not be unconcerned for us who in conversion did not. Some have found it by a second work. For these we give thanks, and we are assured you rejoice with us.

My precious brethren, let us cease our wrangling over minor and insignificant points and join hands in a high purpose henceforth to love the Lord our God with all our heart, and with all our soul, and with all our mind, and our neighbor as ourselves.

CHAPTER III.

Wesley and the Higher Christian Life.

[An address delivered before the Methodist Social Union, Chicago, by Rev. R. Crawford Johnson (of Belfast, Ireland), secretary of the Irish Conference and delegate to the General Conference of the M. E. Church.]

There is a remarkable man in England who calls himself "Father Ignatius, a monk of the Church of England." With all his eccentricity some of his sayings are well worth recording. On one occasion, when visiting a cottager in Wales, Father Ignatius said to her on leaving the door: "Don't take a half Christ, take a whole Christ." Now that is exactly what many do; they want to be saved from hell rather than from sin. Paul had three wishes. He wanted to be in Christ; to be with Christ; but he also wanted to be like Christ. Many want to be in Christ here, that they may be with Christ by and by, but they have no ambition to be like Christ; and yet what is Christianity if it be not likeness to Jesus Christ? On one occasion Cromwell asked his private chaplain, "What is the lowest evidence of regeneration?" and on receiving the answer, he replied, "Then I'm safe." Yes, there it is. Safety, not assimilation, is the aim of multitudes. They want the minimum, not the maximum of grace.

"To qualify contents their heart's desire,
They ask no angel's wing, no seraph's fire."

One reason of this low idea of religion was the prominence given to the doctrine of justification by faith for nearly two centuries. Emphasis often runs into error, and the reformers so emphasized the privilege of justification that they lost sight of the corresponding privilege of sanctification. But, as God raised up Luther to preach the one doctrine, he raised John Wesley to preach the other, and show that we can be saved from a present as well as a future hell. John Wesley declared that the mission of Methodism was to spread scriptural holiness throughout the land.

Dr. Dale used to say that it took fifteen years to get a new idea into his church. It has taken more than a hundred years to get John Wesley's idea of holiness into some of the churches. Thank God, a remarkable change has come over Christendom of late, and a desire for more abundant life is one special feature of the religious history of the present day.

Holiness is a many-sided subject, and I want to confine myself to one aspect of it on this occasion— the relation of holiness to usefulness.

There is a great deal of loose teaching on the subject of holiness. Some teach that if we enter the Holy of Holies, and are fully consecrated, we shall carry about with us a perpetual Pentecost, and see signs following in the conversion of thousands Now, this is certainly an error, and, like every other error, is a source of trouble and condemnation to tender souls. Success in saving souls depends on many things, and while, as we shall see, holiness is one main factor in success, it is not everything. Take two other factors, on which the issue and result will very largely depend—natural gifts and sphere of labor.

1. *Natural Gifts.*—"'There are diversities of gifts." We see this in the ministry. One man is a son of thunder, another a son of consolation—the one has the gift of rousing souls from slumber, the other of soothing, comforting, healing. But Barnabas may be as fully consecrated as Boanerges, though he can only count his converts by units, while the man of thunder can reckon his by thousands. George Whitefield was like the angel in the Apocalypse, flying over land and sea with the everlasting gospel in its hands. No preacher ever addressed such crowds, and no preacher ever counted so many converts. He was largely instrumental in leading two hemispheres to Christ. Samuel Rutherford, on the other hand, mourned over the barrenness of his ministry; his notes on the subject were always in the minor key. Listen to his lamentation: "I see exceedingly small fruits of my ministry." "I would be glad of one soul to be a crown of joy and rejoicing in the day of Christ." "I have a sad heart daily in my ministerial calling." Was George Whitefield a better man than Samuel Rutherford? Certainly not! Rutherford was at once a saint, a hero, and a martyr. His spirit was as pure as a breath of prayer, his life lofty as a psalm of praise; and the church, with true unerring instinct, calls him to-day, "holy Samuel Rutherford." The difference was largely a difference of natural gifts, and the magnetism and oratory of Whitefield went far to lift him, like Saul, head and shoulders above many of his

brethren. The sequel of their lives contains a bit of comfort for the depressed; the musty, dusty sermons of Whitefield are never read, while the aroma of Samuel Rutherford's letters fills all the churches of the present day. "He being dead, yet speaketh."

2. *Sphere of Labor.*—Sphere of labor is another circumstance that will account for the inequalities of success in those who may be equally consecrated. Take two farmers. Put one down on a farm in Connemara; put the other down in the golden vale of Limerick and Tipperary. The one has a miserable tract of mountain and bog, the other has a rich, fertile soil. Now suppose that these two men possess equal skill, equal industry, equal appliances, will they have equal crops and equal remuneration for their toil? Of course not! The poor farmer in Galway and Mayo can hardly eke out a living, while his more favored countryman in the golden vale can easily fill his barn with plenty. Precisely so in the Church of Christ. One man toils painfully in some moral and spiritual Connemara, where souls are few and light is dim, while another puts his sickle in some golden vale and reaps abundantly. The difference is not in gifts, not in zeal, not in holiness; it is simply in the soil. We read in an old book of a very remarkable Preacher. His voice was music, his presence magnetic, divine. He spent whole nights in prayer, and spake as never man spake; he added miracles to sermons, healed the sick, cleansed the leper, raised the dead, but yet in some places Jesus Christ himself could not do many mighty works because of their unbelief. The pew is

responsible, as well as the pulpit; a proud, icy church; an obstructive officialism; two quarrelsome sisters, like Euodias and Syntyche; nay, a solitary Achan, with his accursed wedge of gold, or one ambitious Diotrephes (male or female), with a domineering love of pre-eminence, may make the labor of the most holy apostle barren, and even limit and paralyze the arm of Omnipotence itself.

Here, then, are two things which go to make up success in work quite apart from the element of sanctity—diversity in gifts, and difference in our sphere of labor. Do not applaud the Whitefields, Moodys, or Crossleys and Hunters of the church at the expense of the pastors who lead the flocks to the green pastures and the still waters. Don't worry about results, and don't write bitter things against yourself because you have not gathered the sheaves of some brilliant saint whose biography you have read. Success is not the criterion of piety; and, thank God, success will not be the measure of our reward in heaven! Goodness and faithfulness are the only standards and measurements of God. ''Well done, good and faithful servant, enter thou into the joy of thy Lord.''

I shall now attempt to show that, other things being equal, holiness and usefulness go together, and that while the highest sanctity may not enable us to reap the harvests of Whitefield and Moody, it will certainly increase our own power and make us more successful than we would otherwise be. The reason for this is very obvious. There are many ways of doing good, and holiness gives increasing power to all.

20

1. *It gives increased power to my life.*—'' I will bless thee and thou shalt be a blessing.'' Please note the verb *be.*

Holiness and usefulness. We sometimes make a false distinction here. At any rate we emphasize the distinction too much; holiness *is* usefulness. This is beautifully taught by Hosea in describing the effect produced by the dews of grace. ''His beauty shall be as the olive tree; and his smell as Lebanon.'' The two things mentioned here seldom go together—beauty and fragrance. The dahlia captivates the eye, but possesses no sweet smell, while homely flowers, like verbena, musk, and mignonette fill the air with fragrance. Truth surpasses type, and it requires the double figure to show what a man of God may be. Now, when the Christian is at once beautiful and fragrant in his character, what is the result? ''They that dwell under his shadow shall return.'' Children, servants, friends shall feel the power of his life and ''return '' to God.

In estimating the value of Christian work we think too much of our efforts, too little of our spirit and life; but our character is really of more importance than our work. There are two sets of influences flowing out from every one of us; the influence of what we are, and the influence of what we say. Sometimes these influences clash, and the result is most disastrous. There is nothing more fatal to our usefulness than inconsistency. Men begin by doubting our piety; they end by denying the reality of all religion. On the other hand, when these two influences combine they are simply omnipotent. Carlyle says: "Words have weight when there is a man behind them." Yes! our words weigh lightly when we weigh lightly ourselves. But when they have the power of a holy life behind them, they are veritable thunderbolts.

Brethren, let us be holy men, and we shall be useful men. Sanctify yourselves; your work may be obscure, your talents few, but your life will be a benediction, and like Christ in the retirement of Tyre and Sidon, the aroma of your presence will betray you. You can not be "hid." The want of to-day is holy living. Men will not read "Paley's Evidences" and "Butler's Analogy," but they will read you. Visible rhetoric is the only rhetoric that tells in this age of facts. Remember, while we preach for an hour, you are preaching all the week in mill and factory and shop; your business is a rostrum, and your life a sermon. Be sweet, noble, pure, honest, unselfish, true, and those who dwell under your shadow will live to call you blessed, for holiness *is* usefulness; and the measure of holiness will be the measure of your power.

2. *It will purify and elevate our motives in Christian service.* Our motives in Christian work are pitched too low. Secondary motives are made supreme, and unworthy motives are sometimes the only source of zeal. There is a species of animalcule, living in tufts of moss, which is clear as crystal; when placed under the microscope you see all its organs as clearly as you can see the works of a watch under a cover of glass.

Now, if we were as transparent as that little creature, and if men could read the various motives that prompt us, what revelations would be made! Some work merely to please a friend.   Mr. So-and-So has asked us to take a class in Sunday-school, and we have yielded to the claims of friendship, but feel no inspiration in our work.   Some work to serve a party. We have a zeal for some particular church, and will make any sacrifice or effort to swell its numbers and promote its glory.   This motive is legitimate when kept within its proper limits.   No one admires the patriot who is

> "A friend of every country but his own;
> A patriot of the world alone."

And no one has a deep respect for the religionist of that type.   No! the Church is the army of the living God; and while we should feel the warmest interest in the affairs of every regiment, we prove ourselves unthankful traitors if we feel no special glow when the colors of our own are floating in the air.   But do we?   Do we thrill with interest when we hear of the prosperity of a neighboring church? or does Ephraim envy Judah? No! the prosperity of our brethren is often galling to our denominational ambition and pride, proving that there is a good deal of dross in our motives and zeal. Sometimes we labor from a selfish motive.   "All of self and none of thee."   I speak with trembling and shame!   How often does this motive obtrude itself in the pulpit, and we parade self instead of preaching Jesus Christ!   How much of self mingles with our public charities?.   I knew a tottering firm that gave £500 to a public charity on one occasion to hoodwink the public and restore its failing credit.   This is what

St. Augustine would call a "splendid sin." Yes, vanity and other sins have as much to do with the erection of asylums or cathedrals as either pity or piety, and men have even courted death in the heroic days of the Church to pose as martyrs and secure a niche in the temple of fame. Dear brethren, when we look into our motives and see how self dominates in our holiest services, do we not feel like one of God's servants who said, when congratulated on his virtues, "I take my good works and my bad works, and, casting them into one heap, fly from both to Christ, and fall at his feet saying, ' Lord, save, or I perish!' "

Now, if a man purge himself from these low motives and make God supreme, two results will follow, both of which will intensify our power of doing good. It will give thoroughness to our work. When a Grecian sculptor was engaged in carving a statue, his friends noticed that he took as much pains with the back part of the statue as the front, and thinking it was "sheer waste of time," they said, "Why are you so careful about the back part, it won't be seen?" "The gods will see it," was the grand reply. How slovenly and slipshod is much of our work! How little preparation some Sunday-school teachers make, and how often does a passing shower make the tract distributer stay at home. If men were as lax and careless about their business as they are sometimes about the sacred engagements of the sanctuary, they would soon be in the bankruptcy court, or in the parish workhouse. But when we feel the inspiration of the cross, then we put conscience into everything, and make our vocation a passion and our work a study. It will give constancy. The low motives that often prevail go far to account for the fickleness of Christian zeal. When we work to please a friend our labor ceases when the friendship dies. When we work to swell or serve a sect, if offenses come, we grow sulky and desert our post. When we work to exalt and glorify self, if we are eclipsed by others, our zeal collapses. But when we rise above self and party, and even friendship, and work for the Christ who bought us with his blood, then duty is transfigured into delight, the meanest service is ennobled by its lofty motive, and we are steadfast, unmovable, always abounding in the work of the Lord.

2. *It will give us moral courage to speak and work for Christ.* "Add to your faith courage!" There is hardly anything more lacking in the Church than moral courage. The want of this arises from several causes. Take two, and see the influence of a higher Christian life in relation to them.

Perfect love will not change our temperament— mark you! I do not say our temper. Grace will baptize us with gentleness. It sweetens while it sanctifies—but our natural temperament will remain the same. The phlegmatic will not become sanguine; the sanguine will not grow phlegmatic; Melancthon will still be timid; Luther still bold and fiery; John Wesley will still be calm and logical; Whitefield magnetic and impetuous still.

But while perfect love will not change our temperament, it will nevertheless help the timid and nervous.

How? By what Thomas Chalmers calls "the expulsive power of a new affection"—love will cast out fear. Take an illustration: Perhaps some of you heard Mother Stewart. She was the leader of the crusade against whisky in Ohio. When in Ireland she related a thrilling incident of her work. In one of the towns a' liquor dealer, who expected the crusaders, prepared himself for their visit by hiring a band of rowdies and arming them with revolvers for the occasion. On came the noble band, weak in themselves, but strong in the might of God, and knelt down on the pavement. "Now," said the saloon-keeper (a coarse, powerful man), "I want no praying here; and I give you notice that the first woman who opens her lips in prayer will be shot down." The minister's wife, who headed the crusade, was a fragile-looking, delicate lady, but with more moral courage than it takes to face an army in the heat of battle. In relating the incident she said: "I never felt safer in my own drawing-room than I did when those revolvers were pointed at my head. It seemed as if a voice came from the excellent glory, saying: 'He shall cover thee with his feathers, and under his wing shalt thou trust.'" She felt that God as surely sent his angel as he did when Daniel was in the lion's den. She commenced to pray with closed eyes, and when she had done, the rowdies had dropped their revolvers, and the saloon-keeper, with the tears running down his cheeks, said he never thought his trade was a bad one before, and they were at liberty to come and do what they liked with the liquor, and he helped them to pour it into the street, which they did amid songs of rejoicing.   Now we see here, that faith completely cast out fear; and so with us.   Perfect love will not make the timid brazen, but it will make them brave, and in the sacred presence of duty will strip them, as completely as faith stripped this fragile lady, of the fear of man that bringeth the snare.

Archbishop Whately, in his book on rhetoric, gives tnis as the chief cause of fear in public speaking: The speaker is too much occupied with thoughts about himself—his voice, his gestures, his reputation—in one word, about himself.   The archbishop then points out the absurdity of the advice which is sometimes given to timid speakers.   They are told to reflect upon the ridicule to which they expose themselves by their awkward manners.   This only pours oil on the flame which you want to quench.   No! if undue consciousness of self is the cause of fear, then forgetfulness of self is the true and only cure.   Now perfect love gives us this sweet oblivion.   Oh! how self haunts us!   It desecrates our prayer.   How often in prayer are we thinking so much about the choice of words, the arrangement of parts, the polish of periods, that we are almost oblivious to the presence of God, instead of being so absorbed and swallowed up in the thought of God that we are oblivious to the presence and paltry criticisms of man!   It mars our sermons.   "The Rev. So-and-So ably sustained his reputation."   Ably sustained his reputation!   This is what damns so many sermons—I fear I must add, so many souls.   We are too much concerned about our miserable reputation, and often, like Jonah, think more of it than of the souls that are perishing in sin. We may sing with Faber:

"O miserable omnipresence, stretching
    Over all time and space,
How have I run from thee, yet found thee reaching
    The goal in every race!

"Inevitable self! Vile imitation
    Of universal light—
Within our hearts a dreadful usurpation
    Of God's exclusive right!"

There are three crucifixions spoken of in the epistle to the Galatians—crucifixion to the law, crucifixion to the world—but there is a third, deeper and diviner still —crucifixion to self. When this takes place all our miserable self-consciousness is gone and we are completely emancipated from the lust of praise and the fear of man. Yes! perfect love enthrones Christ. In preaching, souls take the place of critics, and in prayer we see no man save Jesus only. When Christ is on the throne, self is in the dust. It is no longer "some of self and some of thee;" it is "none of self and all of thee," and with Paul of Tarsus, we can say, "I am crucified with Christ, nevertheless I live; yet not I, but Christ liveth in me."

4. *It will endue us with more power from on high.* There are three special rays in the sunlight—the yellow, the red and the blue. The yellow gives light, the red gives heat, but the blue gives life. Take the blue ray away from our conservatory, and there is no fruit on the plant and no blossom on the flower. We need in like manner the fructifying power of the Holy Ghost to give the bud, the blossom, and the fruit. Take the

case of Apollos. He had light. He was "mighty in
the scriptures;" as an old version puts it, "steeped in
the scriptures." He had the warm glow of enthusiasm. He was "fervent in the spirit," literally, "boil-
ing in spirit," but Aquila and Priscilla felt there was
something wanting, and expounded unto him "the
way of God more perfectly." The orator sat at the
feet of the saints, and he now received the baptism of
Christ. "Like priest, like people." Apollos was
pastor of the church at Ephesus, and as the stream can
not rise above its level, the people of the church had,
up to this time, known only the baptism of John. A
minor Pentecost soon followed, and now the whole of
Asia Minor was filled with the music of the cross, and
the Word of God grew mightily and prevailed.

The revised version makes a significant change in
a passage which I have already quoted; it turns the
indicative into the imperative mood. "I will bless
thee, *and be thou a blessing.*" What is *privilege*, so
far as we personally are concerned, becomes *duty*, when
we consider our sacred relationship to others. "Be
filled with the Spirit:" as the French say, "Be intoxi-
cated with God." Then, and only then, shalt thou
be a blessing in Pentecostal plenitude and fervor.

> "The soul must overflow
> If thou another's soul would reach;
> It needs the overflow of heart
> To give the lips full speech."

The great interest in this subject felt by other
Churches has a solemn moral for the people called
Methodists. The special Mission of Methodism, accord-

ing to John Wesley, was to spread scriptural holiness through the world. The teaching of holiness has been at once its offence and glory. Well, then, what about our experience and life? Creed implies responsibility; creed should find its counterpart in life. We expect a purer life in a Christian than in a Mohammedan, because he has a loftier creed. We believe in holiness. Do we enjoy it? Do we embody it in our life? That was a searching question put to the Rev. Joseph Bush at the Brighton convention. A German minister was speaking to Mr. Bush about the teaching of the convention and asked him if he had ever heard it before. "Oh, yes," said Mr. Bush; "we Methodists have always believed in this privilege." "Indeed!" said the stranger. Mr. Bush then read him some of our hymns, such as—

"Lord, I believe a rest remains
  To all thy people known;
A rest where pure enjoyment reigns,
  And thou art loved alone.

"A rest, where all our soul's desire
  Is fixed on things above;
Where fear and sin and grief expire,
  Cast out by perfect love."

"That's beautiful!" exclaimed the German. "And do your people believe this?" "Yes," said Mr. Bush. Then, quite naturally, he added, "And do your people enjoy this?" Ay, there's the rub—do we live our creed? We rehearse it; we preach it; we argue and wrangle about it; we examine our workers on it; we glory in it. Do we enjoy and embody it? We say that John Wesley was raised to revive this truth:

Charles Wesley to sing it; John Fletcher to defend it; we call it the *peculium* of Methodism.   But is it a mere theological relic that we guard with reverence and care; or is it a living, vitalizing power in our hearts and lives?   Thank God we have no monopoly of the doctrine now; and all the Churches are thrilling with desire of a more abundant life.   Let their zeal rekindle ours, and let us pray with our friends of the Church of England: "Almighty God, unto whom all hearts are open, all desires known, and from whom no secrets are hid; cleanse the thoughts of our hearts by the inspiration of the Holy Spirit, that we may perfectly love thee. and worthily magnify thy holy name through Chris' ur Lord.   Amen."

CHAPTER IV.

Purity and Peace.

REV. JOHN J. TIGERT, D. D., LL. D.

We have never been specially wedded to the much-ridiculed phrase, "second blessing;" but we have always contended that better than any other single phrase it sums up the essentials of the Wesleyan and scriptural doctrine—namely, (1) the incompleteness of regeneration; (2) the ordinary necessity of a second work, both gradual and instantaneous; and (3) its completeness and attainableness in this life. In the second stanza of Hymn 444 of our present hymn book, the doctrine is clearly stated by Charles Wesley:

> Breathe, O breathe thy loving Spirit
> Into every troubled breast!
> Let us all in Thee inherit,
> Let us find that second rest:
> Take away our bent to sinning;
> Alpha and Omega be;
> End of faith, as its beginning,
> Set our hearts at liberty.

Dr. Miley definitely accepts the phrase, "second blessing," as the formula of the Wesleyan doctrine, and under the caption, "The Second-Blessing View," gives his full and positive account of the doctrine and experience. It so nearly coincides with what seems to us to be the true view that, with the possible exception of a sentiment or two, we give it our hearty indorsement, and reproduce it in full for the benefit of our readers:

"The doctrinal views of the second blessing, as definitely held, consists of two parts, one of which has already been stated, but which may here be restated in connection with the other. The doctrine will thus be presented the more clearly.

"Underlying the definite second-blessing view is the doctrine of a common incompleteness of the work of regeneration. Herein the soul is renewed, but not wholly; purified, but not thoroughly. Somewhat of depravity remains which wars against the new spiritual life; not strong enough to bring that life into bondage to itself, yet strong enough to impose a burden upon the work of its maintenance. Such is the first part. The doctrine in the second part is that the regenerate shall come to the consciousness of this incompleteness, and to a deep sense of the need of a fullness of the spiritual life; that these experiences shall be analogous to those which preceded the attainment of regeneration and be just as deep and thorough. The fullness of sanctification shall be instantly attained; and there shall be a new experience of a great and gracious change, and just as consciously as the experience in regeneration.

"That Mr. Wesley held and taught such views, there can be no doubt; though we think it would be a wrong to him to say that he allowed no instances of entire sanctification except in this definite mode. We see no perplexity for faith in the possibility of such an instant subjective purification. Through the divine

...̱acy the soul may be as quickly cleansed as the
̱per, as quickly purified in whole as in part. We
admit an instant partial sanctification in regeneration,
and therefore may admit the possibility of an instant
entire sanctification.

"Such a view of sanctification does not mean that
there need be no preparation for its attainment. The
necessity of such a preparation is uniformly held, even
by such as hold strongly the second-blessing view.
The idea of such a preparation is inseparable from the
process of experience through which, according to
this view, the regenerate must pass in order to the
attainment of entire sanctification.

"However, this process of preparation need not be
chronologically long No assumption of such a necessity could be true to the soteriology of the scriptures.
Let it be recalled that the question here is, not the
maturity of the Christian life, but the purification of
the nature. For the attainment of the former there
must be growth, and growth requires time. But
while the subjective purification may be progressively
wrought, it is not subject to the law of growth: and
it is so thoroughly and solely the work of God that it
may be quickly wrought. Neither is there any necessity that the mental process of preparation shall be
chronologically a long one. Here, as in many other
spheres, the mental movement may be very rapid. It
is often so in conversion. In many instances the
whole mental process has been crowded into an hour,
or even less time. Even heathen have been saved,
born of the Spirit through faith in Christ, under the

first sermon they ever heard. But there is as really a necessary process of preparation for regeneration as for entire sanctification, and such preparation need require no more time in the latter case than in the former.

"That a subjective purification may be attained according to the definite second blessing view, does not limit the possibility to this single mode. There is no ground for such limitation. Indeed, the attainableness of sanctification according to this definitely wrought doctrine, as above stated, is a truth which lies in the soteriology of the scriptures as a whole and not in any definite teaching on the question. While they are full of the idea of entire sanctification according, they are quite empty of any such teaching respecting the mode of its attainment. Hence any insistence upon such a mode as the only possible mode of sanctification must be without definite warrant of scripture. Further, we think it a serious objection to this view, as thus rigidly held, that it can not consistently allow any preaching of holiness, or any seeking after it, or any expectation of its attainment, except in this definite mode.

"Mr. Wesley held strongly the view of an instant subjective sanctification; and we fully agree with him, not only in its possibility, but also in its frequent actuality; but his own illustrations of his doctrine points to a possible attainment in a gradual mode. It is given in his answer to the question: "Is this death to sin, and renewal in love, gradual or instantaneous?' His answer is: 'A man may be dying for sometime, yet he does not, properly speaking, die till the instant the soul is separated from the body, and in that instant he lives the life of eternity. In like manner, he may be dying to sin for sometime; yet he is not dead to sin till sin is separated from the soul; and in that instant he lives the full life of love.' The instant consummation here emphasized does not exclude the gradual approach to it; so that, according to this illustration, there may be a gradual dying unto sin, until the death is complete; a gradual subjective purification until completeness is attained. Such a view is in the fullest accord with the soteriology of the scriptures.

"The privilege of entire sanctification is at once so thoroughly scriptural and Wesleyan that from it there is among us only the rarest dissent. Yet not a few hesitate respecting the sharply defined second-blessing view. We do not share this hesitation, so far as that view represents a possible mode of entire sanctification; though we object to any insistence that such is the only possible mode. Right here is the occasion of unfortunate differences among us. However, much of the evil consequence might easily be avoided; much of it would be avoided through a spirit of mutual forbearance. Let those who hold rigidly the second-blessing view preach sanctification in their own way, but let them be tolerant of such as preach it in a manner somewhat different; also let such as hesitate respecting that special view be tolerant of those for whom it possesses great interest. All ministers who believe in the privilege of a full salvation ᴠι preach it in good fait'ı. Indeed, they are not at aiberty to omit this preaching."

21

CHAPTER V.

The Second Blessing.

REV. SAM P. JONES.

Psalm 15:2: "And speaking the truth in his heart."

A man is never better than his heart. A clean heart is the need of every Christian man and woman. This should be the cry and the plea and the earnest object of every believing child of God: "Create in me a clean heart, O God!" Thank God that this is our privilege. Thank God that many people seek and obtain it. I don't care what you call it, whether the second or third or the thousandth blessing, it cleans out and then cleans up—purifies the heart, cleans up the life, and, thank God, so benign and wondrous and so needed a work of grace can be possessed by men and women. I welcome it under any name, and have a profound contempt for the spirit which would depreciate the people who possess it, or the great grace which has come to them

You may say what you please about the holiness people, but I want to say this: I have never seen a holiness man that wasn't a Prohibitionist from his hat to his heels. I have never seen one who didn't vote for prohibition always and everywhere. I have never seen one that didn't fight liquor, card playing, and every phase and form of worldliness in the Church. I have never seen a second blessing man or woman that

(322)

believed in or gave card parties, indulged in punch slinging, went to the theatre, or dancing parties, or engaged in or encouraged any phase or form of the deviltry that is cursing the Church to-day. I have never seen a second blessing man or woman that wouldn't pray anywhere and everywhere when called on, and that wasn't ready to stand up and testify for the Lord whenever opportunity offered. I never saw a second blessing person in my life, man or woman, at the head of a family, that didn't get down night and morning and pray for the children in that home and for God's guiding hand in all things pertaining to their sacred home responsibilities.

I will tell you another thing: I never saw a preacher in my life that was fighting the holiness crowd that wasn't a dead dog in his pulpit—can't bite. You may watch it. Every little preacher that you hear fighting the holiness people, is a fellow that hasn't had a revival or a conversion in his ministry in years, unless he got somebody else to hold his meeting. God just won't honor any such a preacher. You never see a man in the Church who fights the holiness people, but what if you will search down far enough, you will find him wrong in his life or rotten in his character.

I will tell you another thing: Whenever you hear one of the sisters in the church just pitching into these "second blessing fanatics," as she calls them, you may set it down she is one of them old gals that either has a punch bowl in her house, or she slips across to her neighbor and just "takes a little," or leads in some form of worldliness.

Sometimes folks have said that I "fit" the second blessing people. I want to say here and now, it is not true. I never do any such thing. I don't fight 'em; I just trim them up sometimes, like I do all the other gangs, and they need trimming just like the balance of you folks need trimming; and you will find that all the fellows that have got the blessing don't mind the trimming. The second blessing people are right in heart; some of them are wrong in the head. There are black sheep in that flock as well as in your flock. Some second blessing people, so-called, haven't got the right spirit, and maybe don't live right. I can say this—such folks haven't got the second blessing, and if they ever had it, they have lost it. And I can say that some of the crowd that is everlastingly fighting the second blessing folks may have had the first blessing when they commenced the fight, but they have fought and fought until they have lost the first blessing.

You have got to have a clean heart if you have a clean a life, and God desires both; and yet some of you worldly gang in the church are whining: "I just, can't live without sin; I just have to sin every day; I am just a poor worm of the dust, and poor human nature is so frail that I just can't live without sin." Well, now, just tell me, What sin is it you are compelled to commit every day? Just sit down and write it out on a piece of paper and look at it, and see which of the commandments you have got to break every day of your life. What sin or sins have you got to commit every day of your life? What a libel on your Savior! What a slander on the atoning blood of the Lamb! For what was the Lamb slain? Why did the crimson tide flow from the side of Divine Innocence if it was not to cleanse us from all sin? Did He not come to save from sin? Where sin abounded, did not grace much more abound? No, brother, sister, thank God, it is false when you say that you *have to sin;* you sin because you want to sin, and you insult your Lord and misrepresent the atonement when you seek to cover your guilt or apologize for your love for something forbidden by pleading a necessity for sin.

Let's suppose a case: Here is a man who has a fine ten-room house which he sells to a friend; makes him a deed in fee simple; receives the cash in payment and turns over to him the property, giving him the keys to nine rooms, but retains the key to one room. The buyer says, "Well, hello, friend, didn't you say there were ten rooms in that house? Why don't you give me the key to the tenth room?" "Oh," says the other, "I've got some snakes and lions and bears locked up in that room, and I don't propose to turn that over to you." "Well, but didn't I buy the whole house; and didn't you deed it to me, and pledge yourself in the deed to deliver the same and to forever warrant and defend the title to the same to me; and do you suppose I am going to move my family into that house, one room of which is filled with snakes and lions and bears to endanger my family and the lives of my children?" Now, brethren, you know that would burst up the whole transaction on the spot. There ain't a man in Christendom that would stand any such a piece of fraud as that, and you know it; and yet there are lots of you folks that profess to make a full consecration, and with a heart thoroughly emptied to invite the Lord to enter and take full possession in all His cleansing power, and you know there is a nook or corner in your heart where you won't let Him enter, and which He has never entered and can never enter because there in that sequestered nook of your nature you are nursing the hissing serpents of envy and jealousy. Roaming around in that dark region are the lions and bears of hate and malice and spite. You know as well as you know that you are living, that there are tempers, carnal passions, and a thousand things unexpelled from your nature which keep your Lord from a full and absolute supremacy in your hearts. And yet you profess to have turned the whole thing over to Him!

Oh brethren and sisters, you have got to turn loose, laying everything on the altar, and sweep out into the ocean of God's infinite love. Thank God that I ever did that. Some of the sweetest memories of my life and the profoundest experiences of my Christian character are connected with these holiness brethren. Never shall I forget an association with a holiness preacher down in a Georgia town a few years ago. That brother had preached this great blessing with all the earnestness and power of his soul. The tidal wave of salvation was sweeping over the people. He was urging a full and uncompromising consecration of all to God, and that accompanying supreme act of faith which procures the downpour of the Spirit in all his fulness. We were walking alone after one of the services had closed, and, turning to me, he said: "Sam, why in the world, brother, don't you turn loose everything that lies between you and God's fulness and lay hold on this great blessing?'' I said: ''Brother P., everything that stands between me and my God and the uttermost which He can do for me is not worth more than a nickle. I wouldn't give a nickle for anything under the burning sun that I wouldn't turn loose in a second that stands between me and God's fulness.'' Brother P. said: ''Then, Sam, you are just within one nickle of the blessing.'' I replied. ''Well, a nickle shan't split such an important matter.'' When I got back to church at the next service the meeting had commenced, and this brother was praying as I entered the church, and knelt down, and he truly had hold of the horns of the altar. Such praying I never heard since I was born in the world. The very windows of heaven seemed open. I felt the very presence of my God: heaven and earth came together. It was a time of heart-searching, heart-emptying, heart-surrendering, and heart-filling. At that meeting, in that solemn and never-to-be-forgotten hour, I turned loose the willows that overhung the banks, and swept out into the very midst of the ocean of God's infinite love; and the joy of that moment lingers sweetly and ineffaceably to-day. Its memory and power have swept over the lapse of years, and it has been my solace in a thousand sorrows, my strength in a thousand struggles, my star of hope through a thousand nights, and like a sheen of glory will canopy with its light and peace and triumph my dying hour. Thank God, there is water enough in the River of Life to cleanse every heart from all sin.

SECTION VI.

WITNESSES TO SANCTIFICATION AS AN EXPERIENCE.

CHAPTER I.

Experience of Mrs. Phoebe Palmer.

I never made much progress in the career of faith, until I most solemnly resolved, in the strength of the Lord Jehovah, that I would do every duty, though I might die in the effort. From that hour my course was onward and upward. I also covenanted with God that I would be a *Bible Christian*, and most carefully seek to know the mind of the Spirit, as recorded in the written WORD, though it might lead to an experience unlike all the world beside. I had often prayed for holiness of heart, but do not remember now that holiness, as a blessing in *name*, was on my mind; my highest and all-engrossing desire was to be a BIBLE CHRISTIAN.

The day of the Lord is near in the Valley of *Decision*. This was an important step, and took me much nearer to God, the Source of Light and Love. In a manner that exceeded all former perceptions, the living WORD said to my heart: "*Ye are not your own, ye are bought with a price; therefore glorify God in your body and spirit, which are God's.*"

From this I saw I could not be a Bible Christian, without being *wholly consecrated*. I arose early, and began every new day with a renewed solemn consecration. In the name and strength of the Triune Deity, I presented myself to the Lord. And every day, and hour, my soul seemed to be pressing hard after God. From the depths of my being, I said,

"My heart-strings groan with deep complaint,
  My flesh is panting, Lord, for Thee;
And every nerve and every joint,
  Stretches for perfect purity."

While in this state of longing expectancy, my pastor came in one morning, and spoke of a lady who, the evening previous, had presented herself at the altar of prayer, as a seeker, and professed to find the Savior. He said that the lady appeared to be an entire stranger, and asked, "Will you not go and see her?" I might have hesitated about going to a stranger thus, but the Holy Spirit whispered, "Did you not consecrate yourself to the Lord this morning; and if so, it is not left optional with yourself whether you will go; the one and only question is, Would the Lord have you go?"

Looking at the question in that light, the duty was clear. I went; found the lady a new creature in Christ Jesus. An unconverted, gay sister was sitting by, who manifested great displeasure. I asked if she did not feel the need of the same grace that her sister had received? In a manner exceedingly repulsive, she answered, "*No!*" Affectionately, I entreated her to be careful of her utterances before God, as she was in danger of sinning as Ananias and Sapphira did — that is, lying against the Holy Ghost.   And here I was withstood.   "How much of *self* in this performance," suggested the tempter.   Though consciously not insincere, yet the accusation was for the moment almost paralyzing, and from the depths of my soul I cried out, "What shall I do?"   The still, small voice whispered, "Stand still, and see the salvation of God!"

"Stand still, and do nothing?"   No.   "Be ye steadfast, unmovable, always abounding in the work of the Lord, forasmuch as ye know that your labor is not in vain in the Lord."   It was thus that the blessed Holy Spirit, through the living WORD, deigned to talk with me, making the written Word spirit and life.

At this point I perceived the privilege of *knowing that my labors were in the Lord*.   Paul must have known it, or he would not have written thus.   And to *know this*, I must be conscious that the spring of every motive is pure.   It was thus I apprehended heart-purity as an absolute *necessity* if I would be *useful*.

On the evening of the third day after this conversation with the young lady, she was powerfully converted, the Spirit having used my lips in convincing her of sin.   Between the hours of eight and nine o'clock the same evening, I was led by the Spirit to the determination that I would never rest, day or night, until I *knew* that the spring of every motive was pure, and that the consecration I made of myself was wholly accepted.

The adversary said, "Don't be rash.   You may

have to wrestle all night, and perhaps all day to-mor-row, and the next day, too. If you do this, it will be your death." I replied, "God demands present holi-ness. I cannot glorify Him without holiness; and if I cannot live to glorify God, let me die and glorify Him."

I was then withstood with the suggestion, "How do you know that this is God's *time ?*" Again the Spirit, through the written WORD, speaking to my in-most soul, said, "*Now* is the accepted time; behold NOW is the day of salvation !"

Had any one asked me, weeks previous to this, "Are you wholly consecrated ?" my answer might have been, as far as I know myself, "I am." Otherwise, I could not understandingly have retained a state of *justification*, for, *how* can one on *Scriptural* principles retain a state of justification, while *knowingly* keeping back anything from God. "To him that knoweth to do good, and doeth it not, to him it is *sin*."

But I was now following hard after God, and to the degree my mind was enlightened, was making daily advances God-ward. Said Jesus, "I have many things to say unto you, but ye cannot bear them now." He had been saying thus to me as His disciple, and following on lovingly after Him, true to the light re-vealed, I was walking in *justification* before Him

In coming to the decision, I *will be holy* NOW, I took a step beyond any I had ever before taken. God is *light*. As I drew nearer to Him than ever before, He drew nearer to me. I had often entered into cove-nant with God before. Now, by the light of the **Holy**

Spirit, I saw that the High and Holy One would have me enter into a covenant with Him, the duration of which would be lasting as eternity, *absolute* and *unconditional*.

I felt that the Spirit was leading into a solemn, most sacred, and inviolable compact between God and the soul that came forth from Him, by which, in the sight of God, angels and men, I was to be united in eternal oneness with the Lord my Redeemer, requiring unquestionable allegiance on my part, and infinite love and everlasting salvation, guidance and protection, on the part of Him who had loved and redeemed me, so that from henceforth He might say to me, "I will betroth thee unto Me forever."

That the covenant might be well ordered and sure, I thought, "Let me *particularize*, taking every step, so that not one may ever have to be retraced." The first object presented to be given up, was one with which every fiber of my being seemed interwoven. With amazement, I asked, "Can it be that the Lord requires that this one beloved object, dearer to me than life itself, be bound to the altar? What shall I have to live for if I give up this object?" The Holy Spirit suggested, "Have you not often said to the Lord, your Redeemer, 'I take Thee as my only portion!' Now, God is taking you at your word."

"What a sacrifice," said the tempter, "Did you ever hear of such a sacrifice being required at the hand of any one?

Here the tender, loving Spirit interposed. " Did Abraham know *why* he was called to give up Isaac at the *time* he gave him up? But he knows *now*. And are you willing to wait till you get to heaven in order to know why the Lord demands this sacrifice at your hand?" My soul replied, " Yes, Lord, I will wait till knowledge is made perfect. Take this object if Thou dost require. Take life or friends away. I am wholly Thine! There is not a tie that binds me to earth. Every tie has been severed."

" Perhaps there is something that you do not know of, not yet given up," whispered the tempter.

" What will not a man give for his life? and I have given up that which is dearer to me than life. I make no provision for future emergencies, resolved here-after, as God shall reveal His will, to say, ' Behold Thy willing servant!' "

Arriving at this point, the enemy had no further ground for questioning, relative to the *consecration,* whether it was *entire, absolute, and unconditional.* From the depths of my being I felt that the consecra-tion was absolute and universal, and in view of all coming time. But at this point I was for a moment perplexed with the question —

" How do you know that God will receive you?" And here I paused and pondered, "*How* may I know that the Lord *does* receive me?" To this, in gentle whispers, the Spirit replied, "It is *written*, I WILL RECEIVE YOU." " Must I believe it, because it simply stands written, without any other *evidence* than the *Word of God?*" I exclaimed.

In answer to these questionings, the ever-blessed Spirit (given to guide us to into all truth) suggested,

"Suppose you should hear a voice, speaking in tones of thunder, from heaven, saying, '*I will receive you,*' would you not believe it then?"   "I could not help believing it then, because I should have the 'evidence of my *senses,*'" was my reply.

In a moment I saw the inconsistency of my position, remembering that I was taught by the Scripture most plainly, and had always known, that the blessing of entire satisfaction was received by *faith*, inasmuch as it stands written, "Sanctify them through Thy truth, THY WORD IS TRUTH."

"But," said the adversary, "suppose, that after you have believed you do not *feel* any different, what will you do?"   Here the blessed WORD again met me, intensifying the truth, "The just SHALL *live by faith.*" I now saw what *faith* was in all its *simplicity.* Such preceptions of the *Divinity* of the WORD I never before had.   So true is it that, "if any man WILL DO His will, he shall know of the doctrine."

I had thought of the doctrine of faith as difficult. Now I saw that it was to believe *heartily*, what in fact I had always professed to believe, that is, that the Bible is the WORD OF GOD, just as truly as though I could hear Him speaking in tones of thunder from Sinai's Mount, and *faith* is to *believe it* '

Still the enemy withstood me, with the suggestion, "Suppose you should be called to live a long life, say till three-score or a hundred years old, and never have any of those manifestations that others enjoy—never have anything but the naked Word of God upon which to rely ; and should die, and come up before your

,udge, without ever having had anything but the naked Word to assure your faith? ''

My reply was, ''I would come up before my Judge, and in the face of an assembled universe, say, ' The foundation of my faith was Thy immutable WORD.' '' The moment I came to this point, the Holy Spirit most assuringly whispered, '' This is just the way in which Abraham, the father of the faithful, walked.'' ''By *faith* he journeyed, not knowing whither he went.''

There is joy in faith. '' Can it be that the Lord of the Way is going to honor me thus, as to permit me all along through life, to tread in the footseps of the father of the faithful?''—was the language of my heart.

It was at this point that the Covenant was consum-mated between God and my soul, that I would live a *life of faith*. That, however diversified life's currents might roll, though I might be called to endure more complicated and long-continued trials of my faith than were ever before conceived of, or even brought to a climax, where, as with the father of the faithful, com-mands and promises might *seem* to conflict, that I would still believe, though I might *die in the effort*, I would hold on in the death-struggle. In the strength of Omnipotence I laid hold on the Word, ''I WILL RECEIVE YOU.''

Faith apprehended the written WORD, not as a *dead letter*, but as the living voice of the living God. '' Holy men of God spake as they were moved by the Holy Ghost.'' The Holy Scriptures were intensified to my mind as the *lively* (or living) *oracles*—the voice of God to me, as truly as though I could every moment hear Him speaking in tones of thunder from Sinai. And now, that through the inworkings of the Holy Spirit, I had presented all my redeemed powers to God, through Christ, how could I doubt His immutable word, "I will receive you?"

O, with what light, clearness and power, were the words invested, "*Sanctify them through thy truth, thy* WORD *is truth!*"

Yet, though I *knew* that it could not be otherwise than that God did receive me, my faith was put to the test. I had expected that some wonderful manifestation would at once follow as the reward of my faith. But I was shut up to faith—*naked faith* in a *naked promise.*

Said the adversary, tauntingly, "Where now is the great joy that you anticipated? Why do you not, from constraining influences, praise the Lord, as many others do who receive the blessing of a clean heart?"

So subtle is Satan, when transformed as an angel of light, that though kept from yielding, I did not perceive that it was the tempter, and, in answer to his subtle suggestion, replied, "I do not feel so much like praising the Lord from impelling influences now, as on some other occasions."

True it is that the kingdom of heaven cometh not by observation. But O, the proneness of the human heart to say, Lo, here, and Lo, there! And how few seem to remember that the ever-blessed, tender, gentle Holy Spirit, is quiet in its influences! He would fain lead the soul into green pastures, and beside the *still* waters—casting down all high imaginations, and whispering soothingly, "In quietness and assurance thy *rest* shall be." And now that Satan would have come in as a flood, the Spirit lifted up a standard thus—

"Through what power were you enabled to enter into the bonds of an everlasting covenant with God, yielding up that which was dearer to you than life?" "It was through the power of Omnipotence. I could no more have done it of myself than I could have created a world. Every step toward the attainment of this grace has been through the direct inspirations of the Holy Spirit."

"And upon whose WORD do you now rely?" "It is on the WORD of the immutable Jehovah. He has given me that WORD." Wonderful, indeed, that the Holy Spirit does thus condescened to reason with the human heart; but through these reasonings I saw with the clearness of a sunbeam, that it was all from first to last the work of the Spirit—"God working in me to will and to do." With the poet, I experimentally apprehended,

> "Thou all our works in us hast wrought,
>   Our good is all Divine;
> The praise of every virtuous thought,
>   And righteous act is *Thine.*"

Now, that I so clearly apprehended that the power to will and to do was all so manifestly of the Lord, I began to reason with myself thus: "Do I wait to thank a friend who does me a great favor, till I feel an *impelling* influence to do it? Do I not do it because it is a *duty?*   And now, if the Lord has enabled me to make an unconditional and absolute surrender of all my redeemed powers and faculties, and has given HIS WORD, assuring me that He *does* receive me, shall I refuse to give Him the glory due to His name, till I feel constraining influences?'' Ashamed of the thought, I took yet another step in the Divine order, without which, a most important and imperative requirement would have been omitted.

There are distinctive steps in the attainment of the great salvation.   In that of ENTIRE CONSECRATION, I had so carefully pondered the path of my feet, that. the way back again to self, or the world in any degree, was returnless.   The next step, FAITH, in regard to Divine acceptance of all, had also been distinctly taken.   And now, as I plainly saw the third step clearly defined in the Word, I took the advance ground--CONFESSION.

Giving God the glory due to his name, I exclaimed, ''Through Thy grace alone I have been enabled to give myself wholly and forever to Thee.   Thou hast given Thy Word, assuring me that Thou dost receive. I believe that WORD! Alleluia! the Lord God Omnipotent reigneth unrivalled in my heart.   Glory be to the Father! Glory be to the Son! Glory be to the Holy Ghost forever!''   O, into what a region of light, glory and purity was my soul at this moment ushered! I felt that I was but as a drop in the ocean of infinite LOVE, and Christ was All in All.

If any one had asked me previous to this, ''Are any of the graces of the Spirit perfected in you?''   I might have said, " I am, indeed greatly deficient in all the gifts and graces of the Holy Spirit; but if one grace is nearer perfected than another, it is the grace of *humility*. But never before did I know the meaning of the word *humility*. How the realization was intensified to my mind: " Not by works of righteousness that we have done!" I saw that I was not sufficient of myself to think a good thought, much less to perform a righteous action. I felt that I could not save myself, even for one moment, and from the depths, my soul cried out,

> "Every moment, Lord, I need
>   The merit of Thy death."

But amid these realizations of utter nothingness, I had such views of the unbounded efficacy of the atonement, that if the guilt of the universe had been concentrated and laid upon my head,

> "The stream of Jesus' precious blood
>   Would wash away the dreadful load."

On the morning of August 10th, 1837, I was blessed in a peculiar manner. About four o'clock I awoke, with an intense breathing after God. I was assured, by the way in which my soul seemed to grasp a signal blessing, that the Lord was about to seal me more fully His. For days previous I had, with unutterable desire, been pleading that the Holy Spirit might continuously urge me onward in the divine life; that I might not be permitted to rest short of any state of grace made possible for me, through the death and present intercession of the Saviour; and to that degree in which it might consist with the will of God, might prove the full power of saving grace, to transform to the uttermost, in heart and in life.

Never before had I such a deep experimental consciousness of the Apostle's meaning: "Likewise the Spirit also helpeth our infirmities, for we know not what we should pray for, as we ought; but the Spirit itself maketh intercession for us with groanings which cannot be uttered. And He that searcheth the heart, knoweth what is the mind of the Spirit, because He maketh intercession for the saints according to the will of God." My special prayer on this eventful occasion was set forth, Ephes. 1 : 13 : "In whom ye also trusted, after that ye heard the word of truth, the gospel of your salvation; in whom also, after ye believed, ye were sealed with that Holy Spirit of promise, which is the earnest of our inheritance, until the redemption of the purchased possession."

Now, my prayer was, "*Lord, seal me unto the day of redemption* !" There was a distinctiveness in the hallowed exercises of that hour which must ever preclude all questioning. The Divine Spirit that inspired those unutterable groanings sealed the truth on my heart, that the work was of God. For about two hours I remained under those peculiarly hallowing influences, breathing forth in inexpressible longing, "O Lord, seal me, seal me unto the day of redemption !" The Spirit itself helped my infirmities, and I was enabled to ask in conscious *faith*, and realize that I had the thing I desired of God.

So sacred was the communion of that hour, so holy and inviolable the covenant entered upon by the ever lasting God, and the Spirit that came forth from Him, that it should be assimilated yet more and more to His own glorious likeness here on earth, and eventually reunited to Him forever, that I had not a temptation to doubt. Glory be to the Father! Glory be to the Son! Glory be to the Holy Spirit!

> "My hope is full, O glorious hope,
> Of immortality,"

Surely it was to me a day to be remembered throughout the untold ages of eternity !

CHAPTER II.

Experience of Rev. T. H. B. Anderson.

Since Dr. Carradine's meetings in San Francisco, and elsewhere in California, fifty or more letters have been received from all parts of the world, making inquiry concerning what Dr. Briggs and myself received. I have answered none, except a few in which "I confessed and denied not" that the Lord had richly, gloriously blessed, not Dr. Briggs and myself only, but Revs. T. A. Atkinson, Jesse Wood, C. E. W. Smith and W. P. Andrews as well. As letters continue to come, and as I have no time to answer all, allow me to reply through your paper to the above inquiry from one of our best missionaries in Japan.

I am a modest man, although I have to tell it before people will believe it. I have an idea that the blessing of sanctification, like that of justification, should not be paraded on every occasion; hence my silence since the Lord did this great thing for me. Silence! I mean that I have not obtruded it upon any one, but have kept it in my heart; but whenever, in sermons, or in conversation with friends, it became necessary, I confessed it.

With your permission I will tell how it occurred under the labors of Dr. Carradine.

1. I was known to be bitterly opposed to the "Second Blessing Theory" of sanctification. I prejudiced many minds against it; and now find it hard

to believe that the "Second Blessing Theory" is the correct one. I think it destroys the continuity of Christian experience ; that the unities in a measure are eliminated by it. I am not disposed, however, to argue the matter here. I am only concerned about the fact—the experience. At some future time, I shall discuss the place sanctification holds in Christian experience—holds not as a "SECOND BLESSING" but as a *work*, wrought in us by the Holy Ghost. I think it can be shown that both justification and regeneration are prophetic of this **work**—point to it as the crowning glory of Christian experience on earth. I was opposed to it all ; and more, I fought it publicly and privately. God forgave me, and now rejoice that I stand where, for the first time, I can understand Christian experience. It's a golden chain, composed of many links—the last being glorification. *Vide* Romans 6 : 22.

2. Many people—of the justified school—doubted seriously my having any great amount of religion. I never had a long face, was always cheerful and generally hopeful. It always gave me pain when such judgments were passed upon me. That I had been converted there was no doubt—in my mind ; that I feared God—I knew ; that I was doing all I could— my almost day and night work was proof. What more did I need ? There was unrest—a lack of continuous peace—of uninterrupted joy. My friends I loved passionately ; my enemies—not any too well. Plainly: My feet were weary ; my heart ached and my present experience not satisfactory. *I had not*

lost ground; this had been my experience for more than thirty years.

But the story must be told how Dr. Briggs and myself came into the experience :

1. We covenanted with each other that, let others profess it, we would not; that we would hear Dr. Carradine, but nothing more. On this we shook hands and parted, feeling that if Atkinson, Wood, Smith and Andrews were weak enough to surrender, we were strong enough to weather the gale.

2. The meeting was held in Centenary Church, San Francisco, eight miles from Asbury Church, Oakland. It is forty minutes from my place to where Dr. Carradine held his meeting ; it ran one week before I attended. On Friday, Dr. C. prayed for the pastor of Centenary Church—Dr. Briggs. At the conclusion of the prayer Dr. Briggs asked the privilege of praying, which was, of course, granted. The prayer is said to have been remarkable for its fervor, eloquence, spirit. As he prayed, he descended into the depths ; the surrender became absolute ; the Fire came down and he was "filled." Hallelujahs came leaping out of his soul ; and for hours he was tossed by tempests of peace and joy. Briggs had fallen !

3. About five o'clock word came to me that he had professed sanctification. "The unexpected always happens," said I. Who would have thought it ? I confess that it gave me pain ; but I braced up and said : "Briggs *always did need religion*. He is a good fellow, eloquent as Demosthenes, but lacked spirituality." Do you see the point ? I made myself

as comfortable as I could that night—think I turned over one hundred times. ''Briggs professed sanctification! Well, well, well! He must be crazy; anyhow he is a good fellow, and always was. Tom Atkinson is impulsive, but Briggs—well! Don't it beat anything?'' Thus I reasoned.

Saturday word came to me from Briggs that he would preach for me Sunday night; that I must go to Centenary and hear Dr. Carradine. I gladly accepted Dr. Briggs' kind offer and went over on Sabbath evening. The sermon by Dr. Carradine, songs and prayers, all made a good impression; but far from what they seemed to make on others. Indeed, there was intense feeling in the house. Tears, shouts, amens were everywhere, but I was not equal to the occassion. It was above me; I could not reach it. I went away—sad and thoughtful; went away introspecting my life. What I found I have already told. I returned Monday morning and was present at the nine o'clock service. It was of remarkable power; the Lord was there. At the close of the service Dr. Carradine called for seekers of sanctification. I neither went forward nor stood up; but concluded that I would go away. To me it was a mystery; it was *not* such a meeting as I have often attended. There was lightning in it; the strokes were coming thick and fast. My soul was gradually becoming a storm center; I was being slowly but surely drawn into it by the power of Divine grace.

I took my hat, cane and overcoat and started out of the Church, but found Dr. Briggs at the door, who urged me to remain. He was weeping. I was neither

cold nor indifferent to his plea, but treated it with re·
spect. I knew he was in earnest, and earnestness always commands attention. Looking around, I found
Mrs. Glide, a lady whom I had known for many years,
on the same mission, who after speaking a few words
on another subject, said quietly: "Are you going
away?" I had an engagement in Oakland; but concluded to let it go and attend to it later. I went back
into the Church and took my seat. My thoughts, for
a few moments, ran thus: "Lord, what blessings I
have received from you have been good, and I know
all about them. I now take the place of the ox on the
Greek coin—stand between the altar and the plow—
ready for service or sacrifice. I am ready for poverty
or riches, friends or foes, but give me what I need."
This is as near the train of thought as I can give.
Suddenly I found myself falling—falling away from
everything—the Church and the preachers; my family
and friends. I went down into loneliness and deso-
lation. I became unconscious of what was about me
—I could not see—a horror of darknss was around me.
I went down, down; and for the first time I felt *alone*.
O, the sense of loneliness was awful; never to my dying day can I forget it. As I continued to descend
the Fire went crashing down through my body; a sense
of burning as distinct in my flesh as though coals of
fire were laid on it; yet there was no charring—no
pain. By this time I believed that I was dying, and
although I could not see, my mind was active; I felt
my pulse, and found that my heart was beating regularly. Just at the end of the darkness, to my surprise,

I found myself in the arms of the "Wonderful Man." He was the whitest man I ever saw; his face was like the sun. For a moment He held me; and such a bracing, buttressing, and girding of life I never had before. I was, blessed be God, in the arms of Omnipotence. Then the vision seemed to be objective; slowly as I sat there, I saw the Christ pass into my own life, and with the last glimpse of him came bliss unutterable. For hours and hours wave after wave of glory rolled into my soul. At times it seemed to me that I would die; it was more than I could hold. Then there would be a cessation; but as I could get my breath another great wave would come and quite overwhelm me. For forty-eight hours I was tossed by these heavenly gales.

I have said enough; the half I have not nor could I tell. The effect on my life has been peace, quietness, assurance. I found the work wrought in me to be purgative, illuminative, unitive. I love my Church, my brethren, my family—the whole world—better than I did before. Her doctrines, justification, regeneration, sanctification and redemption, stand out in my experience as great lights.

Everything drops to its place; and my experience is delightful. I have no quarrels about terms; no fault to find with other people's experience; only want the privilege of "growing in grace and in the knowledge of our Lord and Saviour."

How did I get it? Have told you all that I know; but looking backward see that my surrender was complete, my consecration perfect. The Lord Jesus came and accepted the sacrifice; and every moment since I have been happy. More: A large number of devout men and women were praying for me — praying that I might be conquered, as I had been an open enemy to the experience. No doubt the great Head of the Church heard their prayers, and for his own sake, theirs and mine gave me this joy.

What effect has it had on my life? It has tranquilized it. The fret, worry, anxiety, all gone; my heart aches no more; my feet so tired, are resting; indeed they feel as if they were in the burning path of the cherubim. Hallelujah!

I am not a dreamer, nor given to hallucinations. It has been hard for me to believe in the supernatural; hence I have preached more on miracles, the new birth and subjects involving supernatural power than most preachers. "Why should you thus preach?" you ask. Because I forced myself by study and by talk to believe that the Holy Ghost was imminent in everything. I know it now. He imported into my life the life of Jesus Christ. "Christ in us," rehabilitating our natures, is my conception of sanctification.

Dr. Beverly Carradine was a blessing to hundreds on the Pacific coast, and the M. E. Church, South, is better for his coming. He sowed no seeds of strife; he divided no churches, but left behind him a name as precious as the name of the good can be.

Now, my dear Brother ——, you are on the outpost. Wainwright and Newton, your colleagues, told me of their own spiritual uplift. The Lord come to you in power; come to your good wife, come to Sister H., and make you all successful in every good work.

I must add: That I do not call it "Second Bles-sing," but sanctification; that is its name, and shall be so long as the New Testament is read.

CHAPTER III.

Frances E. Willard's Experience.

At the age of nineteen, in the month of June, in the year 1859, she was converted. Lingering in the crisis of typhoid fever a voice seemed to speak to her saying, "My child, give me thy heart. I called thee long by joy; I call thee now by chastisement, but I have called thee always and only because I love thee with an everlasting love."

She heard and obeyed this voice and joined the Methodist Church. Of a speculative mind, bold, original, with a hasty temper, and ambitious to be great, with a thirst for knowledge insatiate, a tongue brilliant in repartee but blighting in sarcasm, she had much to lay aside and much to consecrate to her Lord in her new life. This she did, and lived a beautiful Christian life for six years.

"Six years passed by," she says, "during which I grew to love more and more the house of God and the fellowship of the blessed Christian people who were my brothers and sisters in the church." At this time there was placed in her hand, she informs us, the Life of Hester Ann Rogers, Life of Carvosso, Life of Mrs. Fletcher, Wesley's Sermons on Christian Perfection, and Mrs. Palmer's Guide to Holiness. Reading these books led her, to use her own words, "to desire and pray for holiness of heart." About this time D and Mrs. Phœbe Palmer held a meeting at Evanston. She shall tell, in her own words, her passage of this second great crisis in her spiritual life. She says:

"One evening, early in their meetings, when Mrs. Palmer had spoken with marvelous clearness and power, and at the close those desirous of entering into the higher Christian life had been asked to kneel at the altar, another crisis came to me. It was not so tremendous as the first, but it was one that deeply left its impress on my spirit. I turned to my mother (who was converted and joined the church when she was only twelve years old) and whispered, 'Will you go with me to the altar?' She did not hesitate a minute. Kneeling in utter self-abandonment I consecrated myself anew to God. I cannot describe the deep welling up of joy that gradually possessed me. I was utterly free from care. I was blithe as a bird that is good for nothing except to sing. I did not ask myself, 'is this my duty?' but just *intuitively* knew what I was called upon to do. The conscious emotional presence of Christ through the Holy Spirit held me. I ran about His errands *just for love*. Life was a halycon day. All my friends knew and noticed the change, and I would not like to write down the lovely things some of them said to me, but they did me no harm for I was shut in with the Lord."

Miss Willard proceeds then to relate how she lost the glow and joy of this precious experience through failing to testify to it under the advice of a distin-guished and learned minister who was her sincere but mistaken friend. She was elected to take charge of an institution of learning in Lima, New York, at which place there had been trouble on the holiness question. Her learned friends advised her to continue to live and enjoy her great experience, but to be silent on it in Lima for prudential reasons. This she tried to do, but found and confessed it to be a very grave mistake, and admitted she had paid the inevitable penalty. Twenty years and more afterward, writing of this advice of her friend, which advice was corroborated by a leading professor in the college at Lima, she says:

"Young and docile-minded as I was, and revering these two great and true men, I 'kept still' until I soon found I had nothing in particular to keep still about. The experience left me. Since then I sat at the feet of every teacher of holiness whom I could reach, and read their books and compared their views. I love and reverence and am greatly drawn toward all and never feel out of harmony with their spirit. Wonderful uplifts come to me as I pass on—clearer views of the life of God in the souls of men. Indeed, *it is the only life*, and all my being sets toward it as the rivers toward the sea. Celestial things grow dearer to me; the love of Christ is steadfast in my soul; the habitudes of a discipline sit more easily upon me; tenderness toward humanity and the lower orders of being increases with the years; but that sweet pervasiveness, that heaven in the soul, of which I came to know in Mrs. Palmer's meeting, I do not feel."

I have given you in her own words the struggles of a great, true, candid soul in the settlement of its mighty issues with the God of Heaven. Every issue was settled on the side of God. The Holy Spirit was admitted on his every approach to do His office work in the realm of her heart, *and He did it.*

Though she lost the rapture and fervor of this glorious experience of the Spirit's fulness, she did not lose the faith or cease to live the life and show forth its efforts and powers in her labors. I am happy to know that she recovered the experience. Some years ago at Old Orchard Holiness Camp-ground, at a meeting conducted by A. B. Simpson, of New York, she sought and regained and publicly and joyfully testified to this gracious experience, and lived and enjoyed it to her dying day.

In this brief epitome of her heart struggles with God she has disclosed to us the secret of her power. *It was God in her!!!* He found a will submissive—a great heart absolutely open—a wondrously gifted mind wholly given up to God, and thus made meet to think and do for Him.

These facts enable us to understand why it is that Frances Willard's name will remain a household word and continue fresh in the memory of millions so long as helplessness shall continue to need a friend, entrenched wrong need heroes and heroines to make spartan resistance to its havoc of human hearts and homes, and the forsaken of earth, bewailing their pitilessness, shall long for a refuge which will afford a chance of reform.

23

As she "crept in with mother," as she called her dying, she uttered these last words: "*How beautiful to be with God—with God—with God! God—come—come—come——*"

He came, and Frances Willard sweetly rested from labor.

CHAPTER IV.

Experience of Mrs. Margaret Bottome, President of the King's Daughters. She writes an account of her own death.

In the extreme heat on the evening of July 3, 1897, I arrived at Mount Lake Park, where, with my sister, Mrs. Moore, I had gone to attend a holiness camp meeting. I had not been at what is called a holiness camp meeting in twenty-eight years. The last one I attended was at Round Lake. "O! years gone down into the past, what memories ye bring." I could hear Bishop Simpson's voice as he uttered the words, "I beseech you, by the mercies of God, that ye present your bodies a living sacrifice." I could hear the voice of our saintly Alfred Cookman, and see his uplifted hands in intercessory prayer, and, I felt like singing,

> "The holy ones, behold they come,
> I hear the noise of wings."

Ah, how many I thought of who are not now "camping on the old camp ground;" but they are living. And it was very grateful to me one day, after listening to the last hymn written by the one who wrote, "O, bliss of the purified," that was sung for the first time twenty-eight years ago, and now the last hymn he wrote, "The Comforter

Has Come," is sung with the same enthusiasm. As the Rev. Dr. Fowler, the President of the National Association, passed my chair while I was listening to the song as it went on, "The Comforter Has Come," he simply said, "They are yet speaking." I went to the camp meeting rather hungry to see an encampment again. I wanted to see tents, but I saw instead a lovely auditorium, built so that you might think of a huge tent. I met a number of ministers at the Mountain Lake Park Hotel, but I only recognized Dr. Pepper and the saintly, almost angelic, Rev. John Thompson, the leader of the camp meeting, who is now almost totally blind. All the others were new to me.

In the first meeting, I felt the sacred influence that was so wonderful in the early national meetings. I had playfully said to some one who asked me, "Why are you going to a camp meeting? You surely are not going to work?" "Oh, no; I am going to bathe my weary soul in seas of heavenly rest.'" But the meeting was not of a style to rock you to sleep. I found myself listening to the old Methodist theology, after the style of—

> "Break off the yoke of inbred sin,
>   And fully set my spirit free ;
> I cannot rest till pure within,
>   'Till I am wholly lost in Thee."

I listened to a sermon by Dr. Fowler that deeply moved me. The subject of sin was dealt with in a scriptural manner that was not calculated to make some people feel very comfortable. I heard a sermon by a remarkable Quaker preacher, a Rev. Mr. Rees, who preached from, "He shall baptize you with the Holy Ghost and with fire." Never had I heard a sermon on "fire" so searching as that. I soon found I was in a very serious place. The 6th of July (a never to be forgotten day with me), after listening to the Rev. G. A. A. Gardner, of the Protestant Episcopal Church, of New York City, when it seemed as he took his text, "Are ye able to be baptized with the baptism I am baptized with?" as if we were in the immediate presence of God. The Holy Ghost showed me myself in God's sight as I had not seen myself before. The altar service was led by the Quaker preacher, Rev. Seth Rees; and he invited those to come forward who wanted to die—needed to die—to die to the self. Like I had spoken in the morning from the desk on the more "abundant" life, and now I was confronted with the need of a death. I had known of consecration—of giving up to God, of laying all on the altar, but at this time I saw nothing but the one fact that I was to die to some things. I left my seat and knelt at the altar, and I shall always think of Dr. Fowler and Rev. Mr. Rees as helping me to die. They did not spare me; there are words that will never leave me that I heard in prayer. "Lay the axe to the roots;" and one said she has had everything done to spoil her. We are here not to sympathize with her, nor to flatter her, but to help her die. And all the time I heard the refrain going on that I had known from my childhood—

"Refining fire go through my heart,
    Illuminate my soul,
    Scatter thy light through every part,
    And sanctify the whole."

And I was facing eternity. All thought of work, all thought of more power to be more useful, all was out of sight. O, in that hour how infinitely greater it was to be holy than to be the President of a great Order. or to do anything. All I can say is that I said : "Yes," oh, such a great—yes—to God. I chose in that hour to die. I did not struggle much All that I prayed for seemed to be in that "yes" to God; it was not giving Him anything, either. It was saying "yes" to death. And nothing can be taken from me in the future ; no reproach can come that was not included in that "yes." I must have died, for I was soon in another world (and you have to die to get in another world). How like a little child I became. All the congratulations seemed like flowers brought to my funeral. All I could think or say was " I did die." And I wanted everybody to die. There was nothing so fascinating as the word "die " Then I understood Christ's words: " Except a corn of wheat fall into the ground and die, it abideth alone, but if it die, it shall bring forth much fruit." I had said many times: " Well, we shall have to die to know," but I did not think of *this* death, and yet *this* is the death that makes you enter a place where you *know*. Nothing seemed appropriate but the old funeral anthem : " Blessed are the dead which die in the Lord. Yea, saith the Spirit, that they may rest from their labors; and their works do follow them." It was a great voice from heaven that said this, and it was my funeral anthem. I do not feel particularly interested in what will be called my death some day, but this death is intensely interesting to me, and I find myself so interested in having my friends who are not dead to die in this sense. I want them to be at rest. I want them in a very special sense to depart this life and be with Christ, which is far better. I seemed spoiled for everything but to see people die to the self-life. Oh, the light that falls on a heart and on a face that enters another world! Another world here, and isn't the heavenly life needed here? All I want for the rest of the way is to be in another world while in this,—dead indeed unto sin and alive unto God. I have much more I would like to say, but to take up more space would be selfish. Only let me add, thank God for leading my steps to the Mt. Lake Park Camp Meeting.

CHAPTER V.

How to Keep the Blessing.

REV. B. CARRADINE.

In one sense the blessing of sanctification keeps us. Hence it is very properly called "the keeping blessing." The constant indwelling of Christ, the easy exercise of faith, the restfulness and inner steadfastness of the experience, are all delightful features of the life, and contribute as well to its perpetuity.

The statement that sanctification is more easily kept than regeneration, seems quite incredible to some people. They wonder how a higher life and deeper grace can be more easily retained than a less exalted experience. The explanation is that inbred sin, the disturbing factor and bosom foe of the regenerated man, is cast out in the work of sanctification. The internal war is over. The battle is now on the outside. The life feels as if it was self-perpetuating. There is no fag or let-down in it, because Christ is ever in the heart. Brimful of holy energy it is always aggressive, and in addition has such unfoldings and disclosures of new strength and sudden developments of power which thrill the possessor, and can only be explained by the indwelling presence of the Son of God. At once on awakening in the morning the man feels the blessing stirring in his soul. With every call to duty there is felt a great reserve of strength and a conscious adequacy for the occasion.

Yet, of course, there are things for the sanctified individual to do, and which not to do, would rank him with Antinomians and fanatics and result disastrously and suicidally to the blessing. There are precautions and observances that must be seen to. We never get beyond the need of means of grace while in this world of probation. Self-denial, cross-bearing, watchfulness and prayer are to be practiced up to the portals of the tomb. To deny and neglect these things is to write ourselves down as moral idiots and bring danger and ruin upon the soul.

The sweet grace of sanctification can be retained. Great and gracious as it is, there is no need of losing it. The author has enjoyed the experience for seven years. He knows of a lady who has possessed it unbrokenly for fifty years, and he heard an aged servant of God say once that he had enjoyed it uninterruptedly for sixty-two years.

But these people did something to preserve the grace. For just as neglecting to do certain things has caused the blessing to depart, so the doing of certain things commanded us will retain the gracious experience. There are several things which, if observed and practiced, will prevent all spiritual lapse and plant the blessing in us like a towering and immovable mountain.

The first is faith. We obtain sanctification by faith, but it is also retained by faith. Faith is the vital point of union with Christ, and, of course, Satan makes the strongest assaults at this point. If after the reception of the blessing he can make the soul doubt its presence or continuance, he at once secures a foothold again in the territory from which he was ejected, and will soon rob the heart of its birthright and treasure.

It is noticeable that immediately after a person has received the witness of the Spirit to sanctification, the Adversary charges down upon the soul with his doubts. It is well for all such assaulted individuals to remember that just as soon as the Son of God received the anointing or baptism of the Holy Ghost on the banks of the Jordan, that he was immediately afterwards driven into the wilderness and there tempted forty days by the Devil. He conquered by faith and in the use of the Word of God. We can do the same.

The writer made this discovery on the second day of his sanctification. He found that under the heavy pressure of dark spirits he kept sweet and still in soul by exercising faith and repeating a number of times through the time of spiritual trial the words, "The blood cleanseth me from all sin," and, "The altar sanctifieth the gift." This quiet exercise of faith kept the experience as steady in the soul as a fixed star is in the heaven. He never forgot the victory nor the lesson learned at that time. He found that a quiet, persistent faith will either keep in check or throw off the gloomy and dark influences of Satan as a mountain wall casts off the waves of the sea. That it was a tonic protecting from the malaria of doubt. Fe

discovered that the simple repeating of certain passages of God's Word, as quoted above, had a strange
strengthening effect upon the heart and vitalized the
spirit of faith itself. He saw that there was a wonderful reacting influence on each other, the Word on the
faith and the faith on the Word. Faith grew stronger
by repeating passages of Scripture, and the Word
became sweeter and stronger in its meaning under the
increasing faith. In short, he found that Satan is
powerless to despoil the soul of the pearl of great
price so long as the soul believes God sanctifies it.
That when a man drives a stake down here and says,
Alabama, " Here we rest," he does rest, and the Adversary has to stand with impotent rage and see the
smiling child of God with head anointed, cup running
over and eating joyously in the presence of his enemies, whether they be terrestrial or infernal.

Many of those who have lost the blessing made the
confession, '' I got to doubting.'' Who wonders at
the loss ? As Faith is the condition of the reception
and retention of grace, then, of course, Doubt, which
is its opposite, is the way to lose all we have. All sin
and spiritual lapse is preceded by doubt. It opens the
door to Satan and he rushes in to sow tares in the
wheat, and possess the house again which had been
swept and garnished.

But faith keeps the door of the heart; faith retains
the grace and presence of God, and makes it impossible for the devil to do his work. And so the just not
only shall, but do, live by faith.

A friend of the writer was sanctified one day, and

three days afterward the powers of darkness came
down upon him and the Satanic whisper was fairly
hissed in his soul: "You know you are not sanctified." But this time the great Enemy bore down
upon one who was ready and able through grace to
meet him. His reply was, "Is that so? Then if I
am not sanctified, here goes again. My all is on the
altar; the altar sanctifies the gift. I am the gift and,
therefore, I am sanctified. Hallelujah!" And lo! as
suddenly as he came Satan left him.

From a lady friend he did not so soon depart. For
several days after she received the witness of the Spirit
to her sanctification the devil violently assailed her.
Passing her several times during the time of her faith
trial we saw the hunted, distressed and puzzled look
in her eyes. She could not understand why this tight
spiritual pressure should be on her. She did not
remember that after the glorious experience on the
banks of Jordan came the wilderness trial to Christ.
There was no time to talk with her, so I gave her an
encouraging smile and grasp of the hand, saying,
"All will be well; hold on by faith." She did hold
on, quietly exercising a childlike trust until suddenly
the Saviour appeared, scattered her tormentors, and
angels came and ministered unto her. She obtained
the lesson of her life, and to-day has no trouble in
going through these character tests, but moves calmly
and brightly through them all like a star through the
night.

It is wonderful how quickly the lesson of faith is
learned which retains the experience of holiness. At

first it may be an effort to exercise the belief and go on repeating the Word of God, especially when the joy of the soul may have run low or departed. But in a few hours or days one becomes established in the grace, there is a spirit or whisper of trust in the heart, and the soul settles down with a delightful sense of recumbency upon the love, power and protecting care of the Son of God.

It is now that the man sees the tremendous force of faith as by it he retains the greatest experience of the Christian life. He can now mentally exercise it. It seems to be the breath of his soul and is exhaled like breath. Instead of words being uttered, the thought itself is uppermost, "The blood cleanses me," "Jesus sanctifies me."

Still, while it may be hard at times to repeat those passages of God's Word which bear upon the soul-cleansing power of the blood, yet there is peculiar blessedness in such oral testimony and confession of the lips. In our own experience we have never had to repeat such words as "The blood cleanses me," "The altar sanctifies me," "Jesus saves me now," more than the third time before feeling the sense of victory in the soul, and hearing an inward hallelujah voiced by the answering Spirit who thus assured us that all was well.

The expression, "exercising faith" means much. But it is a simple truth for all the blessedness it brings. Men know what it is to exercise their lungs and arms and body, but seem bewildered when we tell them to exercise faith. If we exercise the voice or limbs, we *use* them. So to exercise faith we use it, trot it out, whirl it around, and propel it upward. Every effort makes it easier to do, and from uttering the words, "The blood cleanses," "Jesus sanctifies me," the soul gets so that, as we said before, it actually *thinks* these sentences of life. The heart literally broods on the atoning blood, and a feeling of trust encompasses the life like the mountains stand about Jerusalem.

One night at a preaching service we noticed the minister, who was a sanctified man, with head bowed and lips moving. It was during a protracted meeting and was one of those times when the air seemed to be full of evil spirits. The congregation appeared frozen, and the very atmosphere depressing. We thought that the preacher was praying, as we observed the motion of his lips and caught indistinct whispers. After the service was over we asked him if this was not the case. His reply was:

"No; I was not praying."

"What, then, were you doing?"

With the greatest seriousness and a tone that deeply impressed us, he replied:

"I was exercising faith!"

In a flash, then, I saw what a battle he had been going through; and that there in the pulpit he had met the devil and whipped him out by whispering passages of the Word of God and by the exercise of faith. There was a great victory that night in the sermon and at the altar, and this was the way it was won. What this brother did in the meeting and vanquishing of the difficulties of that night, we are to do with every spiritual trial and doubt flung in our way by men and devils. We are to *believe through them* into light.

Let no man who ever saw a person flash a lantern up a dark alley and make it a path of light from end to end, say he does not know what it is to exercise faith. It is to throw a headlight of belief on God's Word and work through a tunnel of spiritual gloom. It bores its way through the devil's suggestions and lies. It turns an X-ray on a wall of dark circumstance and reveals God on the other side. It steadily refuses to doubt the statement of God's Word and the witness of His Spirit. It says that light or no light, sensation or no sensation, feeling or no feeling, knowledge, or no knowledge, when God says a thing is so, it is so. That this settles the matter finally and forever.

We fail to see how Satan can find entrance, much less be able to rob the soul of its greatest treasure when such a faith stands guard with unsleeping vigilance at the door. This is the victory that overcometh low spirits, a sinking heart, whispers of the devil and all the discouragements of this lower world—even our faith.

The second thing necessary to keep the blessing of sanctification is obedience.

Faith is the heart condition, obedience is the life condition. If there is true faith within there will be obedience to God without. They walk together and they go down together. When faith fails disobedience sets in. When obedience fails faith sickens and will die if the course is persisted in.

When consciously disobedient to God, faith feels paralyzed for the time, and the lips seem unable to frame the words, "The blood cleanses me now from all sin."

We do not mean to say that the blessing of sanctification is lost by one small act of disobedience, or by two or three such. We certainly believe that by a single act of murder or adultery the blessing would be forfeited. But there are failures of duty that may not be compared to these two sins. Grave as is any act of disobedience, be it small or great in its nature, yet we can not believe that God suddenly leaves a man forsaken and cursed for one such omission or commission. We believe that sanctification, like regeneration, as a rule, departs gradually. As the light fades out of the sky, so the glory leaves the soul. First joy goes, then liberty, and then the testimony. The man has become dumb. Satan has again locked the lips, the daughters of music are gone, and the old heart burden has come back. The blessing has leaked out, as some of them say. Yes, and it leaked out through acts of disobedience.

Disobedience is a grave thing. We know a lady, now eighty years of age, who says that she deliberately disobeyed God fifty years ago, after having been a sanctified woman for several years. She says that while God forgave her and she has not lost the blessing, yet her sanctified experience has never been the same. We believe that she has allowed Satan to keep her crushed down by this memory, when the atonement covers the whole thing and she should have gone free; but the fact that the memory of the act has so burdened her all through life shows the gravity of a single deed of disobedience. If we would keep the blessing of sanctification we must obey God. His Word must be kept. We cannot violate His commandments. We must hearken to His calls and follow His leadings. He can unmistakably impress His will upon us, and if we do it not, we will be certain to get into trouble.

We do not mean that every impression that comes to the mind is of God. Some of them are so far from being of heaven that we will please God by not paying any attention to them. He says, "My sheep know my voice," and that voice will sound in His Word, in His Providence, and in the whisper of the Spirit to the heart, guiding, restraining, teaching and leading.

We must obey God. What a joy it brings to the soul to be thus consciously submissive and doing the whole will of God. What a ring to the voice and what an added power to the life it brings. Satan feels helpless before a man with faith in heart and perfect obedience to God in life. In a word, we must "trust and obey," and in doing so will be invincible.

There is a lovely little hymn which bears the name "Trust and Obey." The chorus runs,—

> "Trust and obey
> For there's no other way,
> To be happy in Jesus
> But to trust and obey."

Neither is there any other way to retain the grace of

sanctification but by this same Faith and Obedience.

The third essential is seen in "The Blood." The instant there is a conscious spiritual hurt we should fly to the blood of Christ and claim its immediate application. It is better not to lose time in argument or inquiry as to whether the act was wrong or not which brought the disturbed state of mind and heart. Better fly at once to the blood, obtain the instantaneous cleansing, and settle the other matters afterward.

Few realize the ever-present power of the blood of Christ. It "cleanseth," says John. It cleanses instantly, and it cleanses now, the very moment we claim its virtue by faith.

There is no need to be in condemnation a moment in case of sins of ignorance and surprise. The blood is available every second. Even in matters of graver nature, it is through lack of knowledge of the present power of the blood, that makes the man postpone his soul-cleansing and recovery until certain mental agonies, fervent supplications and physical humiliations shall have been gone through with.

The Bible does not say that the blood and something else cleanseth, but *The blood!* So, if the world to-day would renounce its beads, pilgrimages and works of righteousness, and look to the blood of Christ, it would be saved. If Christians would turn their gaze from the thought of growth, development and church work to the purifying blood of Jesus, the heart purity and holiness they desire would be instantly given. If sanctified people who have lapsed more or less in the sanctified life, and are trying to work their way back into the old time favor and honor of Heaven, would only look to "The Blood," they would find themselves instantly healed, restored, cleansed, filled and fired again.

In recognition of possible weakness, mistakes and missteps; in view of the fact that some fiery dart of the evil one may pierce the Christian armor, God has provided the ever-present, ever-powerful, ever-cleansing blood of Christ. The instant that the soul is wounded it should fly at once, without the loss of a second, to the Saviour, and cry, Lord Jesus, apply thy blood ; and it should stay at His feet until it is done.

This is not Antinomianism, abusing the grace of God, and sinning that mercy might abound ; but a proper faith that comes at once to the Saviour when betrayed into sin. The spirit that would tarry and bemoan the past with profitless groans and paralyzed activities is not that which is enjoined in the Bible. It is not the act that most exalts God and His plan for our redemption.

That which honors Christ and His salvation is the immediate return to the Lord in case of departure, and the instant appropriation of the blood which cleanses through and through, and now, and for evermore.

www.ingramcontent.com/pod-product-compliance
Lightning Source LLC
Chambersburg PA
CBHW020846090426
42736CB00008B/250